THE PRE-INDUSTRIAL ECONOMY IN ENGLAND
1500-1750

Studies in Economic and Social History

L. A. Clarkson

Senior Lecturer in Economic and Social History
The Queen's University of Belfast

The Pre-Industrial
Economy in England
1500-1750

B. T. BATSFORD LTD London

First published 1971
Second impression 1972
© L. A. Clarkson 1971

Made and printed in Great Britain
by C. Tinling and Co. Ltd, London and Prescot
for the publishers B. T. Batsford Ltd,
4 Fitzhardinge Street, London W.1

7134 1380 8

Contents

Preface

A work of this kind should, properly, be written by an emeritus professor possessing wisdom to guide his judgments, reputation to guard him from the barbs of his critics and senility to excuse his follies. Lacking all these defences, I can plead only that I have written this book because I wanted to and because I thought there was a need for it. On the last point I have on several occasions been encouraged to continue, when the initial desire to write was wearing thin, by students complaining that they did not know where to begin their studies of the pre-industrial economy. I have tried to provide a beginning.

Confronted with a mass of new—and old—scholarship on the economic history of England between 1500 and 1750, I decided to reduce it to a manageable volume by organising it around a few basic economic concepts. In particular, it seems to me that the pre-industrial period is best understood as a market economy hampered by low productivity and poorly developed economic institutions. Possibly economists will claim that my economic concepts are not merely simple, but simple-minded; while historians might complain that I have used them as a straight-jacket to confine an infinite variety of economic and social history over two and a half centuries. I admit the first charge in advance; as to the second, I hope I have avoided the perils of Procrustes, but without some working hypothesis history is merely a tangle of confusing facts.

I have incurred an enormous debt to scholars whose works I have plundered for ideas and information. In order to avoid a

vast undergrowth of references on every page I have not acknowledged sources in footnotes—save for quotations and a few
esoteric references—but have gathered them together in a
bibliography arranged by chapters and sections within chapters.
I am grateful to my colleagues in the Department of Economic
and Social History at Queen's, former colleagues E. H. Hunt
and J. M. Martin, and Dr Joan Thirsk of Oxford, who have been
generous with time and criticism. Comments from under-
graduates, not always complimentary, have proved the best form
of student participation that I know. I am particularly grateful
for help from John Cockerill, David Cocks, Jim McAllister,
Malcolm Thick and Ann Wright. I once thought of including
my bank manager in the acknowledgments but decided that his
usurious $8\frac{1}{2}$ per cent was adequate recompense for his services.
On the other hand, the contribution of my wife cannot adequately
be acknowledged, least of all in the customary place at the end of
a preface. But for her this book would not exist.

I

The Structure of the Economy
1500-1750

(i)

This book is concerned with the pre-industrial economy in England between 1500 and 1750. The dates are arbitrarily chosen, but they are not without economic significance. After a century of factional conflict the accession of the Tudors inaugurated an era of relatively stable government vital to economic development. The geographical discoveries of the late fifteenth century extended the economic horizons of Europe in a way that was to benefit English trade in the two centuries that followed; while the Reformation stimulated religious attitudes favourable to economic development. Of more immediate significance, economically, was the increase in England's population from about 1500 after a century and a half of decline and stagnation. Much of the economic history of the period 1500–1750 can be seen as a response to changes in the rate of population growth.

The choice of 1750 to mark the end of the pre-industrial period is more difficult to justify. It certainly does not mark the precise beginning of the industrial revolution, for harbingers of rapid economic change were evident earlier in the century, while many features of the old economy survived until late into the nineteenth century. But the middle of the eighteenth century is a watershed in British economic development and as he crosses it the historian's task changes from examining the constraints on economic growth to describing and explaining the onset of industrialization.

9

Countries that have not experienced an industrial revolution are frequently described as underdeveloped, a condition which has been defined as 'the failure to provide acceptable levels of living to a large proportion of a country's population, with resulting misery and material privation.'[1] Its main features are a large fraction of a country's labour force employed in agriculture, an absence of sustained increases in *per capita* incomes for the mass of the population, and a high incidence of poverty. The English economy displayed all these features before 1750. A majority of the population obtained its income from agricultural employment, although it is impossible to be precise about the size of the agricultural sector since men frequently combined agriculture with industrial and commercial activities. The pre-industrial economy was also characterized by stagnation: there was some improvement in incomes per head between 1500 and 1750, and more particularly after 1650, but it was painfully slow compared with the years after the transformation of the economy in the late eighteenth and early nineteenth centuries. By modern standards the general level of living was very low and large numbers of people existed in a state of persistent poverty.

But it is at this point that we come up against a major difficulty in applying concepts of underdevelopment to pre-industrial England. By the standards of the time England was not regarded as a poor country. In 1559, for example, Jóhn Aylmer exclaimed patriotically:

> Oh if you knewest thou Englishe man in what welth thou livest and in how plentifull a countrye: Thou wouldst vii times of the day fall flat on thy face before God, and geve him thanks, that thou wart born an Englishe man, and not a french pesant, nor an Italyan, nor Almane.[2]

[1] S. Kuznets, 'Underdeveloped Countries and the Pre-industrial Phase in the Advanced Countries', in *The Economics of Development*, ed. A. N. Agarwala and S. P. Singh, 1958, p. 137.

[2] John Aylmer, *An Harbowe For Faithfull and Trewe Subjectes*, in G. Orwell and R. Reynolds (eds.), *British Pamphleteers*, vol. 1, 1938, pp. 31–2;

And nearly two centuries later Defoe described Britain as 'the most flourishing and opulent country in the world.[1] On the eve of the industrial revolution England was wealthier than many underdeveloped countries today and far more sophisticated in her economic and social structure. As Professor P. T. Bauer has written:

> ... by the eighteenth century Great Britain and western Europe had had centuries of sustained economic development behind them, and had reached a high degree of cultural, technical and economic achievement. Perhaps even more important they had become almost completely pervaded by an exchange economy ... Compare this with the position of underdeveloped countries today, or a few decades ago. Africa south of the Sahara has never invented the wheel; over large parts of Africa ... even fifty years ago most people had never seen one. There was still cannibalism in West Africa towards the end of the last century, and slavery was a recognised institution until well into this century. The position and development of most of the indigenous peoples of Africa and Southeast Asia at the beginning of this century resembled not that of the West in the seventeenth and eighteenth centuries, but, at best, those of northern and western Europe in the sixth and seventh centuries.[2]

Like beauty, underdevelopment lies in the eye of the beholder; and it is less ambiguous to describe the English economy before 1750 as pre-industrial, meaning simply an economy that had not been transformed by industrialization.

The most obvious feature of the economy before 1750 was the importance of agriculture as a basic activity and the most striking contrast with the two centuries after 1750 was the slow pace of economic change. To explain these characteristics it is useful to consider the reasons adduced by economists to account for economic growth in advanced countries of the world today. Not that

[1] D. Defoe, *A Tour Through England and Wales*, Everyman ed., 1928, vol. 1, p. 1.

[2] P. T. Bauer, *Economic Analysis and Policy in Underdeveloped Countries*, 1957, p. 47.

there is any general agreement. A long tradition in economic writing, from the days of Adam Smith, stresses the importance of an increasing rate of capital formation in bringing about economic growth. More recently this factor has been considered in conjunction with the supply of skilled labour and the state of technology; and since the Keynesian revolution there has been a revival of interest, largely dormant since Malthus, in the level of effective demand as a determinant of economic development. Professor W. A. Lewis has focused attention on non-economic reasons for growth by distinguishing between the 'proximate causes of growth' and the 'causes of these causes'. The former include the effort to economize, increases in knowledge and its application to production, and the accumulation of capital. Among the latter are the nature of economic, social and political institutions, attitudes towards material progress, and natural resources. In a recent study Professor D. C. North has classified the factors making for growth in the United States during the nineteenth and twentieth centuries as radical changes in technology, investment in 'human capital' by which the economy is supplied with skilled manpower, and an efficient organization which in the western world is the price system organized around a market economy.[1] This classification will be used in the remainder of this chapter to consider the economic features of pre-industrial England. Discussion of non-economic influences on economic development between 1500 and 1750 is reserved for the next chapter.

(ii)

Continuous technical advance has been a feature of the British economy ever since the industrial revolution. It has taken three main forms: the development of new sources of energy such as coal and steam, electricity and petroleum; the exploitation of new or practically new raw materials; and the subsequent development of new production processes and entirely new products. The technical

[1] D. C. North, *Growth and Welfare in the American Past*, 1966, pp. 6-8.

deficiencies of English industry before 1750 are immediately apparent. Mechanical power was provided by human and animal muscle, supplemented by wind and water. There were improvements in water wheels and pumping machinery during the period and by the end of the seventeenth century steam power was beginning to be used; but the main sources of power in 1750 remained much as they had been in 1500. There was a little progress in the use of raw materials. Coal replaced wood as a domestic fuel for the poor in urban areas and was used increasingly in industry during the sixteenth and seventeenth centuries, but it made very little advance in the iron industry – eventually to be the leading industrial consumer of coal – until the late eighteenth century. Although cotton was introduced into the textile industry in the early seventeenth century its use did not expand significantly for another century and a half. Basic manufacturing techniques in such industries as textiles, leather production and leather working, metal smelting and metal working, building, and food processing altered little in pre-industrial England.

There was a similar lack of technical advance in transport and commerce. Methods of road construction scarcely improved between 1500 and 1750. In many respects, however, inland communications were better in pre-industrial England than in either continental Europe at the same time or underdeveloped countries today. England was a small country possessing a long coast line and long stretches of navigable rivers, advantages that were exploited more and more during the seventeenth and early eighteenth centuries by improvements to river navigations and harbours. A more serious hindrance to commerce was the poor quality of the coinage which arose partly from technical difficulties of producing coins of uniform weight and size. Basic skills of reading, writing and counting were also frequently absent with the result that records of commercial transactions were not kept or were defective. Not that too much should be made of this point. Literacy and numeracy were probably greater in pre-industrial England than in many African and Asian countries today and were, in any case, not an insuperable barrier to commercial enterprise.[1]

The most serious technical shortcomings in pre-industrial England were in agriculture since their ramifications were felt throughout the economy. In any country the level of agricultural production depends on the extent and quality of land available for cultivation, the amount of labour and capital devoted to agriculture, and the techniques of cultivation. As long as agricultural methods remain primitive most people will be engaged in scratching a miserable living from the soil and they will have little, if any, surplus available for sale. If, on the other hand, by better methods of cultivation some farmers can produce food in excess of their own needs, conditions are established for the development of industry and commerce.

Farming techniques were not static in the two and a half centuries before 1750. The picture of unthinking and unchanging agricultural practices following an immutable three-course rotation within a uniform open-field system is a caricature created by eighteenth-century propagandists and perpetuated by twentieth-century textbooks. In no sector of the pre-industrial economy was change more pervasive than in agriculture; and the transformation of the economy after 1750 would have been impossible without the long period of agricultural progress that preceded it. Nevertheless, before the mid-eighteenth century agricultural practices were still sufficiently backward to keep a large and only gradually diminishing proportion of the country's workforce engaged in primary production. Furthermore, technical progress in agriculture occurred very slowly with the result that increases in agricultural

---

[1] The point is illustrated by the case of the farmer in the sixteenth century who agreed, on the payment of £20, to supply a dealer with four corns of wheat in the first week, eight the second week, sixteen the third week, and so on in geometric progression throughout the year. By the time the unfortunate victim realised he was liable to supply over four thousand billion grains by the end of the year, he was doubtless determined not to enter the wicked world of trade again. On the other hand, the dealer stood to make huge profits by exploiting the farmer's arithmetical ignorance. (Alan Everitt, 'The Marketing of Agricultural Produce', in *The Agrarian History of England and Wales, 1500–1640*, vol. IV, ed. Joan Thirsk, 1967, pp. 566–7).

productivity, especially before 1650, tended to be overtaken by increases in population, causing food prices to rise. Agricultural methods advanced further than industrial or commercial techniques between 1500 and 1750 but progress was neither rapid nor revolutionary.

The development of new methods of production depends on invention, that is the discovery of new techniques, and on innovation, or the application of inventions to production for the market. Invention is a reflection of the intellectual activity of society. There is no need to doubt the intellectual achievements of an age stimulated by the Renaissance and the Reformation, but there were great gaps in available knowledge and the results of intellectual enquiry were rarely organized on a systematic basis. As a result, technical progress in all branches of economic life was more a matter of making empirical improvements to production methods than of applying scientific principles. When, for example, the Royal Society investigated tanning methods in the late seventeenth century it was unable to improve on the long-established practices of practical tanners. As late as 1799 Sir Humphry Davy, after conducting a series of investigations into the chemistry of tanning, concluded that 'in general, tanners appear to have arrived in consequence of repeated practical experiments, at a degree of perfection which cannot be very far extended by means of any elucidation of theory that has yet been made known.'[1]

Because organized science rarely had the answer, farmers and manufacturers tended to look overseas for solutions to their technical problems. In farming, land reclamation, mining, metallurgy, glass manufacture, paper-making, textiles and many other industries, new techniques were introduced into England from Europe during the sixteenth and seventeenth centuries. The situation may be compared with that by which underdeveloped countries today import techniques from advanced countries. But the comparison is superficial only. Nowadays technology flows from countries with high levels of cultural and economic achievement to regions with low levels, whereas in the sixteenth and seventeenth centuries

[1] Sir Humphry Davy, *Collected Works*, ed. J. Davy, 1839, vol. II, p. 287.

England was economically and culturally similar to western Europe. Thus the introduction of European production methods into England created relatively few problems of obtaining adequate supplies of capital or skilled labour without which imported processes would be useless.

The availability of European agricultural and industrial techniques suggests that the major factors governing the pace of technical progress in pre-industrial England were those affecting the process of innovation. Innovation depended in part on the willingness of society to accept new ideas, and there was no doubt a good deal of suspicion about new-fangled things. 'It were good . . .', wrote Bacon at the end of the sixteenth century, 'that Men in their Innouations, would follow the Example of Time its selfe; what indeed Innouateth greatly, but quietly, and by degrees, scarce to be perceived . . .' However, suspicion could be broken down and there were enough men with enterprise and capital in the sixteenth and seventeenth centuries to promote new projects when market conditions made them worthwhile. But as long as markets remained static and the growth of demand was limited by small populations, low incomes and poor transport, there was little incentive to change methods of production. It is no accident that the most important technical advances in pre-industrial England occurred in agriculture, since it was this sector of the economy that felt the pressures of increasing demand from the growing population most strongly.

(iii)

The second cause of rapid economic growth in the advanced countries of the world today is the increasing supply of skilled labour of all kinds. Developing skills are as much the product of economic growth as its cause, for just as a technologically sophisticated, market-orientated economy requires scientists, technicians, businessmen and professional people, so it creates opportunities for their employment and the resources that can be devoted to training them. For convenience we can distinguish between three different types of skills necessary for economic growth: technical, entrepreneurial, and managerial or administrative.

In pre-industrial England labour was more evident by its quantity than its high quality. It was generally unskilled, uneducated in a formal way, and frequently undernourished. Practically all production processes involved a great deal of manual labour; yet the productivity of such labour was low. Recurrent harvest failures produced ill-balanced and irregular diets and exposed the population to the risks of endemic illnesses and sporadic epidemics which cut off adults in their working prime and debilitated the survivors. Traditional technical skills were gained through experience. Sons learned the annual cycle of farming from their fathers and in this way past customs often became enshrined as present wisdom. Manufacturing skills were similarly acquired or learnt through apprenticeships. Many basic industrial techniques such as spinning and weaving, wood-working, brewing or baking, were readily mastered by low-grade labour without any formal training: the long apprenticeships common in many crafts in the sixteenth and seventeenth centuries were less a reflection of the high degree of skill involved than a means of providing masters with cheap labour. There were some occupations requiring a high degree of expertise, but this, too, was usually obtained by experience. Huntington Beaumont, for example, an enterprising mining engineer at the turn of the sixteenth and seventeenth centuries, learnt his trade in the coal mines on his father's estates in Leicestershire. Occasionally technical skills were learnt from foreign workmen who settled in England or who visited the country temporarily; or by Englishmen travelling overseas in order to master particular techniques.

In pre-industrial England there was no hard and fast division between technical skills and entrepreneurial and managerial talent, and in marked contrast to present-day underdeveloped countries there was no shortage of entrepreneurs possessing a 'sense of market opportunity combined with the capacity needed to exploit it'.[1] For the most part entrepreneurs were anonymous, their monument

[1] This definition of entrepreneurial functions comes from Charles Wilson, 'The Entrepreneur in the Industrial Revolution in Britain', *Explorations in*

being the achievements they wrought in the economy, although the exploits of the more enterprising of them have caught the eye of historians.[1] English society placed few obstacles in their way. Successful entrepreneurs were able to advance up the social ladder without much difficulty. In certain spheres of activities, it is true, enterprise was frustrated by gilds interested in maintaining the *status quo*, by government-protected monopolies, such as the chartered companies in overseas trade, and sometimes by the government itself which imposed statutory restrictions on industry and trade. But these were not formidable barriers and were often ignored.

The most serious restriction to entrepreneurship was a lack of market opportunities. One of the functions of entrepreneurs is to create, as well as to exploit, market opportunities but in this they were hampered by the same difficulties that retarded innovation – poor transport, low incomes and small populations. The spur to entrepreneurial activity is the desire to make money but this was often frustrated by the restricted markets in pre-industrial England, so the desire turned to more lucrative directions. Sometimes foreign trade or involvement in colonial exploitation appeared more profitable than anything the home market could offer and a good deal of talent and capital found outlets in overseas ventures. Money-lending was an even easier path to profits in an economy where there was a large demand for, but a small supply of, credit. Other attractions lay in the direction of government administration. Many men who in a later age might have become captains of industry found lush grazings among bureaucratic pastures. There were two reasons for this. At the level of the individual business there was little demand for administrative ability when most units of production were small. At the national level there was a ramshackle and cumbersome machine of government regulating the economy at

---

Entrepreneurial History, VII, 3 (Feb. 1955), reprinted in *The Experience of Economic Growth*, ed. B. E. Supple, 1963, p. 176.

[1] Many instances of industrial entrepreneurship between the sixteenth and eighteenth centuries are presented in J. W. Gough, *The Rise of the Entrepreneur*, 1969.

many points and requiring an ever-growing army of officials, ranging from petty collectors of customs in obscure havens to the highest officers of the government at Westminster. Not many of these posts were well paid – many were not paid at all – but they were potentially profitable because of the opportunities they presented for patronage and peculation. The outlets chosen by entrepreneurs for their talents were not always profitable ones for the economy as a whole, but until the market provided greater opportunities, the pre-industrial economy suffered from a haemorrhage, not a dearth, of entrepreneurship.

(iv)

'The engine of economic development before the days of governmental planning was the market.'[1] Professor Kindleberger's aphorism is particularly relevant to pre-industrial England where the pace of economic change was determined by the market. There were of course large pockets of subsistence production in agriculture and many households must have attended to their own needs for clothing, tools, beer, bread and other essential needs. Even so, there is abundant evidence of widespread commercial relationships. Few producers were completely isolated from the market and for a growing majority market prices were the first factors to be considered when organizing production. Similarly, the market, not the state, determined the pattern of activity. The government played almost no part in economic life beyond raising taxes and regulating private enterprise, possessing neither the knowledge nor the means of organizing production and distribution.

A fully-fledged market economy is characterized by four main features: the price mechanism, competition, the institution of private property, and self interest. Prices are the means whereby consumers express their preferences and indicate to producers the quantities and combinations of goods that should be supplied in the future. They are also the means by which goods are allocated to consumers according to income. As the result of competition

[1] C. P. Kindleberger, *Economic Development*, 2nd ed., 1965, p. 150.

among producers prices are forced down and encouragement given to the most efficient forms of production. The institution of private property is necessary to ensure that owners of means of production can use their resources as they please and enjoy the income arising from their profitable employment; while profit maximization or self interest spurs men to produce goods and services for the market.

Before 1750 the market economy fell even further below textbook perfection than it does today. Its proper operation was encumbered in many ways. Poor communications confined trading areas geographically to regions containing relatively small numbers of people, mostly with very low incomes. Producers were thus denied the advantages of economies of scale and the division of labour was frustrated. Restricted markets also made it difficult for producers to increase sales by reducing prices, since demand is more inelastic when there are few consumers than when there are many. These difficulties were reduced as population grew and transport improved. In addition the growth of towns provided farmers and manufacturers with markets both larger and different in character from those of the small market towns and villages.

Poor communications also curtailed the efficiency of the price system in determining production. In extreme cases rising prices brought about no increase in production because suppliers were ignorant of the rise, or were unable to take advantage of it because of high costs of transport or the difficulties of obtaining supplies of raw materials. Bad transport protected local monopolies from the competition of producers from other regions. Institutional factors gave further encouragement to local monopolies. Practically every town possessed gilds which protected local artisans from the competition of foreign workmen, while the central government granted monopolies of trade and manufacture to favoured groups. However monopolies, whether supported by the authority of municipal or national government or created by bad transport, became progressively weaker during the seventeenth century with the gradual improvement of transport and the means of distribution.

Two features of the market economy were relatively well developed even in the sixteenth century. In the first place the doctrine of self interest was firmly entrenched as a guide to economic behaviour even though it was sometimes questioned. This is clearly illustrated by the debate on enclosure in the sixteenth century. When the landlord in the *Discourse of the Common Weal*, written about 1549, asked 'if [landlords] find more proffite [by enclosing] than otherwise, why should they not?' he received the traditional reply: 'I can tell youe well inowgh why they should not, for they maie not purchase them selues proffitt by that that may be hurtfull to others...' Yet it was recognized by the author that the only effective way of preventing enclosure for pasture was 'to make the proffitt of the plow to be as good, rate for rate, as the proffitt of the graisiers and shepmasters.'[1] by the end of the sixteenth century the victory of the gospel of profit maximization was virtually complete. Secondly, the institution of private property was recognized and accepted in the sixteenth century. It was not entirely sacrosanct. Before the Civil War the surviving feudal privileges of the crown, particularly the right of wardship, sometimes encroached on the freedom of landowners to enjoy the full incomes of their estates. More serious was the exercise of the royal prerogative in granting monopolies infringing on already established trades. However the common law strenuously resisted the royal prerogative when it infringed private property. In the early seventeenth century Lord Chief Justice Coke claimed that 'the common law is the best and most common birth-right that the subject hath, for the safeguard and defence, not only of his goods, lands and revenues, but of his wife, children, his body, fame and life also'. Almost a century later a judge admonished a defendant in a case of abduction: 'your offence hath been in a nation where property is better preserved than in any other government in the world...'[2]

[1] *A Discourse of the Common Weal of this Realm of England*, ed. E. Lamond, 1893, pp. 50, 53.

[2] E. W. Ives, 'Social Change and the Law', in *The English Revolution, 1600–1660*, 1968, p. 120; D. Ogg, *England in the Reigns of James II and William III*, 1955, p. 72.

(v)

We have suggested that rapid growth in modern economies depends on a high level of technology, an abundance of skilled labour and an efficient form of economic organization. This approach provides us with a mirror-image of the features of the pre-industrial economy: primitive technology and a very slow rate of technical development, an abundance of unskilled labour, and a market economy that was defective in many respects. Of these three features the last was the most important in accounting for the economic stagnation of the period. Techniques were slow to improve in agriculture, industry and commerce since there was little pressure on producers to alter their production functions. The scarcity of skilled labour in the economy, by comparison with the nineteenth and twentieth centuries, was a consequence of the low state of technology and the backwardness of the economic organization. In relation to the demands for skilled labour in pre-industrial England, there is little evidence of a shortage. But the market was a feeble engine of growth. Because of difficulties of transport and communications; because of institutional barriers; and, above all, because the mass of consumers was poor and their effective demand restricted by low incomes, the market exercised a weak pull on the economy. This situation gradually improved as the growth of population created more consumers and the slow advance of agricultural techniques increased food production and resulted, by the late seventeenth century, in falling food prices and a rise in the demand for non-agricultural goods. Transport improvements extended market areas and the restless exploitation of market opportunities by entrepreneurs simultaneously raised the level of technology and improved economic organization. Nevertheless, the fact remains that English economic history before 1750 is in a large measure the story of economic stagnation.

2

The Environment of Change

The growth of production in pre-industrial England was limited by the extent of the market. There were, nevertheless, advances in all branches of the economy. Some historians, indeed, surveying the progress made in agriculture, industry and commerce between the early sixteenth and early eighteenth centuries, have described it as revolutionary. But unlike the industrial revolution of the eighteenth century, developments in production methods and forms of organization in earlier centuries did not radically transform the structure of the economy. Such economic progress as occurred in pre-industrial England was brought about by entrepreneurs exploiting new patterns of demand and seeking fresh market opportunities. On the whole, their efforts were aided by favourable resource endowments, a relatively secure political framework and a sympathetic social structure. It is these non-economic influences on economic development that form the subject of the present chapter. The achievements themselves will be reviewed in chapters that follow.

Geography and Resources

England was well endowed by nature for economic development. Tudor and Stuart Englishmen believed their homeland to be little inferior to the Garden of Eden. One enthusiast writing in the mid-sixteenth century described the country as 'invironed with the occian seas full of havyns, poortes, and crekes, farre excedying

France', and with 'dyvers goodly rivers'. He noted the 'ryches of bestiall in England ... oxen, kyne, swinne, goates and such other; also we have shepe berying the fynest wool of the worlde ...; and the ryches under the earth ..., many metals, coal, slate and stone'. A century later, Henry Belasyse was more concise: 'England is famous for mountains, bridges, fountains, churches, women and woll.' The women were possibly a distraction to economic progress, being 'by the consent of mankinde held to be the fairest in Europe'; so fair, indeed, that the only English Pope urged that they 'should not be permitted to goe in pilgramage to Rome, lest their beauty might be a tumbling block to others vertu'. Belasyse also had an eye for other beauties as well as a taste for the mixed metaphor:

> whole mountains of fish in our seas; whole clouds of birds in our skyes; whole plaines covered with beeves and cattle; whole regions swarming with sheep; whole provinces cladd with forests and parks; whole forests abounding in game for our gentry; and whole mines of fewell growing underground for the commodity of the poor.... the ayre of England is so temperate, that its neither so hott nor so cold as it is in France ... the neighbourhood of the sea affording cooleings in the summer, and a most warme ayre in winter, which makes our noses dropp but not dropp off as in Muscovie.[1]

Climate exercised a major influence on economic activity in pre-industrial England, affecting the state of the grain harvest, the growth of grass – and hence the size of the livestock population – the supply of wool, hides, tallow, meat and milk, the conditions of roads and the levels of rivers on which industrial power and transport depended. In spite of almost annual meteorological disasters recorded with relish by so many contemporaries, Belasyse's benign views were generally well-founded. Given proper respect, the weather provided good conditions for temperate agriculture. Most

[1] *Tudor Economic Documents*, ed. R. H. Tawney and E. Power, 1924, III, pp. 1–11; H. B[elasyse], *An English Traveler's First Curiosity: or the Knowledge of his owne Countrey*, 1657, in *Hist. Mss. Comm., Various Collections*, II, 1903, pp. 193–4.

regions of England were suitable for crops and animals, and woodlands provided generally adequate supplies of timber, fuel and bark. Of minerals, coal was abundant, and supplies of iron ore and non-ferrous ores sufficient. Only native sources of gold and silver were deficient: hence the importance of overseas trade in acquiring such precious commodities.

Geographically, England was well situated to take part in international trade. In the early sixteenth century she was on the periphery of European trade, but the establishment of European settlements in the New World and the shift of political power and wealth away from the Mediterranean to western Europe placed England at the geographical centre of world trade by the mid-seventeenth century. Her island situation made internal transport relatively easy compared with continental Europe. Rivers were open to anyone who cared to use them and the coast bustled with ports. None of these natural advantages were new in the sixteenth and seventeenth centuries, but their potential was increasingly exploited.

The Growth of Population

Population was the most important of England's resources and variations in its rate of increase were a major influence on the level of economic activity. Table 1 summarizes various estimates that have been made of population in England and Wales between 1500 and 1750. They are not strictly comparable and they vary considerably in quality, but the main features of population history are clear enough. Population doubled between the early sixteenth and early eighteenth centuries, with much of the increase occurring before 1650. Changes in the size of population over shorter periods are less easy to distinguish and regional differences in population growth are difficult to trace. Even more obscure in the present state of demographic studies are the mechanisms by which population increased, for we know very little about the behaviour of fertility and mortality rates in pre-industrial England and the factors influencing them.

When we consider the pattern of population growth more closely, there appears to have been a substantial increase in the first half of the sixteenth century. Most historians believe that the population of England and Wales was between 2.5 million and 3.0 millions

TABLE 1   *Estimates of population, 1480–1750*

Year	England	England and Wales	Source
1480s	2·1m.	—	Cornwall
1500	—	2·5 – 3·0m.	Tucker
1522–5	2·3m.	—	Cornwall
1545	2·8m.	—	Cornwall
1545	—	3·5m.	Tucker, after Russell
1570	2·8m.	3·5m.	*See text*
1603	3·75m.	—	Cornwall
1603	—	4·1m.	Tucker, after Russell
1650	—	5·5m.	Wrigley
1695	—	5·2 – 5·5m.	Glass, after Gregory King
1700	—	5·8m.	Griffith
1710	—	6·01m.	Griffith
1720	—	6·05m.	Griffith
1730	—	6·01m.	Griffith
1740	—	6·01m.	Griffith
1750	—	6·25m.	Griffith

REFERENCES

Julian Cornwall: 'English Population in the Early Sixteenth Century', *Econ. Hist. Rev.*, 2nd ser., vol. XXIII, April 1970, pp. 32–44.
G. S. L. Tucker: 'English Pre-Industrial Population Trends', *Econ. Hist. Rev.*, 2nd ser., vol. XVI, Dec. 1963, pp. 205–8.
J. C. Russell: *British Medieval Population*, 1948.
E. A. Wrigley: 'A Simple Model of London's Importance in Changing English Society and Economy, 1650–1750', *Past and Present*, no. 37, 1967, pp. 48–9, 56.
D. V. Glass: 'Gregory King's Estimate of the Population of England and Wales, 1695', *Population Studies*, vol. III, 1948–9, p. 358.
G. T. Griffith: *Population Problems in the Age of Malthus*, 1926.

in 1500, probably nearer the higher figure than the lower. Professor J. C. Russell has put the population in 1545 at about 3.5 millions although his estimates are not accepted by all historians. Dr Cornwall has recently reckoned that the population for England alone was substantially smaller; but whether we prefer the estimates of Professor Russell or Dr Cornwall we are left with the likelihood that the population increased by roughly three-quarters of a million between the end of the fifteenth and the middle of the sixteenth centuries. This was the first sustained increase since the Black Death; but the growth seems to have outstripped the capacity of agriculture to increase production in pace with the increased demand for food that it generated and by the 1550s there were distinct signs of over-population. Food prices were very high in the first half of the decade and in the second half a severe epidemic of influenza ravaged a population weakened by under-nourishment. The death rate soared high above the birth rate and the population declined – possibly by as much as 20 per cent in some districts.

The setback of the 1550s proved temporary and growth was resumed in the 1560s, although the population was probably no larger by 1570 than it had been in 1545. During the final three decades of the sixteenth century there was a rapid increase in population. On Professor Russell's calculations population in England and Wales went up by about 600,000 and Dr Cornwall's estimates for England alone imply an even greater increase. Again growth was checked during the 1580s and 1590s by high food prices and epidemics; but they caused no more than a falter in the rate of increase and by the mid-seventeenth century the population of England and Wales may have exceeded 5 millions. Dr Wrigley assumes a population of 5.5 million for 1650, a figure that appears high in the light of Gregory King's widely accepted estimate for 1695. But studies of parish registers from many parts of the country leave no doubt that there was a substantial increase in population in the late sixteenth and early seventeenth centuries at a rate comparable with the early decades of the industrial revolution.

Sometime during the second quarter of the seventeenth century the rate of growth of population in England slackened and remained sluggish until the end of the century, although there were marked contrasts between one region and another. An extreme case is probably that of the Devonshire village of Colyton where the number of burials recorded in the parish registers rose above baptisms in the 1640s and remained higher for most of the next century. The registers of many parishes in the north and north-west of England also record persistent surpluses of burials over baptisms, or only very small excesses of births over deaths, in the second half of the seventeenth century, whereas earlier in the century there had been an ample balance in the other direction. On the other hand, population growth in the Midlands recovered its old momentum in the late seventeenth century. After 1670, for example, the population of the village of Wigston Magna in Leicestershire grew rapidly after stagnating from about 1620. Wigston seems to have been typical of many industrializing areas in the Midlands in the late seventeenth and early eighteenth centuries, including the towns of Birmingham and Nottingham and the industrial villages of the east and west Midlands. There was probably also a high rate of growth in the Home Counties where much of the increase was fed into London, the population of which increased by more than 250,000 between 1650 and 1750. After 1720 population growth throughout England slackened once more. The 1730s and 1740s were the last years of 'massacre by epidemics' when infectious diseases such as smallpox and influenza caused heavy mortality. Growth was resumed after 1740 and continued into a new phase of population history coinciding with the industrial revolution.

Population increase in pre-industrial England depended on the excess of births over deaths. Birth and death rates were both high by the standards of modern western communities. In the early eighteenth century the birth rate was normally around 35 per 1,000 and the death rate a little below 30 per 1,000 per annum, but both varied considerably in the short run. The death rate was more volatile than the birth rate. In years of harvest failure or epidemic it might rise to twice the normal level or even higher. Years of high mortality were a recurrent feature of all communities in pre-industrial England. They often occurred when the price of grain was high and people were hungry; and sometimes they were the result of epidemics of plague, influenza, small-pox, typhus or dysentery. When harvest failures and epidemics coincided the result was disastrous. But although the virulence of epidemics was heightened by food shortages, their onset was often independent of economic conditions. For example, the heavy mortalities of the 1730s occurred in a period of generally good harvests. Some of the deaths occurring in bad years anticipated those of later years, and periods of high mortality, therefore, were usually followed by years in which the number of deaths was lower than average.

Short-term variations in birth rates were connected with changes in the death rate. During periods of high mortality the number of marriages might fall, compared with the number in healthier periods, because of the death of prospective partners, or because hard times caused a postponement of marriages, thus bringing about a reduction in the number of conceptions. But in subsequent years postponed marriages were contracted. Perhaps even more important, the scarcity of tenants for holdings, and labour for industrial employment following a period of heavy mortality, created conditions favourable to early marriages and an increased number of births.

In addition to short-term fluctuations, there were also long-term changes in mortality and fertility rates. Dr Wrigley's study of the Devonshire village of Colyton suggests that the expectation of life was higher before 1625 than afterwards, possibly because the incidence of epidemic diseases was lower in the sixteenth and early seventeenth centuries. It is not clear whether the higher mortality at Colyton in the later seventeenth century was repeated in other English parishes, but it is consistent with the reduced rate of population growth found elsewhere. The Colyton study also suggests that there were long-term changes in fertility. From the 1640s women were marrying later and, once married, having fewer children than their predecessors had done in the century before. This situation persisted until the early decades of the eighteenth century. A rise in the age of marriage would itself be sufficient to reduce the number of children born to a marriage, but there is evidence that the inhabitants of Colyton deliberately limited the number of conceptions within their marriages in the second half of the seventeenth and the early eighteenth centuries. Once again, we do not know whether the situation at Colyton was paralleled elsewhere, but 'it is possible that many parishes in England conformed roughly to the Colyton pattern in the sixteenth and seventeenth centuries'.[1] Nor do we know why fertility was deliberately restricted from the mid-seventeenth century; but possibly the vigorous growth of population in the late sixteenth and early seventeenth centuries created a threat to living standards by the 1640s which caused individuals to reduce their rate of increase. If so, a revealing light is thrown on the economic attitudes of people in pre-industrial England, for it suggests that they were not content to allow their levels of living to sink to subsistence levels and were prepared to forgo children in the interest of higher material standards.

Much yet remains to be learnt of the connection between population change and economic development in pre-industrial England. We have already touched on some of the short-run relationships. A bad harvest could produce high mortality and a fall in marriages and fertility, followed in the next period by low mortality, increasing marriages and rising fertility. Increasing numbers might bring about a fall in incomes per head, thus again establishing conditions for a rise in mortality. In the long-run a growing population was the basis of an expanding market for agricultural goods. A mere increase in numbers might not have produced this result: it might merely create more peasant cultivators supplying their own food. But in England rising population created an ever-growing class of landless labourers who were compelled to buy their food. The stimulus thus given to agricultural production varied in its impact from commodity to commodity and also from time to time. Before 1650 when population growth was accompanied by falling real incomes for many people, the increase in demand was chiefly for basic foodstuffs. But after 1650 the rate of population

[1] E. A. Wrigley, *Population in History*, 1969, p. 89.

growth was slower and real incomes were rising among the wage-earning classes, leading to a rising demand for meat and dairy produce, fruit and vegetables. The growth of population also helped to increase the demand for essential manufactured commodities such as clothing and household goods.

The extension of output necessary to meet increasing demand required the employment of more factors of production or the more efficient use of existing ones. Since most production was labour-intensive, output was readily increased by putting more hands to work. Until the late seventeenth century this caused no great difficulty. Not only was population rising, thus increasing the total supply of labour, but there was a good deal of surplus labour in agriculture which could be absorbed, for example, by rural industry. Thus the expansion of production caused little increase in wage rates. Nor was output in the agricultural sector depressed by the movement of labour out of agriculture into industrial production since the value of the marginal product of under-employed agricultural labour was very low.

Population growth also increased the need for houses and social overhead capital. Housebuilding, road construction, river improvements and the extension of ports and harbours were labour-intensive activities which were able to recruit under-employed labour from agriculture and the additional population provided by natural increase. In the long-run, therefore, the growth of population added to the stock of capital in the community, although there is no certainty that stocks increased per head of population. For houses, in fact, the evidence points the other way. By the late sixteenth or early seventeenth century in the large towns and in some country regions the existing supply of dwellings was insufficient for the needs of the growing population. Nevertheless, some growth of capital stock in the economy was possible without undue pressure on consumption and was an important element in helping to raise the productivity of other factors of production.

The increase in economic activity stimulated by population growth suggests that there was a good deal of mobility of labour both between occupations and from one region to another. There was considerable migration from the surrounding countryside to the town. During the second half of the seventeenth century, for example, newcomers were arriving in London possibly at the rate of at least 8,000 a year, compelled to leave their country homes by shortage of land or employment and attracted by the great variety of legitimate and criminal occupations available in the capital. Immigration also made a significant contribution to the doubling of population in Worcester between 1540 and 1640 and to the growth of Wigston Magna in the late sixteenth and the late seventeenth centuries. In Nottingham, migration was responsible for much of the city's growth in the late seventeenth century, and for more than 90 per cent of the population increase in the first forty years of the eighteenth century. Even within rural areas there was a considerable turn-over of population. For example, 153 of the 401 people who lived in the Nottinghamshire village of Clayworth in 1676 had moved away ten years later and had been replaced by others so that the total population remained almost unchanged.

Much of the flow of population to towns was made up of young men going to take up apprenticeships and unskilled labour seeking work; and in rural areas there was a good deal of coming and going as servants changed their place of employment. There was also a movement of people from areas where land was scarce to regions where it was still possible to find a piece of common land or waste on which to eke out a living, and into areas possessing rural industry. Many migrants into the east Midlands at the turn of the seventeenth and eighteenth centuries, for example, were attracted by the opportunities of working in the expanding industry of framework-knitting. No doubt there were non-economic reasons why some men left their native villages while other families remained rooted to the same place for generations. But the widespread nature of labour mobility in pre-industrial England strongly suggests that many people desired to better their living standards.

The Long-term Movement of Prices

Running more or less parallel to secular population trends and

almost certainly connected with them were long-term price movements, which many historians have treated as an exogenous influence on economic development in the sixteenth and seventeenth
centuries. From the beginning of the sixteenth to the middle of the
seventeenth century food prices in England rose approximately
seven times and prices of a selection of industrial products increased
three-fold. These years witnessed the most sustained inflationary
period between the thirteenth and nineteenth century although the
rate of inflation was mild by twentieth century standards. From the
mid-seventeenth to the mid-eighteenth century, by contrast there
was no marked upward trend in prices.

The rise in prices before 1650 has frequently been attributed to
changes in the supply of money resulting from an inflow of bullion
into western Europe from Spanish-America. The argument was
advanced most strongly by Professor E. J. Hamilton who attempted to establish a direct correlation between the import of
Spanish-American treasure and increases in European prices. He
buttressed his case by use of the quantity theory of money which, in
its simplest form, states that changes in the price level are directly
proportional to changes in the quantity of money in circulation.
The thesis appeared to be well documented and provided a general
explanation of inflation that was a European and not merely an
English experience, and was therefore widely accepted.

Unfortunately Professor Hamilton's hypothesis was a good deal
less sound than it first appeared. Prices were influenced by many
factors besides the supply of money, and particularly by variations
in the level of output and demand. Bullion from Spanish-America
added to an already existing stock of coins and to an elusive and
immeasurable volume of credit. There were also additions to the
coinage from the output of European silver mines and the melting
down of plate. It is obviously unrealistic, therefore, to relate changes
in the price level only or even mainly to the supply of coin. There is
a special problem with England in that prices began to rise before
imports of Spanish-American silver into the country became significant.

The most serious weakness of the monetary explanation of the so-called price revolution is that it does not explain why food prices rose faster than industrial prices. This fact suggests that the underlying cause of inflation was a rate of increase of population faster than the rate of increase of farm output. From time to time this long-term tendency was aggravated by harvest failures (for example, in the early 1550s, 1590s, and 1630s); and the debasement of the coinage during the 1540s added a further twist to the inflationary spiral. At other times the price rise was alleviated by good harvests or a temporary check to the growth of population, as occurred for example at the end of the 1550s. But it was not until the second half of the seventeenth century when there was a slower rate of population growth and, possibly, more elastic supply conditions in agriculture, that food prices ceased to rise in the long-term. Industrial prices were less affected by secular population trends, partly because supply conditions were probably more elastic than in farming, but more likely because the inflation of food prices eroded the incomes of many sections of the community, thus depressing the growth of demand for industrial goods.

Monetary explanations of the price revolution have often been extended to a second stage which suggests that inflation stimulated economic growth. It is argued that prices rose faster than both wages and rents, which were the main costs of production, causing profits to rise, thus providing the incentive for new enterprise and funds to finance it. As with the first part of the monetary argument, the second stage is also suspect. For one thing, it is inconsistent with the view that relates changes in the price level to changes in the supply of money, for this relationship holds only by assuming that there are no changes in the velocity of circulation (the rate at which money changes hands) and in the number of transactions occurring in an economy. Yet an increase in enterprise (or 'rise of capitalism' in Professor Hamilton's phrase) necessarily involves an increasing number of transactions. The argument is also suspect on evidential grounds. Although wages lagged behind prices, it is extremely doubtful whether rents did so in general. It is clear, however, that non-farm prices rose less rapidly than food prices. If any group enjoyed the benefits of profit inflation, therefore, it was composed of farmers who held their land on freehold or copyhold with fixed outgoings and who received prices for their products that were rising faster than the wages they paid and the prices of manufactured goods they bought. Whether they used their increasing incomes to finance new enterprises, to improve their standard of living, to work less hard, or to do all three, depended on their attitudes to work and wealth.

It is more realistic to attribute inflation before 1650 to the interaction of long-term shifts in demand and supply, although monetary factors were not entirely insignificant. Without additions to Europe's stocks of monetary metals economic progress might have been hindered by an inadequate supply of coin. But secular changes in price levels were not the product of forces external to the English economy and prices were not an independent cause of economic change. Inflation petered out in the mid-seventeenth century when supplies of silver from Spanish-America were dwindling. But it was also a time when population growth in England began to slacken. From the 1660s the long-term trend of grain prices was downwards, reflecting both increased agricultural capacity and a slower rate of growth of demand for food. Possibly the relative lack of new silver exercised a deflationary influence, although the development of paper money and the more extensive use of credit supplemented the supply of precious metals. In the main, however, price movements after 1650 were the product of market changes rather than of purely monetary influences.

The Political and Social Framework

Pre-industrial England possessed a political and social structure favourable to economic change. As we discussed in the previous chapter, the economy before 1750 was organized around the market which required a stable political climate for its effective operation. Through luck or policy foreign invasion was avoided; there were sporadic internal civil commotions in the sixteenth century, but they probably did less harm to the economic life than the ravages of epidemics or harvest failures. The effects of the Civil War were serious but surprisingly difficult to assess. The economy was depressed for much of the 1640s and 1650s, but it is doubtful whether the Civil War brought about any fundamental change in economic development. Indirectly it was important since it asserted the authority of parliament in the government of the country. Parliament was undemocratic but it represented the interests of landowners and merchants who influenced economic legislation. In 1651 the Venetian ambassador in London noted that English trade 'has made great strides for some time past, and is now improved by the protection it receives from Parliament, the government of the commonwealth and that of its trade being exercised by the same individuals'.[1] The observation was, if anything, even more true by the end of the century by which time parliament had gained control of public finance and evolved a system of taxation that rested lightly on property and profits. Even though parliament lacked a unanimous voice on economic questions, its view could not be ignored on matters affecting the economic life of the country.

In general the English social system permitted the economically successful to rise to the top and so did not act as a barrier to development. The various ranks of society acted as a ladder on which men could ascend and descend and not as a means of keeping them immutably in their place. The fundamental distinction in status lay between the gentry and the non-gentry. The gentlemen were a small group, comprising less than a twentieth of the entire population but possessing practically all the political power and social prestige. The most elevated of the gentry were the nobility. There were fewer than a hundred noble families in the late sixteenth century and no more than two hundred a century later. Below these were baronets, knights and esquires who formed a 'county élite'. In the lowest ranks were several thousand 'parish gentry' with no title other than that of 'gent' but who shared a common bond with all gentlemen in being accepted by society as gentry and living chiefly on the rents from their estates.

The bulk of the population lacked gentle status. The most respected were yeomen and tenant farmers, with their urban

[1] *Cal. S. P. Venetian*, 1647–52, p. 188.

equivalents, the artisans, shopkeepers and small traders. They were bound together by the possession of property, either owned or rented, or of goods used in trade. Beneath these were rural and urban labourers, a growing class in pre-industrial England, whose principal asset was the labour they offered on the market. At the base of society were dependants. They consisted of the very old and very young, the sick and maimed, the widowed and unemployed, all of whom depended on public or private charity for their livelihoods; and also apprentices and living-in servants who lived in their masters' households, and depended on them for their keep, without being fully exposed to the winds of the labour market.

Social status depended ultimately on the possession of wealth, some forms being more acceptable than others. The peerage possessed titles granted to them by the sovereign or inherited from their fathers and the non-titular gentry technically had the right to bear a coat of arms. But as far as society was concerned the true test was the ability, in a famous phrase, to 'bear the port, charge and countenance of a gentleman'. In practice this required the ownership of estates large enough to provide an income from rents sufficient to cover the expenses of living and behaving like gentlemen. Forms of wealth other than land did not fit easily into conventional attitudes and the proper rank of merchants, lawyers and similar professional men was a puzzle to pre-industrial society. As late as 1669 it was argued that 'Tradesmen in all Ages and Nations have been reputed ignoble',[1] but in practice merchants and others were accepted as gentlemen when they translated their profits into acres in the countryside.

Crossing the great divide between gentry and non-gentry was not easy but it was not impossible. Merchants in overseas trade were more likely to make the transition than most since their opportunities for accumulating wealth were great. At all times successful traders bought land and the tendency was particularly marked in the late seventeenth and early eighteenth centuries when rich merchants purchased estates from gentlemen hard-pressed by rising costs of ownership. Occasionally a successful industrialist, such as

[1] Quoted by L. Stone, *The Crisis of the Aristocracy, 1558-1641*, 1965, p. 40.

Sir Ambrose Crowley in the early eighteenth century, broke into society. It was not too unusual, either, for the sons of successful artisans or farmers to become gentlemen. Thus, Robert Brerewood, an illiterate but successful glover in Chester at the end of the sixteenth century, sent a son to Oxford and saw him become professor of astronomy at Gresham College, and, had he lived long enough, would have seen his grandson read for the law, receive a knighthood and become a judge. Earlier in the sixteenth century, the father of Bishop Latimer had been a Leicestershire tenant farmer. Not everyone aspired to be gentlemen: 'it is better to be the head of the yeomanry than the tail of the gentry.' But for those who did, the path was not completely blocked.

There were also movements in the other direction. Among the lower orders younger sons of owner-occupiers sometimes descended to the ranks of landless labourers or industrial wage-earners when it was impossible or impractical to sub-divide the family farm among all the children; and some tenants suffered the same fate through eviction. Among the nobility in the sixteenth and early seventeenth centuries a few land-owners were overtaken by inflation and excessive expenditure and were forced to sell all or part of their estates — in the process providing the means for others to rise. Later in the seventeenth century rising costs of land-ownership spelt downfall for some small land-owners. The gentry were often victims of their own fertility, producing children beyond the capacity of the family estate to support them. The custom of primogeniture was developed to preserve the estate for the eldest son but it placed younger sons in danger of tumbling down the social ladder. If their elder brothers would not provide for them they had to seek their livings by serving at court or in the professions, or even by becoming apprenticed to tradesmen.

> . . . nothing argues the ill breeding of our gentlemen so much as the low employment they betake themselves to as not knowing themselves fitt for higher ones. To be apprenticed in a shop, sitt bare head, sweep the shop and streets is the life of thousands. To serve noblemen in most unnoble offices, to pull off their boots,

brush their cloathes, waite at table with a trencher in their hand, ride with a cloakbag behinde them, dine and sup with footmen and groomes, is the ordinary course of Gentlemen in England, whilst in other countreys they goe to the warres and scorne to sit in a shop or wate upon any one.[1]

But whatever social stigma attached to such sorry decline, it was good for economic progress. Not that younger sons brought special talents or substantial fortunes into business; but they provided a link between the gentry and ruling classes, and commerce and industry. Sweeping with the same broom as sons of farmers or artisans, younger sons came to share their outlook on life. If they wished to re-establish themselves in the ranks of the gentry, a swift route back was to be successful in business and purchase an estate or, quicker still, contract a judicious marriage with the widow or daughter of a wealthy merchant. Many gentry families were connected by marriage with mercantile families in the towns. These relationships did much to create sympathetic attitudes towards business in the minds of those possessing political power which contrasted sharply with the situation in seventeenth-century France. There, society held that:

> The *raison d'être* of the merchant was the acquisition of material wealth, his dominant motive personal gain. For his base and calculating virtues a fortune was ample recompense. Social prestige, on the other hand, should be preserved for those who displayed valour or piety, and who devoted themselves without remuneration or distraction to serve the community on the battlefield or in the chancel.

Attempts by French ministers in the seventeenth century to break down these attitudes failed and they remained an 'important obstacle to French commercial expansion'.[2]

The English social system before 1750 possessed one inbuilt feature

[1] H. Belasyse, *op. cit.*, p. 204.

[2] R. B. Grassby, 'Social Status and Commercial Enterprise under Louis xiv', *Econ. Hist. Rev.* 2nd ser., vol. xiii, 1960, pp. 19–20.

that might conceivably have acted as an impediment to economic progress. This was the stress placed on land as a source of wealth and badge of prestige which tended to direct capital away from commerce and industry into the purchase of estates. Since land was socially acceptable it was good security for loans and the ease with which money could be raised on land may have forced up the rate of interest on borrowing for other purposes. It is difficult to measure the importance of the obsession with land as a symbol of status. Mercantile wealth certainly flowed into land-ownership, but merchants presumably brought the methods of the counting house to the management of their newly acquired estates, to the benefit of the latter. Money borrowed on the security of land in the late sixteenth and early seventeenth centuries was sometimes used to finance a frenzy of conspicuous consumption in which case it represented a diversion of investment funds away from more productive uses. But landlords also borrowed in order to improve their estates. Insofar as loans were cheaper on security of land than other forms of collateral, the lower rate of interest reflected the lower risks of investment in land and the solid economic and social advantages it afforded.

But if the preoccupation with land was an obstacle to economic progress – and it is not clear that it was – in one other respect the structure of society in pre-industrial England was very well suited to economic development. In marked contrast to many under-developed societies today, Englishmen of all ranks usually lived in conjugal family units made up of parents and unmarried children, and not in extended families composed of several generations and including an ever-widening circle of hazily defined relations. Too little is known of this aspect of pre-industrial society to allow any statement about its origins; but it had important demographic and economic implications. In the first place, marriage meant the creation of a new household. Married children did not normally live with their parents except when an aged or widowed mother or father was taken into the home. In order to set up house there had to be a farm available or industrial or commercial work that would provide an income. In this way there was a close connection between the marriage rate and economic conditions.[1] Secondly, the family was an economic unit as well as a social institution, its members working on the family farm or in the family workshop, or employed in some kind of putting-out industry. Immediate family labour was sometimes supplemented by journeymen, labourers, apprentices and servants living in as part of the family. These people formed an extension of the conjugal family, but there were usually only one or two of them, and in many households none at all. Thirdly, the restricted family was less likely to consume all it produced than the extended family of present-day under-developed society. Whatever the social benefits of the extended family, it tends to prevent the accumulation of surpluses for the market and inhibits the accumulation of capital since all the family's resources go on supporting an army of relations, many of whom contribute nothing to production. In sixteenth and seventeenth century England the conjugal family forced even near relations into the world to earn their livings. No doubt this helped to swell the great numbers of poor and destitute relying on public charity who were a feature of the age, but it also stimulated the creation of a mobile labour force and enlarged the supply of entrepreneurial talent. Even more important for economic progress, the restricted family was able to produce marketable surpluses. It was an essential element in the growth of a market economy.

Attitudes towards Economic Development

Implicit throughout this chapter has been the assumption that attitudes in pre-industrial England were favourable to economic development. As Professor Fisher has written: 'The late sixteenth and early seventeenth centuries constitute perhaps the last period in English history in which economic appetites were remarkably vigorous but in which economic expansion was still slow.'[2] This vigour, it is often suggested, was increased by the Protestant Re-

[1] See above p. 29.
[2] F. J. Fisher, 'Tawney's Century', in *Essays in the Economic and Social History of Tudor and Stuart England*, ed. F. J. Fisher, 1961, p. 2.

41

formation. According to the German scholar, Max Weber, the 'spirit of capitalism', which he defined as the 'pursuit of profit, and forever renewed profit, by means of rational, capitalistic enterprise', was stimulated by the Protestant ethic in a way that it was not by Catholic economic teaching with its condemnation of profit-making. At the heart of the Protestant ethic was the doctrine of the calling which regarded every-day work, however menial, as a task appointed by God. Since work was divinely ordained, it had to be done successfully for the glorification of God and as a way to salvation. From here it was a short step to believing that the rewards for work well done – treasures on earth – were the outward and visible sign of treasures in heaven.

The Weber thesis has been extensively criticized. It is doubtful whether there was any sharp dichotomy between Catholic and Protestant economic teaching: Luther at least, was an arch-conservative in such matters, condemning money-making more forcefully than all the fathers of the medieval church. Neither does the historical record demonstrate that economic development was more rapid in Protestant than Catholic countries. Calvinistic Scotland, for example, lagged far behind Catholic Flanders. And, 'if by the capitalistic spirit is meant the temper which is prepared to sacrifice all moral scruples to the pursuit of profit, it had been only too familiar to the saints and sages of the Middle Ages.'[1] Yet the critics sometimes overlooked the fact that Weber claimed only that Protestant teaching provided a climate of thought in which capitalistic attitudes could flourish. 'There is nothing in protestantism', Christopher Hill has written, 'which leads automatically to capitalism ...' but, 'the protestant revolt melted down the iron ideological framework of the institutional church which held society h its ancient mould. Where capitalism already existed, it had henceforth freer scope.'[2] During the sixteenth and seventeenth centuries religious beliefs in England evolved slowly from a general suspicion of economic endeavour to a position where they

[1] R. F. Tawney, *Religion and the Rise of Capitalism*, Penguin ed., 1938, p. 93.
[2] Christopher Hill, 'Protestantism and Capitalism', in *Essays in the Economic and Social History of Tudor and Stuart England*, p. 36.

were either indifferent to or sometimes sympathetic with the desire to make money.

For the mass of the population the views of the institutional church on money matters were probably less important than the harsh realities of economic conditions which condemned all but a few to a life of unremitting toil. This is perhaps why many contemporaries believed that the poor were more inclined to idleness than profit-maximization, for when life was hard leisure was a prized possession. Sir William Petty voiced a common complaint when he wrote in the 1670s:

> It is observed by Clothiers and others, who employ great numbers of poor people, that when corn is extremely plentiful, that the labour of the poor is proportionately dear: and scarce to be had at all (so licentious are they who labour only to eat, or rather to drink).[1]

This view implies a high leisure preference and stereotyped consumption patterns which are familiar features of backward economies today, creating formidable barriers to economic development. Yet we may wonder whether they were such important obstacles to progress in pre-industrial England. Even in present-day underdeveloped countries attitudes to consumption, leisure and work can change quite quickly as economic opportunities become available. In England many forces broke down traditional attitudes to work and leisure. The hierarchical structure of society ensured that the lower ranks aspired to match the consumption habits of their social superiors. There were many complaints in the sixteenth, seventeenth and eighteenth centuries that the poor were attempting to ape their betters, not at all consistent with other observations implying static demands. Traditional habits of work and consumption were particularly liable to be cast aside in the cities where foreign goods enticed consumers, rich merchants and gentlemen set new fashions, and foreigners behaved in outlandish ways. London was especially important in this respect since so many

[1] Sir William Petty, *Political Arithmetic* (1690), in *The Economic Writings of Sir William Petty*, ed. C. H. Hull, 1899, vol. I, p. 274.

43

people came to the capital to be exposed to new goods that created new wants. Even when Petty wrote, other economic writers were wondering whether men did not respond to high wages by working more in order to raise their standards of living. The attitudes of people at the base of the social pyramid, who provided the bulk of the labour necessary in what was essentially a labour-intensive economy, were, it may be thought, coloured by the absence or presence of economic opportunities, and did not seriously retard the pace of economic development. In attitudes, as in other matters, the environment for economic progress in pre-industrial England was healthy.

3

Agriculture

The Demand for Agricultural Products

Before 1750 agriculture provided virtually all the food and drink consumed by Englishmen and the bulk of the raw materials used in industry. The demand for agricultural commodities provided farmers in pre-industrial England with opportunities of producing for the market which attracted more and more of them during the period. There were always those who produced crops only for household consumption; but the subsistence sector did not dominate agriculture and few farmers were completely divorced from the market, if only because of the need to pay rent which compelled the cultivation of cash crops. Naturally, all farmers produced certain commodities intended mainly for consumption on the farm. In grazing areas where livestock and livestock products were produced for sale, grain was grown for domestic use. Elsewhere arable products were cultivated for the market and a cow or two kept to supply the farmer with butter and milk. The essentially commercial nature of English agriculture between 1500 and 1750 contrasts sharply with the subsistence farming widespread in many parts of Africa and Asia until recent times.

Grain was the most important agricultural commodity produced for the market in pre-industrial England, and among the grains barley was the most important. It was hardier than wheat and suited to a wider range of soils and climatic conditions. It served as the bread-corn of the poor and as fodder for animals; but its main use was in brewing and distilling. Barley accounted for roughly half the grain traded in public markets between 1500 and 1640, and malt made from barley for another third. Not until well into the eighteenth century was it displaced from its supremacy by wheat. Oats were probably grown more extensively than wheat before the eighteenth century. They did well on the cold, wet soils of the north where they were used for oatcakes and bread, and also for malting. In the south they were fed to animals. Rye was also grown on poor soils, either by itself or sown with wheat as 'maslin' for human and animal consumption. Wheat occupied only a small part of the sown area of many regions before 1700, but it was a valuable source of income for many farmers because of the relatively high price it commanded.

Livestock was reared for the market in breeding regions of the country, while livestock products – meat, milk and butter – were major sources of farm incomes, their combined value possibly exceeding the value of corn in the late seventeenth century. The demand for these commodities was more elastic than for grain so they became more important in the late seventeenth century when real incomes were rising. Animal by-products, too, were an extremely important source of revenue. Wool had been a cash crop for centuries. At the end of the seventeenth century the value of wool production on the market may have been in the region of £2 million a year, which was roughly the same as the value of wheat; but wool should not be allowed to obscure the importance of other by-products. The value of hides and skins used by English leather manufacturers was between £500,000 and £600,000 a year in the 1720s. Tallow was sold to soap and candle manufacturers, hair was used by plasterers and painters, and bones were turned into glue. One animal product, manure, was not usually produced for sale, but to many farmers it was the most important by-product of all.

All regions had their own specialities. Casual sales of fallen timber provided a little income nearly everywhere, even when arable farming predominated, and in wooded districts fuel, building timber, and bark were important earners of income. Other local specialities included textile materials such as flax, hemp, woad, weld, madder, saffron and teasels, fruit and vegetables for the table, hops, poultry and rabbits. In addition all farmers grew grasses, fodder and forage crops, not for sale, but for feeding to animals.

Between 1500 and 1750 the home demand for agricultural goods grew. The basis of this increase was the growth of population which was accompanied by urbanization, and the enlargement of a wage-earning class obliged to buy its food requirements on the market. London was the most spectacular example of urban growth, its population rising from 50,000 or 60,000 in 1500 to 675,000 in 1750, when it was the largest city in Europe. Its demand for food stretched in all directions. Inevitably the Home Counties were the main source of supply, particularly for perishable goods such as fruit and vegetables, milk and butter, veal, lamb, beef, bacon, pork and poultry. But as the population of the capital grew its demands were felt in more distant parts of the country. Yet London was unique only in the absolute size of its increase. Birmingham grew proportionately even more from less than 2,000 in the mid-sixteenth century to between 30,000 and 50,000 two centuries later. The growth of Birmingham was particularly pronounced in the late seventeenth and early eighteenth centuries when other non-corporate towns such as Manchester and Liverpool were also expanding quickly. But the old-established towns also grew more rapidly than the population as a whole. Between the mid-sixteenth and mid-seventeenth century several towns in the western part of the country including Worcester, Exeter, Tiverton and Plymouth all doubled in size. The population of Nottingham doubled between 1660 and 1740 and Bristol grew from 50,000 to 100,000 in the first half of the eighteenth century. Even Norwich, once the second city in England, increased in size four and a half times, from 12,000 to 56,000 between the early sixteenth and the mid-eighteenth century.

Probably 50 per cent or more of the population of towns were wage-earners in the early sixteenth century and were dependent on the market for their food. In rural areas, too, there were many people who possessed little or no land. Between one quarter and one-third of the rural population were wage-earners in the late sixteenth and early seventeenth centuries and the proportion possibly approached one-half by the end of the seventeenth century. Many of them worked as farm labourers; others were employed in rural industry. Either way, they were unable to grow their own food and so were obliged to buy what they needed.

The growth of a class of food consumers has to be considered in conjunction with changes in the levels of individual purchasing power. Before 1650 population grew more quickly than agricultural production with the result that food prices rose faster than wages. Thus the growth of a wage-earning (and hence food-purchasing) class did not produce a proportionate increase in the demand for food. Even so, food consumption per head probably fell to a smaller extent than the fall in real incomes, since the demand for basic food tends to be income-inelastic. A large part of the population, of course, received incomes from sources other than wages, and there is little evidence to suggest that such people suffered a loss of purchasing power between 1500 and 1650. All in all, total demand for food rose during the sixteenth and early seventeenth centuries despite the fall in the purchasing power of wage-earners. After 1650 real wages rose. Agricultural capacity had been increased during the previous century, and after 1650 population grew more slowly. The long-term trend of grain prices in the late seventeenth and early eighteenth century was downwards at the same time as the demand for labour was rising. Judging from the complaints of depression by cereal farmers in the early eighteenth century not a great deal of this increase in purchasing power spilt over into grain consumption but it was felt by producers of milk, cheese and butter, meat and fruit.

The demand for industrial products also increased between 1500 and 1750, bringing about a derived demand for raw materials such as wool, hemp, flax, dyestuffs, hides and skins, tallow and timber. Some of this demand was met by increased imports, but much was supplied from domestic sources. Pastoral farmers benefited particularly from the growing demand for cloth and leather.

Since well over half of the output of leather went to make essential consumer goods such as boots and shoes the demand for hides and skins roughly followed the curve of population growth. There is only impressionistic evidence of the rise in demand for other raw materials. The needs of a growing population stimulated the demand for wood fuel and building timber and caused local shortages of these materials. However, the shortages were not general and by the end of the century coppices were supplying the needs of industry. Indeed, their cultivation had extended so much that there were complaints of over-production of timber in some parts of the country by the 1720s and '30s.

The home demand for English farm products was supplemented by a demand from overseas. Wool and woollen cloth were exported in large quantities from the Middle Ages and fluctuations in the level of cloth exports probably had some influence on decisions whether or not to concentrate on wool production on marginal land. Only small quantities of other agricultural products were exported. A little grain was shipped during the sixteenth century. The trade declined in the early years of the seventeenth century but after 1700 corn exports increased and became for a time a significant item in the total export trade. A few animal products were sent overseas, chiefly hides and skins in the form of leather. The trade grew after leather exports were legalized in the 1660s, but exports never accounted for more than about one-tenth of the output of the leather industry.

Supply Conditions: the Land and its Uses

The response of farmers to increasing demand was conditioned by the nature of the soil and climate which varied considerably throughout the country. The summers of the south are warmer than those of the north and the winters of the east more severe than in the west. Rainfall is heavier in the western side of England and in Wales than in the eastern counties. Soil and subsoil are even more diverse than the climate. As a result husbandry systems, even today, vary greatly from one part of the country to another. In the sixteenth and seventeenth centuries regional differences were even more pronounced since poor communications and the force of custom restricted the diffusion of new methods of cultivation, and farmers were less able to modify the influences of the environment than they are today.

Climate and geography divided pre-industrial England into two major regions. To the north and west were uplands with poor soils and a cool, wet, climate. This was grass-growing country supporting predominantly pastoral farming. On the south and eastern lowlands soils were generally richer, the rainfall lower, and summer temperatures higher. This was corn-and-grass country following a variety of mixed husbandry systems in which arable products were more important than livestock. The boundary between the two regions ran approximately from Teesmouth in the north-east to Weymouth in the south-west although there were many exceptions to the general pattern on both sides of the line. In the north and west mixed-farming economies were located in valleys and coastal plains, and the south and east contained many districts where livestock or livestock products were the main focus of interest. Nevertheless, the basic distinction existed between the pastoral country of the north and west and the mixed husbandry of the south and east.

Pastoral farming was broadly of two kinds. On the northern highlands, running from the Peak District to the Scottish border and extending westwards into the Lake District and eastwards to the north-eastern moors, and also on the Welsh mountains and the moorlands of the West Country, there were extensive open pastures for sheep and cattle. Soils were barren, the climate cold and wet, and human settlements were huddled on valley bottoms where there were a few arable fields and enclosed meadows. Some of these districts specialized in rearing store cattle for sale to lowland farmers. The cattle were grazed on the upland pastures during the summer, and in winter were brought down to the valleys, housed in byres and hand-fed with hay. In other regions, such as the Lake District, large numbers of sheep were kept principally for their wool. They were run throughout the year on the fells, in flocks several thousand strong, and brought down to the valleys at lambing time and for shearing. Another kind of pasture farming was found in the 'wood-pasture' districts of the lowland vales of western England and also in parts of the south and east. Here the fields had originally been enclosed direct from the woodland and were farmed without common rights. The main purpose of husbandry was either the rearing of store cattle, as in the Vale of Herefordshire, or the production of butter and cheese, as in Cheshire and High Suffolk, according to the quality of the grass and the accessibility of markets.

The corn-and-grass districts displayed a greater variety of conditions than pastoral regions but a useful distinction may be drawn between the scarplands that cut across lowland England with their thin soils of chalk, gravel, sands and light loams, and the heavier soils of the vales between. The light soils were free-draining and easy to work but they needed constant manuring to keep them fertile. On this type of land the sheep-fold was 'the sheet-anchor of husbandry'.[1] For example, on the chalk lands radiating from Salisbury Plain large flocks of sheep were grazed on the downs during the day and were brought down to the arable fields at night and penned or 'folded' among the arable fields where they dropped their dung. Hurdles were used to pen the sheep on different parts of the arable land night by night. By day the flocks were returned to the chalk pastures to fill their stomachs in preparation for their nocturnal task. Wheat and barley were grown for the market, usually cultivated in arable fields farmed in common on a four-course rotation. Variations of the sheep fold were found on all the chalk soils of south and eastern England and also on the heaths and brecklands of Norfolk, the heaths of Ascot and Aldershot and in other areas of poor soils.

The soils of the vales ranged from rich, fertile loams to heavy, intractable clays which baked hard in the sun and became waterlogged in wet weather. The husbandry regimes on these soils varied a good deal but they virtually all combined crop and stock. On the Midland Plain, for example, which ran from the Cotswolds

[1] E. Kerridge, *The Agricultural Revolution*, 1967, p. 43.

and Chilterns in the south to the Peak District and eastwards into Yorkshire, most of the land was in tillage in the sixteenth century, usually managed on a three-course rotation, although both longer and shorter rotations were often found. Farmers owned or rented intermingled strips scattered in common fields, but they were free to cultivate whatever crops they pleased on their strips as long as they observed the communally imposed rotations. Barley was the main cash crop, and many farmers grew a considerable amount of peas and beans for fodder. Wheat became rather more important during the seventeenth century. A fallow year was essential in the cultivation of this kind of land. Properly managed fallows restored fertility, improved soil structure and cleared the land of weeds.

Livestock was an important part of husbandry systems in the vales even where the main interest lay in producing crops for the market. Animals supplied household needs for meat, dairy and wool, but above all they provided the manure necessary to maintain the fertility of the soil. In many parts of the Midlands, pasture land was scarce and grazing rights on the fallow and in the arable fields after harvest time were jealously guarded by local cultivators. There were constant attempts to increase the amount of grazing available, including the formation of temporary grass leys within the arable fields which were used for hay or for grazing, and the introduction of convertible husbandry methods which increased livestock production without depressing the output of arable crops.[1] In some cases, when soil and market conditions allowed, arable land was turned over to permanent pasture. By such means parts of the Midlands became increasingly pastoral in character during the seventeenth century. At the beginning of the eighteenth century, for example, Defoe noted of Leicestershire, which a century earlier had been predominately an area of mixed farming that:

> the whole county seems to be taken up in country business ... particularly in breeding and feeding cattle; the largest sheep and horses are found here, and hence it comes to pass too, that

[1] See below, pp. 55–6, 60.

they are in consequence a vast magazine of wool for the rest of the nation.[1]

Elsewhere in lowland England differences in climate and topography and access to markets dictated variations in farming systems. On fens and marshes there was much grazing for store cattle, fatstock, dairy produce and wool. Where soils were particularly bad, husbandry was possible only on the basis of shifting cultivation in which land was cropped for a year or two and then left to revert to grass. The only safe generalization that can be made about farming in pre-industrial England is that it was far from the text-book stereotype of uniform and unthinking methods. Farming methods had been adapted to cope with local conditions of soil, climate and demand. Pre-industrial England no doubt had its share of bad and conservative farmers, but if farmers as a class inclined to traditional practices, it was because those practices had a rational justification.

A feature of agriculture before 1750 in the Midlands, and to a lesser extent in other parts of the country, was the practice of farming in open or common fields. The main elements of common-field agriculture have been described as follows:

First, the arable and meadow is divided into strips among the cultivators, each of whom may occupy a number of strips scattered about the fields. Secondly, both arable and meadow are thrown open for common pasturing by the stock of all the commoners after harvest and in fallow seasons. In the arable fields this means necessarily that some rules about cropping are observed so that spring and winter-sown crops may be grown in separate fields or furlongs. Thirdly, there is common pasturage and waste, where cultivators of strips enjoy the right to graze stock and gather timber, peat and other commodities ... Fourthly, the ordering of these activities is regulated by an assembly of cultivators – the manorial court ... or, where more than one manor was present in a township, a village meeting.[2]

[1] Quoted by W. G. Hoskins, 'The Leicestershire Farmer in the Seventeenth Century', in *Provincial England*, paperback ed. 1965, p. 165.

[2] Joan Thirsk, 'The Common Fields', *Past and Present*, 29, Dec. 1964, p. 3.

Not all these characteristics necessarily existed together. There were some open fields still composed of scattered strips over which common rights had been extinguished. In many parts of the Midlands common pasture had dwindled to vanishing point by the sixteenth century. In some places the manorial court or village meeting had ceased to function, in which case it is impossible to determine how, or whether, crop rotations were communally agreed.

Common-field farming was the result of a gradual development of a social organization centred on the nucleated village, usually possessing a strong manorial structure. As a method of farming it had considerable advantages. Communal farming spread the cost of capital equipment such as ploughs across the whole community. The scattered strips meant that all cultivators benefited from the dung dropped by animals as they grazed the stubble and fallow; and common rights on the meadow enabled all to share the limited supplies of grass and so keep the animals necessary for tillage. Since rotations were determined by common agreement, the lazy or inefficient farmer was kept in line with the accepted practice of the community and there is no reason for believing that standards of farming were set by the worst cultivator. At the same time enterprise was not stifled, for, as we have mentioned, farmers were at liberty to choose what crops they grew within the framework of the field-course. As with the techniques practised within them, the common fields were a rational form of organization suited to conditions of the time.

Supply Conditions: New Techniques

Faced with rising demand farmers increased production with traditional methods and forms of organization. They also experimented with new techniques, improved the organization of their farms and brought new land into cultivation. Frequently one could not be done without the other, for new methods required changes in organization and waste land could be put under the plough only with the aid of new techniques.

On the heavy soils of lowland England the most pressing need was to increase the amount of grazing available. Short of wholesale conversion of farms from arable to pasture, the most effective method of extending the grassland was to introduce techniques of convertible or 'up-and-down' husbandry. In 'up-and-down husbandry everything hinged on the arable fields ... being laid down to grass for a few years and then ploughed up and tilled for a time ...'[1] The land was kept under grass usually for between seven and twelve years during which time it was used for breeding, dairying and grazing for meat and wool. It was then ploughed and kept in tillage, occasionally for as little as two or as long as twelve years, although more often for between five and seven years, depending on soil conditions. The first grain crop after ploughing was often oats, followed by barley and wheat. At the end of the tillage period the land was allowed to grass over naturally. The land could not be kept under crop for too many years nor ploughed too many times in a year, otherwise the roots of the natural grass were destroyed.

The chief advantage of convertible husbandry was that it provided more grass than land farmed on traditional lines without depressing the output of arable crops. At any one time roughly three-quarters of a farm was under grass, the quality of which was higher than the grass of permanent pastures. Animals dropped their dung and urine while grazing, continuously raising the fertility in the soil so that when it was eventually ploughed it yielded perhaps double the quantity of crops that could be obtained from similar land in permanent tillage. Thus, although the acreage of arable was smaller with convertible husbandry, the production of crops was at least maintained, while the quality and quantity of livestock were increased. There was also an increased supply of commodities such as woad, which was frequently sown as a clearing crop on permanent grassland which had been ploughed for the first time and incorporated into a system of convertible husbandry.

The use of convertible husbandry methods spread in the Midlands from about 1560 until, a hundred years later, possibly half

[1] Kerridge, *op. cit.*, p. 181.

the land in this region was farmed in this way. It was also used on former fen and marshland after draining. The technique penetrated into wood-pasture districts and regions of permanent grass such as the Vale of Evesham where the meadows were ploughed for the first time; and it replaced techniques of shifting cultivation on the lowlands of Northumberland and Durham. Convertible husbandry even made limited advances into the chalk country where it occasionally replaced the sheep-fold.

A second major method of increasing output in the sixteenth and seventeenth centuries was by draining the extensive fens, marshes and saltings lying along lengths of the English coastline, estuaries and inland rivers and putting the land to more productive use. The drainage techniques employed varied with the nature of the problem to be tackled. Where land was drowned by the sea or tidal rivers, walls were built to keep the water at bay and ditches were dug to carry away the surface water. The reclaimed land was improved and consolidated by grazing sheep and perhaps by sowing grasses until it reached a condition where it could bear crops. On inland areas such as the Fens, more substantial drainage works were needed, comprising networks of ditches and larger cuts leading to rivers and so to the sea, with perhaps wind pumps to assist the sluggish flow of the water. Reclamation on this scale was expensive and the greatest period of activity was between the late sixteenth and the middle of the seventeenth century when farm incomes were swollen by rising prices.

Reclamation was not always successful. Schemes sometimes came to grief because of poorly planned or poorly executed drainage channels. Often water was taken off one area only to be discharged on land elsewhere. Reclaimed land was apt to be exposed to erosion by wind or to lose fertility when deprived of alluvial deposits that periodic flooding had provided. But, when successful, the reclamation of marsh and fen increased the crop-carrying capacity of the land. Before draining, fens and marshes had specialized in stock, fishing and fowling. Afterwards the acreage of arable was much enlarged, but the level of pastoral production could be maintained by the use of convertible husbandry methods.

The reverse of reclamation was the floating of water meadows. This technique involved damming a river or stream in the late autumn and digging channels to carry the water over adjacent meadows in order to flood them. The flood waters deposited silt and protected the ground from frost. Early in March the water was run off and the meadows left to dry for a few days before being opened to sheep which grazed on the early grass that flooding had produced. The meadows were then floated again in preparation for the hay crop, and repeated flooding could produce two or even three crops. In the late summer the meadows provided valuable grazing for dairy cattle and about November the cycle began again. Floating was practised in the vales of Shropshire, Herefordshire and Somerset at the end of the sixteenth century and became well established during the next fifty or sixty years. It was particularly suited to lowlands watered by streams running off chalk hills which deposited chalky sediment on the meadows. The purpose of floating was to increase the supply of fodder, particularly in the difficult months of the early spring.

Convertible husbandry, reclamation and the water meadows were all innovations introduced in the lowlands between the late sixteenth and late seventeenth century as means of raising farm output, primarily by extending the livestock-carrying capacity of the land. There was also an introduction of new crops, mainly from the mid-seventeenth century onwards, more suited to the lighter soils of the scarp lands. Carrots and turnips had been grown as garden crops in the sixteenth century but were used as field crops in High Suffolk in the mid-seventeenth century. Thereafter turnip cultivation spread steadily on light soils replacing bare fallows, but it could not be used on heavy or very shallow soils and fallows persisted into the nineteenth century in such conditions. Legumes and improved grasses such as sainfoin, ryegrass, clover, trefoil and lucerne were also widely introduced on lighter soils from the mid-seventeenth century, although some of them had been known to farmers in the sixteenth century. They replaced bare fallows or were sown instead of, or mixed with, pulses and grains. They were also incorporated into convertible husbandry regimes in the second half of the seventeenth century replacing natural grass to sward over tillage land when it reverted to pasture.

The new crops improved the fertility of light soils, directly by the nitrogen-fixing ability of the legumes and indirectly by increasing the volume of fodder and forage available to support animals. Light soils were cheaper to cultivate than the heavy vales and had a decided advantage in the production of grain in conditions of falling prices in the late seventeenth and early eighteenth centuries. Consequently corn output increased considerably in these districts after 1660, whereas it declined in heavy soil regions. Roots, legumes and grasses were relatively cheap to introduce so their use spread in spite of falling cereal prices. They had a further advantage, too, in that they provided farmers with richer and more abundant feed for their sheep and breeders were able to pay more attention to raising beasts yielding more and better meat, the demand for which was rising. There is little evidence of substantial improvements in the quality of cattle before the early eighteenth century but the increased amount of fodder and forage available meant that a much larger livestock population could be supported.

How widespread were these new techniques? There is an obvious risk of fastening on novel methods and exaggerating them far beyond their contemporary importance, and the very act of describing them may give them an inflated value. During the sixteenth and seventeenth centuries new methods had to make their way against old and trusted ways in a country where communications were poor and society was by nature conservative. In the mid-seventeenth century Aubrey observed that:

> even to attempt an improvement in Husbandry (though it succeeded with profit) was look'd upon with an ill Eie, their Neighbours did scorne to follow it, though not to doe it, was to their own Detriment.[1]

Even when the benefits of new techniques were appreciated, many farmers could not afford the capital outlay involved and most

[1] Quoted by E. L. Jones, 'The Condition of English Agriculture, 1500–1640', *Econ. Hist. Rev.* 2nd ser., vol. xxi, no. 3, 1968, p. 618.

were suitable only in certain conditions of soil and climate. Convertible husbandry, for example, was suited to relatively heavy soils, but it was expensive to establish and, by the early eighteenth century, it had conquered barely half the Midland lowlands and had made even less advance elsewhere. Reclamation of flooded land was even more expensive and necessarily limited geographically; while the water meadows were not only costly to establish but required a high degree of skill. Their use was confined mainly to the estates of wealthy landowners in the west of England. Sainfoin, clover, other improved grasses and root crops, were widely grown in the late seventeenth and early eighteenth centuries, but chiefly on light soils. Nevertheless, new methods of farming were used increasingly in English agriculture from about the third quarter of the sixteenth century and played a valuable part in expanding agricultural production in pre-industrial England.[1]

Supply Conditions: Re-organization and the Extension of Cultivation.

New farming methods were accompanied by the re-organization of farms. This took two forms: enclosing and engrossing. The main purpose of enclosing was to secure the advantages which might follow extinction of common rights over arable and pasture. When arable land was enclosed it was normally accompanied by the re-arrangement of scattered strips into compact holdings which were then fenced or hedged. Engrossing involved the amalgamation of two or more farms into a single, larger unit. Both practices were normally intended to increase the area of land under grass and both accompanied the conversion of arable land to pasture and the introduction of convertible husbandry.

[1] There is a considerable difference of emphasis between Dr Kerridge, *op. cit.* and Dr Joan Thirsk, writing in *The Agrarian History of England and Wales,* vol. IV, *1500–1640*, ed. Joan Thirsk, 1967, on the importance of new techniques as compared to the extension of cultivation as a means of increasing production. But the latter work does not support, and the former obviously contradicts, Dr Jones's contention that there 'was little in the way of change in the mode of farming' between 1500 and 1640 (E. L. Jones, *op. cit.,* p. 618).

Grass was important in all farming systems, not only for the raising of livestock and the production of livestock products, but also as grazing for animals kept primarily for their manure so necessary to the cultivation of crops. The growth of the export trade in wool and woollen cloth in the late fifteenth and early sixteenth century heightened the demand for pasture. Even more important, population growth increased the demand for crops – and hence for manure – and for meat and livestock products. In regions possessing abundant grazing land the resulting demand for pasture posed no problems, but where pasture was scarce livestock numbers could be increased significantly only by upsetting existing farming arrangements. A partial solution to the problem adopted in the second half of the sixteenth century was the establishment of grass leys on strips in the open fields on which animals were kept, but the difficulties of hurdling or tethering large numbers of animals amid the growing crops imposed limits on this practice. More drastic solutions were the conversion of tillage land into permanent pasture, or the introduction of convertible husbandry, not just on the odd strip, but over a whole farm. Either way spelt the end of common rights. Conversion of tillage land to permanent pasture affected common rights over the meadow as well as the arable since the commoners use of the meadow had hinged on their rights in the arable fields; while convertible husbandry required compact farms and so was usually preceded by engrossing. It also replaced the short rotations of the common fields by a grass-arable rotation stretching over a dozen years or more. The planning of farming practices over such an extended period was difficult if not impossible by an assembly of all the cultivators, many of whom could not afford the capital outlays of introducing 'up-and-down' husbandry. Convertible husbandry, therefore, was incompatible with common-field farming.

Enclosing and engrossing had been taking place for centuries. By the beginning of the sixteenth century common fields had already disappeared from many areas of western and eastern England or survived only in scattered pockets. The main region of common-field farming by 1500 was the Midland Plain and it was this area that was most affected by enclosure during the sixteenth and seventeenth centuries, not merely because there was more land in common fields here than anywhere else, but also because the economic benefits of re-organization were greatest; for much of the land was suitable for farming with a system of convertible husbandry or for permanent pasture. Enclosures in the Midlands provoked a great deal of hostile reaction in the sixteenth century because they caused the loss of already scarce commons on which the livelihoods of many of the poor depended. The movement of land into pasture farming also raised fears for the country's corn supplies. When accompanied by engrossing, enclosures caused depopulation and the dispossessed swelled the numbers of landless, impoverished and dissatisfied people whose existence threatened the security of the state. Most of the anxiety about enclosing and engrossing arose from conditions in counties such as Leicestershire where roughly one-tenth of the land was enclosed during the sixteenth century. An even greater proportion was enclosed in the following century, but the outcry against enclosure died down as its benefits to agricultural production were gradually appreciated.

By itself enclosure did nothing to raise the production of cultivated areas; its effectiveness lay in its association with better methods of stock management and the arable-grass rotations of convertible husbandry. It was also a means of bringing waste or little used land into more intensive cultivation. It is impossible to judge the extent to which the cultivated area was extended since enclosure attracted little comment in regions where waste land was plentiful. But as the result of enclosure, fen, forest, marsh and moors were made to yield greater quantities of crop and livestock. The extension of cultivation and the use of better methods went hand in hand in raising agricultural production in pre-industrial England.

Enterprise and Finance

So far we have said nothing of the enterprise and capital needed to establish new techniques and undertake re-organization. Indeed there is little that can be said with certainty. Historians have recently devoted a great deal of research into the manner in which the land was farmed, and such knowledge was greatly needed since an earlier generation of writers was much more concerned with delineating legal niceties of tenurial arrangements. But, so far, little attention has been given to questions of enterprise and finance in the agricultural sector of pre-industrial England. It is clear, however, from the experience of underdeveloped countries in the twentieth century, that advances in agriculture are greatly affected by the nature of agricultural institutions. In pre-industrial England agrarian organization was apparently favourable to agricultural development and it is to this subject we must look for clues to the sources of enterprise and capital.

Most land in early modern England was farmed by people who did not own it. Land was owned by the crown and church, the great secular landlords, and the gentry and freeholders or owner-occupiers. It was cultivated by an army of tenants differing greatly from one another in the nature of their tenures, size of holdings and wealth, but united in that their occupancy of the land was not absolute. There was a third and growing class in agrarian society, the farm labourers, who possessed little or no land but worked for tenant farmers or owner-occupiers.

The amount of land owned by the crown and the church fell during the sixteenth and seventeenth centuries. The crown was forced by inflation and bad management to sacrifice future income from rents by selling land. Between 1561 and 1640 its share of more than 2,500 manors in various parts of England examined by Professor Tawney declined from 9.5 per cent to 2.0 per cent. Ecclesiastical holdings declined after the dissolution of the monasteries. Before the dissolution, the monasteries and secular clergy together had owned possibly one-fifth of all landed estates in England. After the dissolution only 7 per cent of manors investigated by Professor Tawney remained in ecclesiastical ownership. Even allowing for the fact that the number of manors is not a precise measure of acres or income, it is clear that the church ceased to be a dominant figure in English landed society.

The most important landowners were the large secular landlords with estates of between 10,000 and 20,000 acres. The share of the cultivated land owned by this group rose very gradually between the late fifteenth and mid-eighteenth century from possibly 15 or 20 per cent of the total to 20 or 25 per cent. The great landlords included most of the titled aristocracy as well as several non-titled landowners, but the composition of this category changed a good deal over time as some families accumulated wealth and others fell on hard times. After the dissolution of the monasteries and in the inflationary years of the late sixteenth and early seventeenth centuries less substantial landowners were sometimes able to accumulate large estates by buying church and crown land or even, on occasions, land belonging to aristocratic landowners over-whelmed by debt. During this period, the total number of great landowners probably increased, but there were never more than a few hundred at any one time. In the late seventeenth and eight-eenth centuries the numbers may have fallen slightly, but there was an increase in the size of individual estates as the rising costs of land-ownership forced some of the smaller landowners to sell out to men with more ample resources.

The county and parish gentry owned possibly 30 or 40 per cent of all land in England in the sixteenth century. Their share in-creased to about 50 per cent by the middle of the seventeenth century but then declined. The number of gentry landowners is difficult to assess, but by 1700 there may have been between 10,000 and 20,000 of them. Before the Civil War resourceful gentlemen were able to buy land from the church and crown and a few of them graduated to the class of great landlords. At the other end of the scale yeomen farmers, by dint of careful manage-ment, were sometimes able to accumulate sufficient land to enable them to live as gentlemen. These were joined by successful trades-men, aspiring to status as well as profits, who purchased country estates. In the late seventeenth century, on the other hand, the rising expense of owning land obliged some of the smaller gentry to sell out to large landowners or wealthy merchants.

Turning to the various classes of tenants, the first to be considered are the freeholders, a term fraught with ambiguity. Freehold was a type of tenure 'free' from servile status that had attached to various kinds of customary tenures during the Middle Ages. Freeholders held their land from the king or from a lord of the manor and were obliged to pay various forms of rent, often of a purely nominal kind. Freeholds were inheritable and could be enforced at common law. To all intents and purposes therefore, freeholders were owner-occupiers, unless of course they chose to lease their land to sub-tenants. Together with tenants possessing inheritable copyholds they were often known by the amorphous title of yeomen.

Freeholders were more numerous in eastern than in western England but their numbers varied greatly from manor to manor. According to Gregory King there were between 140,000 and 180,000 freeholders at the end of the seventeenth century, but in this number he included the better sort of copyholders as well. If we think of owner-occupiers, ignoring the distinction between freehold and inheritable copyhold, they probably occupied between 20 and 25 per cent of the cultivated land during the sixteenth and seventeenth centuries. Their share of land increased before 1650 as inflation forced the crown and some secular landlords to sell land. This was a prosperous period for freeholders since the outgoings on their land was fixed while the prices they received for farm products were rising. After 1650 the position was reversed. Costs were increasing, as taxes and wages rose, while grain prices fell in the long run. There was a slow but persistent decline both in the number of owner-occupiers and the amount of land they held. The size of their holdings varied greatly. In parts of East Anglia many holdings were so small that their owners resorted to part-time industrial employment or worked as labourers for large farmers. More substantial owner-occupiers in the sixteenth century had farms of 30 to 100 acres. By 1750 owner-occupiers with holdings of about 150 acres were a small minority; most had farms no more than a third or a fifth of that size.

The majority of farms in the sixteenth century were held on customary tenures, the most important of which was copyhold.

The conditions of these tenures were determined by the custom of the manor and written into the rolls of the manorial court a copy of which was held by the tenant. Since their nature was governed by customary law, copyhold tenures could vary from place to place. The most secure copyholds were inheritable and both the annual rent and the entry fine – the sum payable when a new life entered the tenancy – were fixed. Such copyholds were indistinguishable economically from freehold tenures. Other types of inheritable copyholds were subject to variable entry fines, although any alteration was subject to ratification by the manorial court. Rather more common, particularly in the west, were copyholds for life or lives. These were usually for three lives, but other arrangements also prevailed. Although the annual rent was normally fixed, the entry fines were arbitrary and not subject to the custom of the manor. A small proportion of customary tenants possessed no copy, but their tenures were still subject to customary law.

Important changes occurred in tenurial arrangements during the sixteenth and seventeenth centuries. As prices rose before 1650 landlords had an obvious interest in increasing entry fines and similar payments. William Harrison voiced a familiar complaint in the late sixteenth century when he spoke of the:

> dailie oppression of copiholders, whose lords seeke to bring their poore tenants almost into plaine seruitude and miserie, dailie deuising new meanes, and seeking vp all the old, how to cut them shorter and shorter, doubling trebling, and now and then seuen times increasing their fines . . .[1]

Copyholders for lives were most subject to this sort of pressure since their entry fines were variable. However upward revisions were often done by mutual agreement between landlord and tenant; and Harrison also noted that despite the increase of fines farmers were more prosperous than they had been earlier in the century, thinking their 'gaines verie small toward the end of [their] terme, if [they] have not six or seuen yeares rent lieing by [them], therewith to purchase a new lease . . .'

[1] *Tudor Economic Documents,* ed. R. H. Tawney and E. Power, 1924, III, p. 71.

The sixteenth and seventeenth centuries also saw an increased use of leasehold tenures limited to a term of years and subject to an economic rent instead of the nominal rents of customary tenures. It was in the interests of landlords to substitute flexible leases in place of more rigid customary tenures as prices rose during the sixteenth century so as to share in the rising farm incomes. As copyholds fell in tenants could sometimes be persuaded to accept a lease. Disputes with copyholders also provided landlords with opportunities to tidy up the tangle of customary tenures by replacing them with leases, and occasionally landlords resorted to eviction, although they had to reckon with the protection that customary tenants enjoyed at both customary and common law. Freeholders and copyholders themselves contributed to the growth of leaseholds by sub-letting their holdings for limited periods.

Whatever the form of tenure, most farms in pre-industrial England were small by modern standards. There was of course a great deal of variation from district to district. At the end of the sixteenth century in the common-field districts of the Midlands farms averaged about forty or fifty acres. In Northumberland forty per cent of tenant farms were between thirty and forty acres. In the wood-pasture district of East Anglia many farms were smaller than ten acres although larger holdings were more usual in the neighbouring sheep-corn districts. There was a gradual tendency for farms to become larger, at least in the grain-growing areas. Several reasons encouraged the trend. Enclosing and engrossing created larger units of production which enjoyed the advantages of economies of scale. Landlords usually preferred large farms to small ones since they simplified the tasks of estate management and, by the early eighteenth century, landlords took considerable care to find suitable tenants for large farms. On the other hand, the growth of population encouraged the sub-division of holdings and it was not always easy to consolidate small farms into large ones or to find tenants who could afford to rent them. In addition, some types of agriculture, such as market-gardening, were suited to small holdings and contributed to their survival. As late as 1830 two-thirds of English tenant farms were smaller than 100 acres.

Given the widespread importance of tenant farms in pre-industrial England, the relationship between landlord and tenant was critical to agricultural progress. This is not to say that the contribution of owner-occupiers was unimportant. In the sixteenth and seventeenth centuries they enjoyed comfortable profits, some of which they used to develop their farms: nearly one-fifth of the enclosure taking place in Leicestershire in the second half of the sixteenth century, for example, was initiated by owner-occupiers. But their contribution was minor compared with the progress achieved by landlords in conjunction with their tenants. Although the role of landlords in promoting agricultural improvements awaits thorough investigation, we can, broadly, see them exercising their influence in two ways. First they often financed improvements such as enclosure, the introduction of convertible husbandry and water meadows, and land reclamation. Possibly the initiative for enclosure came mainly from the gentry who relied on the incomes from their estates to a greater extent than the great landowners, but the latter were closely involved in schemes such as fen drainage requiring large outlays of capital. By the late seventeenth century, if not earlier, landlords also seem to have taken on a good deal of the responsibility of providing the fixed capital used on farms and, occasionally, some of the working capital as well. The willingness of landlords to maintain and renew farm buildings, pay land tax and even allow rent arrears, was an important method of helping grain farmers in heavy soil districts to weather the difficulties caused by falling corn prices in the late seventeenth and early eighteenth century.

In the second place, landlords affected farming methods by their leasing policies. As long as they permitted their customary tenants before 1650 to pay fixed annual rents unadjusted to rising prices, there was little pressure on farmers to change their methods of cultivation. But where landlords increased their incomes by raising rents and introduced leases in place of customary tenures, as many did, tenants were compelled to farm in the most efficient way possible in order to meet the higher rent charges. Of course if rents were pushed too high or the conditions of leases were so uncertain that tenants were not able to enjoy the benefits of the improvements that they made, progressive farming was hindered and not encouraged, so a great deal depended on the terms of the leases. In the early seventeenth century some landlords wrote clauses into leases regulating husbandry methods and by the end of the century the practice had extended a good deal.

By 1700:

> ... the skeleton at least of a manorial structure still survived, and, in other circumstances – such as long prevailed in France – the subject might have been vexed and burdened by the dead hand of seignorial jurisdiction. But already the skeleton was covered by the flesh and blood of new life – a life of enterprise and profit, in contrast with which, the old franchise revenues that might still have been squeezed from tenants must have seemed ludicrously small.[1]

The causes of this metamorphosis are obscure; its results were important. It created in England a landlord class ready to exploit their estates for income, but willing to invest part of that income in agricultural improvements. It created also a class of tenants freed from the burden of relying on their own resources entirely for financing development. It created the means whereby the agricultural sector of the economy was able to respond to rising demand.

The Achievement and its Consequences

If we think of the agricultural sector of pre-industrial England as composed of three related parts concerned with the production of corn, pastoral products, and specialized crops such as fruit, vegetables, timber and industrial crops, then we can see advances occurring in all three. Corn production increased as a result of the extension of cultivation and increased yields. Evidence on the second point is scanty, but both Professor Hoskins and Dr Kerridge have suggested substantial increases in yields between 1500 and 1650. During the second half of the seventeenth century there

[1] D. Ogg, *England in the Reigns of James II and William III*, 1955, pp. 69–70

was a switch in the centre of gravity of grain farming away from the heavier clays towards the lighter soils of the scarplands of lowland England, made possible by the introduction of roots and improved grasses on such soils. A growth in the relative importance of wheat is also apparent by the early eighteenth century, the outcome of generally falling grain prices which encouraged farmers to concentrate on the grain commanding the highest price in the market.

But the outstanding feature of corn production between 1500 and 1750 was its relative decline compared with pastoral farming. During the first half of the sixteenth century the demands of the export trade may have encouraged a shift of factors of production into wool growing. In the second half of the sixteenth and the early years of the seventeenth century the balance probably swung back in favour of grain because of the growth of population. Even so, there was no decline in pastoral farming, for the demand for meat and dairy products and industrial raw materials continued to increase, while the output of corn could be raised only as supplies of manure were increased. The trend towards pastoral production was intensified from the middle of the seventeenth century as long-term grain prices ceased to rise, and then fell, and as the demand for animal products grew stronger.

The increase in production of specialized commodities was stimulated by influences on the side of both demand and supply. Urbanization encouraged the establishment of market-gardens, orchards and hay farms, while industrial expansion stimulated arboriculture and the cultivation of dyeing and finishing materials for the textile industry. On the supply side, the spread of convertible husbandry increased the cultivation of various industrial crops, particularly woad. More generally, the fragmentation of holdings in some regions as the result of population increase created farms too small to be economically viable unless used for the production of labour-intensive crops for which there existed a growing demand.

An assessment of the economic consequences of agricultural expansion in pre-industrial England is made difficult by the absence of quantitative measures either of agricultural progress or the rate of economic change in general. Most obviously, the growth of agricultural production provided food and raw materials demanded by a population that doubled during the period. If output had not expanded, the population growth would have been restricted – and there is some evidence, indeed, that by the 1630s or '40s growth was checked by insufficient agricultural expansion – or there would have been recourse to increased imports of food, assuming that supplies were available in western Europe. In these circumstances the balance of trade, always somewhat delicately poised between surplus and deficit before the late seventeenth century, would have been more adverse than it was, with a resulting outward deflationary drain of bullion that might have depressed the level of economic activity. As it was, the import of grain was never necessary for any length of time, and by the early eighteenth century agriculture itself contributed to export earnings.

Not only did population increase. More significantly the non-agricultural proportion of the population became larger. Measurement is impossible, and it must always be remembered that on the eve of the industrial revolution a majority of Englishmen was still employed mainly in primary production. But the evidence of urban growth and industrialization points unquestionably to a decline in the proportion of the workforce in agriculture which was possible only because of increased agricultural productivity. The movement of population from agriculture was accompanied by a fall in the consumption standards of wage earners before 1650, mainly because agricultural productivity did not rise sufficiently, although the situation was probably aggravated by the high costs of food distribution to the towns. Had the growth of agricultural productivity been greater, food prices might have been lower and there would have been a greater effective demand for industrial goods. After 1650 agricultural capacity more than kept pace with the growth of demand and the continued growth of non-agricultural employments was accompanied by rising standards of consumption.

It is more difficult to be certain about the release of other factors of production from agriculture. Some land was used for building particularly in the metropolitan area, and urban and industrial expansion nibbled a little into agricultural land elsewhere. But such losses were more than compensated by the extension of farming onto wastes and commons. As far as capital is concerned, the agricultural sector was probably a net provider of capital to other sectors of the economy despite the fact that a good deal of mercantile wealth flowed into land. During the inflationary years before 1650 the relatively greater increase in agricultural prices compared with non-agricultural prices altered the distribution of income in favour of farmers and landlords, thus facilitating the investment of landed wealth in industry and commerce. Even during the different price conditions prevailing after 1650 agricultural income was probably sufficient to finance capital formation in the agricultural sector and also to contribute to investment projects in other parts of the economy. For example, even the sales of minor by-products such as bark, hides and skins totalled more than three-quarters of a million pounds a year in the early eighteenth century; and they cost virtually nothing to produce since the production costs were incurred in producing the main products of timber, meat and wool. It is not inconceivable that such revenues exceeded, in total, the entire cost of enclosure in the eighteenth century.

Discussion of the contribution of agriculture to capital supplies raises the whole question of the relationship between agricultural incomes and prices and general economic development. In the late seventeenth and early eighteenth centuries agriculture possibly generated between 40 and 50 per cent of total national income although its share of the work force was probably larger. Earlier in the sixteenth and seventeenth centuries agriculture's contribution to income and employment must have been greater. Obviously the expenditure of incomes earned in agriculture had a large impact on the level of activity in other sectors of the economy. For example, as rents and farm incomes rose between 1500 and 1650 landlords and tenants alike increased their expenditure on housing and furnishings and on consumer goods generally. Manufacturing and the import trades were thus stimulated, although against this stimulus must be set the fall in demand from wage earners whose real incomes were reduced by the rise in food prices. Even though incomes generated in agriculture declined as a proportion of total national income in the late seventeenth and early eighteenth centuries, they remained the largest part of national income and continued to exercise a major influence on the economy until well into the nineteenth century.

The point has already been made that real wages rose in the late seventeenth and early eighteenth centuries as grain prices fell and money wages rose, these changes being linked with increased agricultural productivity, sluggish population growth and a buoyant demand for labour. The rise in real wages was significant in two ways. First, any improvement in the real incomes of wage earners made a significant contribution to the level of effective demand in the economy, since wage earners constituted a large and growing proportion of the population. Secondly, rising real incomes resulted not only in an increased demand for commodities already being consumed, but in a diversification of demand. As wage-earners became more prosperous they consumed more meat and dairy produce, more imported commodities such as tobacco, tea and sugar, and more and better manufactured goods.

Yet the advances in agriculture did not shatter the traditional framework of the pre-industrial economy; agriculture remained the most important economic activity before 1750 and, indeed, for many years after. Why was this so? There is some reason for believing that, in spite of the advances made in agriculture, England was a country of expensive food by comparison with Europe at the end of the seventeenth century.[1] Furthermore, the fall in food prices since 1660 had not been consistent. Although the cost of basic food in southern England was as much as 25 per cent lower in the 1740s than it had been in the 1660s, poor harvests pushed up prices in the 1690s and again in the 1710s to levels approaching those prevailing in the 1660s. The improvement in

[1] *See* F. P. Braudel and F. Spooner, 'Prices in Europe from 1450 to 1750', ch. VII of *The Cambridge Economic History of Europe*, vol. IV, ed. E. E. Rich and C. H. Wilson, 1967, pp. 399–400, 473.

real incomes, therefore, although significant, may not have been sufficient to generate a pressure of demand before 1750 strong enough to bring about a fundamental breakthrough in economic development. It must be remembered, too, that virtually the whole burden of raising effective demand in the economy after 1700 rested on the growth of incomes at home, since neither population nor the export trades were growing very much. The real transformation of the economy came after 1750 when growing agricultural productivity, accelerating population growth and the expansion of overseas trade occurred simultaneously.

By itself agricultural expansion in pre-industrial England did not provide a strong stimulus to economic development. Even modern experiences of economic growth offer few examples of countries developing rapidly on the basis of advances in primary production, not even in nineteenth century Australia where economic development came about more through urbanization and industrialization than the growth of agriculture. Agriculture failed to provide a powerful incentive to growth, for it did not cater for an elastic demand. True enough the demand for meat and dairy produce was more elastic than the demand for bread grains; even so, the limitations of the human stomach imposed fairly definite restrictions on the extent to which consumption of such products could be increased. The demand for raw materials was possibly more elastic, but the major raw material, wool, was produced for an industry that itself grew sluggishly. Thus the introduction of improved methods of production into agriculture did not open up the possibility of rapidly increasing sales. Neither did agriculture possess strong links with other branches of the economy. It provided virtually all its own raw materials such as seed corn, breeding animals and manure, and we have already argued that agriculture was able to cope with its own capital requirements. Agriculture made little contribution to urban growth – apart from its indirect contribution of feeding the town dwellers. Towns were of course centres of trade in primary products, but the most rapidly growing towns in pre-industrial England were ports such as London, Bristol and Liverpool whose growth depended to a large extent on overseas trade, or manufacturing centres such as Worcester in the sixteenth and early seventeenth centuries and Birmingham in the seventeenth and eighteenth centuries. Agricultural expansion helped generate additional demands for transport and communications; but here again other economic activities also stimulated developments in the economic infrastructure. To take just one example, the most dynamic element in the coastal trade in pre-industrial England was the expansion of coal shipments between London and Newcastle.

Thus the very considerable developments in agricultural techniques and organization that occurred in pre-industrial England and the resulting increase in agricultural output did not transform the economy before 1750. Instead, it prepared the way for the industrial revolution of the late eighteenth century by permitting the gradual release of factors of production into industry and commerce, by contributing to a modest rise in effective demand among wage-earners and receivers of incomes from non-agricultural sources, and by fostering the growth of a market economy. By 1750 the agrarian yoke on the economy had been eased: it was not removed until the nineteenth century.

4

Industry

The Composition of The Industrial Sector

Industry exists in even the most underdeveloped economies to meet basic needs of processed foods, clothing and shelter. In many parts of Africa and Asia today industry employs between about 4 and 28 per cent of the workforce; while for pre-industrial England Gregory King classified a quarter of a million people as artisans and handicraftsmen out of a total population of 5.5 million people. His figures greatly understate the importance of industry in late seventeenth century England for they do not take account of the large numbers of those he described as 'labouring people and servants' and 'cottagers and paupers' who earned at least a fraction of their livings from industry, nor of the many farmers, traders and shopkeepers with interests in manufacture. There was no sharp division between manufacturing on the one hand and farming and commerce on the other.

In this chapter industry is taken to include mining and building as well as manufacturing. In pre-industrial England the requirements of the market determined the leading industrial activities. The demand for food gave rise to butchers, brewers, bakers, distillers, millers and similar occupations. The demand for clothing supported a large number of textile, clothing and leather crafts; and the need for houses created employment for a myriad of workers in the many branches of the building industry. Metal workers, as well as craftsmen working in wood and leather, sup-

75

plied the demand for tools and utensils used around the house and farm, and the harnesses, saddles, carts and boats needed for travel and transport.

The importance of these industries producing consumer goods was appreciated by writers on economic matters in the sixteenth and seventeenth centuries. The author of the *Discourse of the Common Weal* (1549) grouped artificers into three categories. The first group included, not manufacturers, but men engaged in the distribution of imported goods. In the second category were 'shoe-makers, tailors, carpenters, masons, tilers, bowchers, brewers, bakers, vitailers of all sortes', who produced commodities for consumption in the home market. The third group was composed of craftsmen supplying the export trade as well as home demand and who were, therefore, in the opinion of the author, especially to be cherished: 'clothiars, tanners, cappers, and worsted makers ...'[1] There was no mention of metal workers. In the mid-seventeenth century Henry Belasyse noted the 'chiefe ryches' of England:

> The cheife and first is cloth, which maketh all Europe almost England's servant and weare our livary. The next is out tinn or pewter, which is excellent in Cornwall ... Leather is excellent in England, and of great asteeme abroad ... Stockings belong to shooes and our worsted stockings are in great request all Europe over ... Coales is another great necessary commodity which Smiths at least cannot be without, and as men are shodd with our leather, so horses by our iron and coales. For even iron too which locks up all other treasure, comes out of England.[2]

As with the author of the *Discourse,* Belasyse judged the importance of an industry according to its place in the export trade. It is not clear what evidence was used by a writer in 1783 who rated industries according to the value of their output as follows:[3]

---

[1] *A Discourse of the Common Weal of this Realm of England,* ed. E. Lamond, 1893, pp. 91–92.

[2] H. B[elasyse], *An English Traveler's First Curiosity: or the Knowledge of his owne Country,* 1657, in *Hist. Mss. Comm., Various Collections,* II, 1903, p. 200.

[3] D. Macpherson, *Annals of Commerce,* vol. IV, 1805, p. 15.

Woollen textiles	£16·8 millions
Leather	£10·5 millions
Iron	£ 8·7 millions
Steel and plating	£ 3·4 millions
Tin	£ 1·0 millions

The actual valuations are guesswork, but the importance given to the textile, leather and metallurgical industries is amply confirmed by other evidence.

The most useful way of examining the composition of the industrial sector of pre-industrial England is by studying particular regions of the country. Despite pioneer work of scholars such as Professors Tawney and W. G. Hoskins little has been done in this regard for, in the main, when considering industry historians have been obsessed by the woollen industry to the exclusion of almost everything else. Yet sources such as freemen's rolls, parish registers, taxation lists, muster rolls and probate inventories can be made to yield a great deal of information about the nature of industrial activity, some of which is presented in Table 2 (pp. 88–92).

The evidence and the manner in which it has been analysed is discussed in the notes to the Table. It must be stressed, however, that occupational specialization was not highly developed in pre-industrial England and that any classification of the workforce into particular categories of employment involves a considerable simplification of the actual situation and can be misleading. Many craftsmen and traders were also farmers or farm labourers and for some of them agriculture provided a larger part of their income than other activities. The principle adopted in Table 2 has been to allocate persons to non-agricultural occupations if there are reasonable grounds for believing that they followed that occupation for the purpose of producing for the market even though agriculture may have been their major source of income. This procedure inevitably produces statistics that understate the importance of agriculture in some parts of the country. But the alternative course of action, of classifying people to agriculture if farming was their chief occupation, conceals the considerable diversity of economic activity in early-modern England and obscures important regional differences. Statistics of occupational distribution in pre-industrial England thus share the weaknesses of similar statistics relating to underdeveloped countries today, and for the same reasons:

> The weakness ... is apparent when one considers that in most under-developed countries many of the so-called farmers spend a large part of their time in small-scale transport, porterage and trade both during the farming season and much more so outside the season. They may trade not only in the goods they themselves have produced, but also in goods purchased by them for re-sale ... The imperfect specialization may extend to other classes as well ... The economic activity of many people in under-developed countries is better described as the performance of a number of different tasks than as a pursuit of a definite occupation.[1]

It might be concluded that because of the conceptual problems involved, as well as any difficulties arising from the quality of the evidence relating to occupational distribution in pre-industrial England, statistics should be eschewed altogether. However, for all its faults, Table 2 suggests some interesting features of the occupational landscape of England before the industrial revolution.

In the first place the importance of agriculture as an occupation is apparent, even though the mode of constructing the table does not fully reflect the extent of farming activity. In rural areas anything between 50 and 80 per cent of the workforce was more or less fully employed in agriculture. The lower proportions were found in regions of rural industry such as textiles or metal-working, but it is clear even from the limited evidence presented in Table 2 that rural industry was not a feature of every part of the country. Mid-Essex, in this respect, is especially interesting: here was a region not far distant from the East Anglian textile district of

[1] P. T. Bauer and B. S. Yamey, *The Economics of Under-developed Countries,* 1957, pp. 34-5.

south-central Suffolk and north Essex, yet the manufacture of cloth for the market left hardly a mark on the local economy which was almost completely agrarian. In the towns, on the other hand, agriculture was a minor occupation, although Ashby-de-la-Zouch suggests that the smaller towns had quite strong farming links; and even in the larger towns these links may have been stronger than the figures reveal.

Turning to non-agricultural occupations, there were marked contrasts between town and country areas, particularly in the location of food processing, distribution, and transport which were very largely urban occupations. Thirty per cent of the population of Gloucester, Tewkesbury and Cirencester, for example, were engaged in these activities in the early seventeenth century compared with only nine per cent for rural Gloucestershire. Towns were, in the words of Professor Tawney:

> primarily . . . finishing and distributing centres, which gathered around them rather more than the ordinary number of workers in other industries. They handled such products of the surrounding countryside as required to be worked up and supplied the agricultural districts with wares that could not be produced locally, and served as a link between them and the distant world of London.[1]

This was also a characteristic of towns in other pre-industrial societies. In eighteenth-century Pennsylvania, 'commerce, transportation, public administration and processing were the chief economic sectors' of towns; while in suburban Kampala in the 1950s 51 per cent of the African population were employed in retail trade or skilled crafts of one sort or another.[2] The emphasis on distribution was, in fact, greater than Table 2 suggests since many craftsmen in the clothing, leather and other trades not only made consumer goods but sold them from their own shops or market stalls.

[1] A. J. and R. H. Tawney, 'An Occupational Census of the Seventeenth Century', *Econ. Hist. Rev.*, vol. v, 1934, p. 38.
[2] J. T. Lemon, 'Urbanization and the Development of Eighteenth-century

Likewise, manufacturing employment was more concentrated in towns than in the countryside. The point is worth stressing because of the common assumption that, before 1750, the English countryside, alone, was the important seat of industrial production. There was certainly much manufacturing carried on in farm houses and cottages throughout the country for household consumption, but rural industry supplying regional, national, and international markets, was restricted to particular districts for reasons to be discussed later.

Half a dozen groups of crafts – textiles, clothing, leather, metalworking, building, and the processing of food and drink – provided employment for roughly three-quarters of the urban workforce and also accounted for most of the non-agricultural occupations in the country regions. The statistics of employment in the textile industry presented in Table 2 somewhat modify the impression of the importance of the industry given by most modern economic historians. Woollen cloth held unquestioned supremacy in England's export trade from the sixteenth to the eighteenth century and consequently it was at the centre of discussions of economic policy. Yet the textile industry was no more important as a source of employment than other crafts, except in a few well-defined regions. One such area is represented in Table 2 by Gloucestershire, part of which lay within the west of England cloth manufacturing district. Almost 17 per cent of the county's male population was employed in the textile industry in the early seventeenth century and in five hundreds of the county more than a quarter of the male workforce worked in the industry; although, by contrast, there were ten hundreds where textile production employed only between 5 and 10 per cent of the working population. There were also probably high concentrations of textile workers in parts of Wiltshire and

South-eastern Pennsylvania and Adjacent Delaware', *William and Mary Quarterly*, 3rd ser., vol. xxiv, no. 4, Oct. 1967, p. 502; A. W. Southall and P. C. W. Gutkind, 'Townsmen in the Making: Kampala and its Suburbs', *East African Studies*, no. 9, East African Institute of Social Research, Kampala, Uganda, 1957, p. 51. (I owe these references to Mr A. C. Davies and Dr C. Ehrlich).

Somerset bordering on Gloucestershire, as well as in parts of East Anglia and the West Riding of Yorkshire, two other major cloth-producing regions. Devon also possessed a textile industry producing for national and international markets, which is reflected to some extent in Table 2. It should be noted, however, that specialization in woollen production was not exclusively a country phenomenon. The city of Worcester concentrated very heavily on the manufacture of cloth, and Coventry and Norwich were both important textile towns in the sixteenth and seventeenth centuries. In other towns, though, the textile crafts were unimportant.

The clothing trades – hatters, cappers, tailors and so on – were large employers of labour in towns but they were less important in rural areas except as household pastimes serving family requirements. Towns supplied the local farming populations with clothing when they came to the weekly market. The bigger towns such as York and Norwich had relatively high concentrations of clothing workers in order to supply their larger populations and because they served as market areas for larger areas than the smaller provincial towns. There must have been a great deal of clothing made in country areas for household needs and these skills were sometimes harnessed to the market. In the seventeenth and eighteenth centuries, for example, the hand-knitting of stockings and other garments was an important supplement to farm incomes in parts of northern England, the finished items being sold in London and elsewhere. In the late seventeenth and early eighteenth centuries, framework-knitting became established in many villages in the East Midlands.

One of the most important groups of occupations in pre-industrial towns was the manufacture of leather and leather goods which frequently accounted for around one fifth of the urban working population. The leather crafts were less important in rural areas, although we know from other evidence that certain country regions were centres of leather production for national markets, including parts of western England specializing in the production of light leather and gloves, the dairying region of High Suffolk producing tanned leather for the London shoemakers, the Weald which exported leather through the ports of East Sussex, and Northamptonshire which developed as a boot- and shoe-producing region in the second half of the seventeenth century. In all, possibly 150,000 people were employed in the manufacture of leather and leather goods in England in the early eighteenth century. The importance of the leather crafts reflects the ubiquity of a commodity suitable for boots and bookbindings, buckets and bed hangings. More than half the output of leather was used for footwear and most of the rest for saddles and harnesses and various household and industrial purposes.

Metal-working craftsmen were sprinkled throughout the country. In rural areas blacksmiths were needed to make and repair iron tools and utensils. High concentrations of metal-workers were found in towns where they supplied both the urban population and the local farming community. Practically every household inventory of the sixteenth-century lists fireside and cooking utensils, usually of iron, and many mention brass and pewter-ware, farm tools made partly of iron, lead weights and other metal goods. Most of these things were probably made locally, but by the sixteenth century some parts of the country were specializing in the production of nails, scythes, locks, and other metal goods and supplying a national market. As can be seen from Table 2 a substantial proportion of the population in the west Midlands was employed in the metal trades. Sheffield's specialization in cutlery had been noted by Chaucer in the fourteenth century and by the mid-seventeenth century the parish had assumed a decidedly industrial character. The Forest of Dean was another region with a large number of metal works.

The building industry showed no tendency towards geographical concentration although building workers were more numerous in towns than the countryside. In most villages building must have been very much a part-time occupation which almost everyone engaged in from time to time, for the majority of rural cottages were simple and could be constructed with few special skills. The

more elaborate houses of prosperous yeomen farmers and gentlemen created a demand for bricklayers, masons, glaziers, plasterers
and similar workmen, and the 'rebuilding of rural England' in the
late sixteenth and early seventeenth centuries presumably produced larger numbers of specialized building craftsmen. Towns
possessed substantial buildings such as market halls, merchants'
houses, warehouses and shops, and so it is not surprising that between roughly 5 and 10 per cent of the urban workforce were
building craftsmen.

An important group of crafts in all towns was concerned with
the processing of food and drink. This category overlapped with
workers engaged in distribution. Innkeepers, for example, have been
classified as processers of drink on the assumption that most of them
brewed their own beer. This was the normal situation for beer
was bulky, expensive to transport and did not stand up to long and
bumpy journeys. However, the development of porter in the early
eighteenth century, a more stable beverage than traditional lighter
beers, coupled with improvements in internal transport, encouraged
the growth of innkeepers who were exclusively retailers of beer. Innkeepers and brewers were numerous in pre-industrial England, for
beer and ale was the usual drink in most parts of the country,
but was fairly complicated to make and so was often bought. Even
when brewing was done at home – and many inventories show
evidence of brewing equipment in houses – the malt was frequently
purchased, giving rise to the maltsters, another widespread drink
processing craft. Distilling was not a cottage industry to any extent
in pre-industrial England – unlike Ireland – and most distilling
was done for a cash market. The most numerous craftsmen in the
food, as opposed to the drink, trades were butchers. They were
mainly town dwellers, although they often owned or rented grazing pastures in the nearby countryside. Butchers supplied local
needs but many of them in the Midland towns were also links in
the trade supplying distant markets such as London, buying animals from the breeding counties and fattening them in local pastures for sale to metropolitan butchers.

The half dozen groups of manufacturing occupations discussed so far fail to do justice to the infinite variety of industrial occupations existing in pre-industrial England. In many corners of England men were employed in coal and metal mines and not a few colliers and 'grubbers' are hidden in the 'miscellaneous' column of Table 2 particularly in places like Ashby, the west Midlands and Sheffield. In 1608 between 7 and 11 per cent of the adult males living in coal-mining districts in the Forest of Dean were described as coal miners in the musters roll. The main coal-producing region of pre-industrial England lay in the valleys of the rivers Tyne and Wear in the north-east, and there were other important districts in south Yorkshire, the west Midlands, west Cumberland and Wales. All told, coalmining in England possibly provided direct employment for between 12,000 to 15,000 men in the late seventeenth century. This was only a quarter of the number of men employed as merchant seamen and only one-tenth of those engaged in the production of leather and leather goods. For all its much-vaunted growth in the sixteenth and seventeenth centuries coal-mining gave little employment. Other branches of mining probably employed even fewer people, mostly on a part-time basis. The production of cast and wrought iron and non-ferrous metals can in total have employed only a few thousand people, despite the considerable expansion of the metallurgical industry during the pre-industrial period.

Considerably more important than miners and makers of metals were woodworkers, not only the carpenters and joiners who have been classified as part of the building industry, but coopers, fletchers, basket makers and others. In Norwich they comprised between 2 and 3 per cent of the employed population during the sixteenth century. More than a third of the farm labourers in the Midland forest areas carried on a woodland craft as a secondary employment of agriculture in the sixteenth and early seventeenth centuries, and in a single village in the Rockingham Forest in Northamptonshire, roughly 10 per cent of the able-bodied men were wood turners in the mid-eighteenth century. 'Forest areas were the natural workshops of an agrarian civilization largely dependent on wooden tools and implements for its work: the number and variety of local crafts, often highly specialized and recondite, was legion.'[1]

Occupations connected with the sea clustered around the coastal towns and villages. The most important was shipbuilding. Tiny yards, employing no more than a carpenter or two and turning out vessels of a few score tons, were located in practically every haven in the country. The building of bigger ships was more confined geographically. In the early seventeenth century the main areas were the East Anglian coast and the Thames; but the East Anglian yards declined in the face of competition from Dutch-built vessels and the products of the expanding shipyards of the north-east coast between Hull and Newcastle. By the end of the seventeenth century north Kent possessed four great dockyards – Chatham, Deptford, Woolwich and Sheerness – building ships for the navy and the distant trades and between them employing several thousand men. Shipbuilding stimulated ancillary industries such as sailmaking, ropemaking and the like. Goods brought into the ports gave rise to import-processing industries such as sugar refining, tobacco processing and minor industries such as the manufacture of clay smoking-pipes.

Many minor industries, each employing a few score or a few hundred people, added diversity to the industrial scene of pre-industrial England: salt manufacture in Worcestershire and Cheshire and on the north-east coast, paper-making in the Home Counties and elsewhere, glass manufacture in the Weald and west Midlands, an embryonic chemical industry producing alum, salt-petre, soap, copperas, vitriol and other materials, and many more. The importance of such occupations was slight before 1750 and they were completely overshadowed by the urban and rural crafts catering for the needs of consumers in a basically agrarian economy.

[1] A. Everitt, 'Farm Labourers', ch. vii of *The Agrarian History of England and Wales*, vol. iv, 1500–1650, ed. Joan Thirsk, 1967, p. 427.

The Location of Industries

No single reason explains industrial location, but in an economy bedevilled by poor communications, access to markets was obviously a very strong influence. The majority of craftsmen lived in towns for the simple reason that urban centres had the greatest concentrations of population and the best links with the villages in the neighbouring countryside:

> In most villages of the realme there is some one dresser or worker of leather, and for the supplies of such as have not there are in most of the market townes iij, iiij, or v, and in many great townes and cities x or xx^{te}.'[1]

This description of the leather industry in the late sixteenth century applies equally to many other occupations in pre-industrial England. Industries were situated very largely where their customers were and the degree of geographical specialization in particular branches of manufacture was low. Good water transport, however, might encourage the development of industry in one area rather than another, particularly if the commodity produced was bulky. For example the importance of coal mining on Tyneside, compared to coal fields elsewhere in England, in the sixteenth and seventeenth centuries owed much to direct communications by coastal shipping with London. By contrast, attempts to expand sales of coal to London from the land-locked pits of the Nottinghamshire-Derbyshire border in the early seventeenth century foundered on the sandbanks of the river Trent and the costs of the long haul via Hull and the east coast.

Access to markets, nevertheless, cannot explain all features of industrial location. Often the costs of transporting bulky raw materials was the decisive factor. Practically every industry using wood or charcoal as a fuel, for example, was irrevocably confined to wooded regions since these materials were bulky, friable, and too expensive to be carried over long distances. The location of iron-smelting and forging, in particular, was largely influenced by the

[1] B. M. *Lans. Ms.* 74, p. 154.

availability of fuel supplies, for well over a ton of charcoal was needed to smelt a ton of pig iron (the ratio was 3 : 2 in the Forest of Dean in the seventeenth century) and even greater quantities of wood were required to make that amount of charcoal. The main area of iron production in England in the early sixteenth century was the Sussex Weald and as production expanded the industry spread into the neighbouring regions of Kent and Surrey. By 1574 51 out of the 58 furnaces in blast in England were situated in the Weald which, in addition to wood, possessed ample supplies of iron stone and plenty of fast-flowing streams to operate the bellows and forge hammers. The region also enjoyed good communications with London via the east Sussex ports and the navigable rivers running northwards into the Thames. In the early seventeenth century the Weald gave ground to other parts of the country as costs of wood-fuel and labour in the area rose. By 1653 the number of furnaces in the Weald had fallen to 36 (although furnace capacity may have risen), barely half the total for the whole country. By contrast, the Forest of Dean, south Wales, Yorkshire and the west Midlands all expanded as regions of iron production and they were joined by the Furness district of Lancashire in the early eighteenth century. These regions were well supplied with fuel and there were fewer competing demands for wood from other industries and domestic uses than in Sussex and Kent and so fuel costs – and probably labour costs as well – were lower.

Other wood-burning industries included the manufacture of glass, bricks and tiles, the production of salt, coppers and other chemicals, malting and dyeing. During the seventeenth century some of these industries broke away from their dependence on wood and used coal instead. But one industry that could not turn its back on wood was shipbuilding, although the timber it required was not the same commodity as the wood demanded by industrial and domestic customers. Wood fuel came from underwoods and coppices of young trees twelve to thirty years old, whereas shipbuilders required oaks often more than a century old and of appropriate shape and dimensions. Furthermore, transport costs restricted the area on which shipbuilders could draw to within

TABLE 2 *Occupational*

Place	Date	Type	Nature of Evidence
Ashby-de-la-Zouch	1637–1643	Town	Parish Registers
Ashby-de-la-Zouch	1658–1661	Town	Parish Registers
Chester	1558–1603	Town and Port	Freemen's Rolls
Chester	1603–1625	Town and Port	Freemen's Rolls
Coventry	1522	Town	Muster Roll 635 occupations
Devonshire	1531–1699	County	Inventories (215)*
Gloucestershire	1608	County	Muster Rolls Adult Males 16,000 entries
Gloucester, Tewkesbury and Cirencester	1608	Towns	Muster Rolls Adult Males 1,200 entries
Kirdford, Sussex	1611–1776	Rural Parish	Inventories (121)
Leicester	1559–1603	Town	Freemen's Rolls
Mid-Essex	1635–1749	County (Part)	Inventories (207)
Northampton	1524	Town	Taxation List 390 occupation
Norwich	1558–1603	Town	Freemen's Rolls
Oxfordshire	1550–1590	County	Inventories (209)
Sheffield	1655–1659	Parish	Parish Registers 311 entries
Sheffield	1700–1709	Parish	Parish Registers 2,681 entries
West Midlands	1541–1685	Parishes—Dudley and Stourbridge	Inventories (125)
West Midlands	1614–1787	Parish—Sedgley	Inventories (122)
Worcester	Before 1589	Town	Inventories
Worcester	1590–1620	Town	Inventories
Worcestershire	1550–1600	County	Inventories and Wills (4280)
Worcestershire	1601–1650	County	Inventories and Wills (4434)
York	1558–1603	Town	Freemen's Rolls
York	1603–1625	Town	Freemen's Rolls

* Includes Woodworkers   ? Indicates the informa

Distribution of work force – per Cent

Agriculture	Textiles	Clothing	Leather and Allied	Metal-Working	Building and Allied	Food and Drink Processing	Distribution and Transport	Miscellaneous
.9	2·9	5·6	20·5	5·6	8·2	8·7	7·2	2·7
·1	7·4	5·1	25·0	4·4	4·4	14·0	3·7	10·3
?	10·6	9·3	22·6	?	5·9	12·6	?	?
?	13·3	11·9	21·2	?	4·7	15·5	?	?
?	16·9	16·3	11·0	8·0	4·5	15·5	8·5	?
·4	8·4	0	1·9	0·5	0·9	4·7	5·1	1·4
·5	16·9	4·6	4·7	3·6	5·2	5·2	3·7	2·6
·0	11·3	20·8		6·1	8·4*	29·4		13·3
·6	4·1	2·5	1·7	2·5	4·1	2·5	1·7	4·1
·8	6·6	10·0	22·0	4·6	5·9	18·6	6·7	17·8
·7	0·5	0·5	2·4	2·4	3·9	5·3	3·9	—
?	10·5	5·1	23·0	3·0	7·5	15·0	6·2	?
—	16·2	17·1	13·4	6·2	10·4	12·4	19·8	2·8
·4	2·4	1·0	4·8	2·4	4·3	6·2	3·3	2·8
·2	10·3		7·4	50·0	6·1	4·2	—	8·7
·0	8·1		2·6	54·6	5·4	4·8	1·2	14·9
·8	1·6	1·6	3·2	29·6	0·8	3·2	1·6	3·2
·6	—	1·6	—	37·7	1·6	4·1	0·8	2·5
—	42·0	4·0	11·0	7·0	2·0	12·0	13·0	9·0
—	54·0	1·0	7·0	5·0	3·0	14·0	3·0	11·0
·3	4·3	2·5	3·8	3·4	1·5	2·7	2·5	1·9
·2	6·7	2·5	3·2	3·6	2·5	2·6	1·6	1·2
·6	5·4	17·2	13·9	10·9	8·1	16·6	16·7	5·4
—	9·3	14·2	15·2	7·9	4·3	16·5	21·7	7·2

ilable — Indicates the figure is insignificant

1. *Sources*

The five sources used as evidence of occupational distribution are parish registers, freemen's rolls, muster rolls, taxation records and probate material. They do not yield precisely comparable information. Parish registers record occupations of persons involved in the Anglican rites of baptism, burial and marriage. Provided the registers were carefully kept a wide cross-section of occupations in the community can be obtained, although parish registers do not indicate the extent to which persons were involved in more than one occupation. Freemen's rolls list the names and occupations of men, and occasionally women, made free of a city (i.e. granted the right to practise a trade or occupation in the city), usually by apprenticeship or patrimony. Their value as evidence of occupational distribution depends on the extent to which the obligation to take out freedoms in cities was enforced and whether or not freemen followed the occupation to which they had been nominally admitted. Although gentlemen and yeomen were sometimes entered on the freemen's rolls, it is likely that these sources understate the extent to which city dwellers had interests in agriculture or followed occupations not traditionally represented in the city. Neither do they include labourers and unapprenticed workmen. Muster rolls list able-bodied men available for military service and, when they record occupations, provide valuable information about adult male occupations in rural and urban areas. Similarly taxation records, such as subsidy roles, list householders liable to tax or exempt through poverty and sometimes give their occupations. Probate materials include printed lists of wills, which sometimes give the occupations as well as the names of the testators, and printed and manuscript inventories drawn up for the purpose of proving wills. Such material covers a wide social range but very often occupations are not specifically stated on inventories and special problems arise in inferring occupations from the content of inventories (*see* note 2). Wills and inventories cover both rural and urban areas and are frequently the only evidence available for country regions.

2. *Classifications*

(a) The occupational groupings follow, with slight modifications, those used by J. F. Pound, 'The Social and Trade Structure of Norwich, 1525–1575', *Past and Present*, no. 34 (1966), pp. 67–9. In brief, the groupings are as follows: *Gentry and Professional:* all those described as gentlemen unless they can reasonably be allocated to some other category, e.g. to agriculture, if their inventories suggest that they derived substantial income from direct farming; clergymen, teachers, etc. are also included in this group. *Agriculture:* farmers, husbandmen, farm labourers and farm servants, yeomen unless they had obvious economic interests in trade or manufacture. *Textiles:* all workers employed in the various stages of manufacture of woollen and other textiles, dyers and others in the finishing processes; but not manufacturers of clothing nor mercers, drapers, etc. engaged in distribution. *Clothing:* manufacturers of all clothing from textile materials, but not from leather. *Leather and allied:* workers engaged in the manufacture of leather and leather goods, including footwear, gloves and points; also skinners. *Metal-working:* craftsmen working in ferrous and non-ferrous metals, but not those engaged in metal mining or smelting. *Building and allied:* bricklayers, tilers, masons, glaziers and similar workers; also brickmakers etc.; carpenters and joiners included, but not other woodworkers. *Food and drink processing:* persons employed in the processing and sale of food and drink, e.g. butchers, bakers, brewers, distillers, vintners, innkeepers, millers, fishermen, etc.; but not those engaged exclusively in handling, such as grocers or fishmongers. *Distribution and transport:* persons engaged in wholesale and retail trade, e.g. grocers, apothecaries, drapers, mercers, haberdashers, merchants etc.; transport workers include carriers, watermen, sailors, oastlers etc.; wheelwrights are also included in this group. There is obviously a good deal of overlap between this group and the previous one. *Miscellaneous:* included here are woodworkers, not elsewhere specified, and other miscellaneous craftsmen.

(b) All unidentifiable references have been excluded. These include unspecified labourers and servants and, in the case of inventories, all instances where the source of livelihood cannot be deduced.

(c) Probate inventories have been classified as follows:
   (i) Where the testator's occupation is stated, he has been assigned to that occupation even though the inventory may list no goods belonging to that occupation.
   (ii) Where no occupation is stated the inventory has been classified according to its content. Frequently there is no difficulty in identifying a testator as a farmer. Difficulty arises when there is evidence that a testator had manufacturing or trading interests as well as farming. When it can be reasonably assumed that a trade or craft was followed *for the market,* the inventory has been classified according to the occupation concerned, *whether or not the value of the craft or trade goods listed in the inventory exceed the value of agricultural goods.*
   (iii) All doubtful cases have been excluded.

3. *Interpretation*

Occupations in pre-industrial England were much less specialized than they are today and this table must not be used as evidence of rigid distinctions between one occupation and another. It may be reasonably assumed that persons included in the category of agriculture did not regularly follow any other occupation for the purpose of market production; but this was not the case with industrial craftsmen. The table should therefore be read in the following way. In Oxfordshire, for example, roughly 70 per cent of the population in the late sixteenth century were engaged in agriculture; the remaining 30 per cent of the population may also have had agricultural interests, but they possessed significant economic interests in various branches of manufacture or trade. In the case of the west Midland parishes listed, roughly one-third of the population was engaged in some aspect of metal manufacture for the market; these people may or may not have been involved in agriculture as well. The table, therefore, rather understates the importance of agriculture in rural districts which contained a substantial amount of industry. It does, however, reveal considerable differences in the regional distribution of industry. There is no way of telling from the table whether manufacturing was the only, or the main, or a subsidiary source of income for the craftsmen concerned; but it does reflect the extent to which the working population in various districts were to some degree involved in non-agricultural employments for the purpose of market production.

4. *References*

ASHBY-DE-LA-ZOUCH: Calculated from information provided by Mr C. J. Moxon, Balliol College, Oxford.

CHESTER: D. M. Woodward, 'The Chester Leather Industry, 1558–1625', *Trans. Historic Soc. Lancs. and Cheshire*, vol. 119, 1967, pp. 66–7.

COVENTRY: Calculated from W. G. Hoskins, *Provincial England*, 1963, pp. 78–80.

DEVONSHIRE: Calculated from *Devon Inventories of the Sixteenth and Seventeenth Centuries*, ed. M. Cash, *Devon and Cornwall R.S.*, new ser., vol. 11, Torquay, 1966.

GLOUCESTERSHIRE: Calculated from A. J. and R. H. Tawney, 'An Occupational Census of the Seventeenth Century', *Econ. Hist. Rev.*, vol. v, 1934, pp. 59–61.

GLOUCESTER, TEWKESBURY AND CIRENCESTER: *ibid.*, p. 36.

KIRDFORD: G. H. Kenyon, 'Kirdford Inventories, 1611–1776', *Sussex Archaeological Collections*, vol. 93, 1954, pp. 79–80.

LEICESTER: Calculated from W. G. Hoskins, *op. cit.* pp. 94–6.

MID-ESSEX: Calculated from F. W. Steer, *Farm and Cottage Inventories of Mid-Essex 1634–1749*, Essex Record Office Publication no. 8, 1950.

NORTHAMPTON: Calculated from W. G. Hoskins, *op. cit.*, pp. 79–80.

NORWICH: J. F. Pound, 'The Social and Trade Structure of Norwich, 1525–1575', *Past and Present*, no. 34, 1966, pp. 67–9.

OXFORDSHIRE: Calculated from *Household and Farm Inventories in Oxfordshire, 1550–1590*, ed. M. A. Havinden, Hist. Mss. Comm. JP 10, 1965.

SHEFFIELD: Calculated from E. J. Buckatzch, 'Occupations in the Parish Registers of Sheffield, 1655–1719', *Econ. Hist. Rev.*, 2nd ser., vol. I, 1949, pp. 145–6.

WEST MIDLANDS: Calculated from *Dudley Probate Inventories*, ed. and trnscr. by J. S. Roper, 1st ser., *1544–1603*, Dudley, 1965; 2nd ser., *1605–1685*, Dudley, 1966; 3rd series (Dudley, 1968); *Stourbridge Probate Inventories, 1541–1558*, ed. and trnscr. by J. S. Roper, Dudley, 1966; *Sedgley Probate* Inventories, 1614–1787, ed. and trnscr. by J. S. Roper, Dudley, 1966.

WORCESTER: A. D. Dyer, *The City of Worcester in the Sixteenth Century*, unpub. Ph.D. thesis, Univ. of Birmingham, 1966, p. 474.

WORCESTERSHIRE: Calculated from J. West, *Village Records*, 1962, pp. 125–7.

YORK: Calculated from *Register of the Freemen of the City of York*, vol. II, *1559–1759*, *Surtees Society*, vol. CII, 1899.

twenty miles or so of the coast. This factor accounted for the concentration of great dockyards in north Kent and also explains why there were complaints of timber shortages in southern England in the late sixteenth century, for although iron-masters and ship-builders did not use the same material, they both competed for the same wood-land which was itself subject to competition from other forms of land-use.

Supplies of raw materials also influenced the location of the leather industry, particularly tanning. The raw materials concerned were hides and skins, oak bark and water. Tanning was admittedly concentrated in the towns but the reason was less the nearness of markets – this was more important to shoemakers and other leather-using craftsmen – than the fact that towns were centres of meat production and hence sources of supply of hides and skins. The hide markets of Leadenhall and Southwark in London supplied the tanners and leatherdressers of London – who produced approximately 10 per cent of all leather made in England at the end of the seventeenth century – and also manufacturers in other parts of the country. In High Suffolk a tanning industry developed using skins produced as by-products of the region's dairying industry; and the prevalence of leatherdressing in the pastoral counties of western England was based on locally produced skins, supplemented by sheep and calf skins imported from Ireland. The supply of bark for tanning was also important in influencing location. London tanners were supplied with bark from the woodlands of Surrey, Kent and Sussex. As supplies in the immediate neighbourhood of London became exhausted, it sometimes became more economical to send raw hides and skins to the bark rather than bring the bark to the hides and skins. Thus hides from London were transported to iron-working districts such as the Weald and south Yorkshire where bark came from the trees felled for use in the furnaces and forges. The finished leather was often sent back to London to be sold. Tanners and leatherdressers also needed large quantities of water so they required river-side sites. Since access to markets was not the prime consideration, most tanners and leatherdressers settled on the outskirts of towns where rents were low and where they were less likely to pollute the supplies of drinking water.

Supplies of raw materials influenced the location of other industries as well. The concentration of metal-working in the west Midlands, south Yorkshire and the Forest of Dean, for example, owed something to the presence of bar iron and wood fuel in those regions. Woollen manufacture for the market was more likely to be found in areas where there were good supplies of wool, fullers' earth and water. Yet the availability of raw materials cannot be a complete explanation of the location of the cloth industry. The main cloth-producing districts all supplemented local wool with supplies imported from other parts of England or from Ireland and continental Europe. On the other hand the Midland counties of Northamptonshire and Leicestershire which did produce wool on a large scale were not important centres of cloth production themselves. Nor were the leading cloth producing regions in the sixteenth century the original centres of textile manufacture for the market. In medieval England cloth production for the market had been an urban industry; the development of specialized rural-industrial regions came later. In the west the industry spread into the countryside during the fourteenth and fifteenth centuries; in East Anglia, the West Riding of Yorkshire and the lesser regions of central and north Wales, the Weald and Westmorland, rural expansion occurred in the fifteenth and early sixteenth centuries. In part the growth of rural specialization in cloth production followed the development and innovation of the fulling mill from the thirteenth century onward. In part, too, restrictive attitudes of urban gilds encouraged more enterprising producers to set up business away from the towns. But the most important reason for the growth of the woollen industry in certain parts of the countryside was the search for cheap labour.

Labour was the main factor of production in most industries in pre-industrial England and producers selling in competitive national and international markets were very conscious of their labour costs. The countryside was attractive to employers seeking cheap labour for it frequently contained under-employed agricultural labourers willing to accept some form of secondary employment to supplement their agricultural incomes. Spinning, weaving and the other textile operations were traditional skills among the rural population. Spinning wheels and looms were common pieces of household equipment or could be purchased cheaply and they fitted into rural cottages without difficulty. Rural production, it is true, involved manufacturers in higher distribution costs than urban production but these were offset by the low cost of rural labour.

It has already been pointed out that industrial production for the market was not an important feature of all country regions, although some form of manufacturing was found in practically every farmhouse and cottage to supply household needs. But where conditions were right industrial production for national and international markets developed. In the west of England an important woollen industry became established in the river valleys radiating from the Cotswolds and Mendip hills producing high-quality cloth for export; and there was a secondary region in west Somerset and east Devon specializing in cheap kersies. In East Anglia there were also two centres. One, concentrating on worsteds, was based on Norwich and the surrounding villages. The other, producing a variety of good quality undyed broadcloths and cheap coloured cloths, was located in south-central Suffolk, reaching across the river Stour to include parishes in north Essex. In the West Riding of Yorkshire the woollen industry was confined to an area commencing just north of the river Aire, stretching to Leeds and Wakefield in the east, Huddersfield in the south and the Lancashire border in the west. The main products of the area were coarse woollens although worsteds became important in the late seventeenth century. Less important areas with an interest in national and overseas markets included Berkshire, the Weald of Kent, central and north Wales and Westmorland. Almost without exception the manufacture of cloth was located in densely populated parishes where the farms were too small to provide an adequate income from agriculture alone. In lowland England such parishes were usually in wood-pasture districts of small dairy farms, more heavily populated than the neighbouring fielden parishes. In Wiltshire, for example, the cloth industry was concentrated in the pastoral region of the north-west and was not found on the sheep-corn country of the chalk. In East Anglia, south-central Suffolk was a densely populated dairying region. The worsted industry of Norfolk, on the other hand, was situated in a predominantly arable region, but it probably owed much to the supplies of cheap labour in Norwich, the second largest city in England. The Weald of Kent, like High Suffolk and the Wiltshire region, was a heavily populated pastoral district. In the West Riding and Westmorland the woollen industry was concentrated in large parishes where the soil was too poor to support most of the population by agriculture. In Halifax, for example,

> . . . and other places thereonto adjoyning, being planted in grete wastes and Moores where the fertilitie of the Grounde is not apte to bringe forthe any corne nor good Grasse, but in rare places, and by exceading and great Industrye of thinhabitauntes; and the same Inhabitauntes altogether doo lyve by Clothemaking . . .[1]

Behind differences in population densities in rural England lie a complex of reasons that historians have scarcely begun to explore. The most heavily populated parishes in lowland England had at one time been, and sometimes still were densely wooded. They had contained plenty of unused land waiting to be cleared which had attracted migrants from areas where land was more difficult to get. By the sixteenth century they were still centres of immigration, not because there was still land to be settled – on the contrary they were by now often congested – but because, being regions of late settlement, manorial organization was weak or did not exist at all, and there were few, if any, communal regulations designed to keep newcomers from arriving in the hope of finding a scrap of land on which to settle. These areas were a reservoir of cheap labour for rural industry which, once established, attracted the jobless from elsewhere. Rural industry also promoted population growth

[1] 2 and 3 Philip & Mary, c. 13, preamble.

through natural increase by providing an economic base for early marriage independent of the availability of land. In the northern upland parishes, also, there were few restraints on immigration with the result that population growth outran the capacity of the limited amount of arable land to support people by farming. Thus over-population created a pool of cheap labour in these regions that could survive only by engaging in industrial production.

This discussion of the influence of population densities on the location of industries has been confined to the case of woollen cloth, but it is also relevant to other industries. The rural-industrial villages of the west Midlands with their army of metal workers were located in forest regions which were more heavily populated than the neighbouring fielden districts. The particular specialization in metal-working rather than textiles is explained by the presence of iron and wood-fuel in the vicinity. Specialization in the manufacture of gloves and other light leather goods in pastoral regions of western England occurred in villages where there was 'a great number of Poor, many of which are incapable of following any other employ'.[1] Stocking-knitting supported the numerous poor in the barren parishes of the Pennines. At the end of the seventeenth century London manufacturers of hosiery and footwear were attracted by the cheap labour found in the overpopulated villages of the East Midlands, both in forest areas and in fielden districts where manorial restraints on immigration had collapsed. Rural industries supplying distant markets, in short, developed continuously in pre-industrial England as the market opened up fresh opportunities and producers sought out the cheapest labour available.

Industrial Organization

The diversity of manufacturing in pre-industrial England was matched by a considerable uniformity in organization. Most manufacturers operated on a small scale, used little fixed capital and employed labour-intensive methods. Neither the nature of industrial

---

[1] *House of Commons Journals,* vol. XI, pp. 766–7.

technology nor the size of the market made extensive investment of capital necessary. Machinery was usually small and operated manually. Few production techniques required specialized buildings and when premises were needed to house machines or workers, or for warehouses, they could usually be rented cheaply. Tanners, for example, required more space and equipment than many crafts-men, yet at the end of the sixteenth century a tanyard complete with vats, storehouses and living accommodation could be leased for a few pounds a year. Fixed capital requirements were even further reduced when industry was organized on a putting-out basis since production was carried out in the homes of employees who usually owned their own tools.

A few occupations demanded more than the common run of fixed plant. Collieries, for example, could be omnivorous consumers of capital. Huntington Beaumont spent between £6,000 and £7,000 developing coal mines in north-east England during the early years of the seventeenth century; although some of this was working capital, a good deal was invested in boring and drainage equipment, always expensive items in deep mining. Yet for every pit sunk deep there were a dozen shallow shafts worked with little expense beyond the purchase of a mining lease, a stock of pit props and a few simple tools. In the iron industry the erection of a furnace and forge together with the necessary equipment and out-building cost perhaps £100 or £200 in the late sixteenth century and £400 or £500 or more by the middle of the seventeenth century. Large though these sums were, they were small compared with the capital bound up in raw material and fuel. In the metal-working industries expenditure on fixed plant was usually very low. Ambrose Crowley was a most exceptional case with buildings and equipment worth £12,000 in 1728; even so, fixed capital represented only twelve per cent of his total capital assets.

The amount of fixed capital invested in industry probably in-creased during the course of the sixteenth and seventeenth centuries as new techniques were introduced and widening markets made large-scale production worthwhile. In the early eighteenth century industrial giants like Crowley were surpassed by brewers such as

Whitbread who employed fixed plant worth £20,000 in the 1740s to satisfy the thirst of three quarters of a million Londoners. But it is easy to exaggerate the amount of large-scale enterprise in pre-industrial England and overlook the fact that most forms of manu-facturing were small-scale, labour-intensive crafts.

Circulating capital was more important than investment in building and machinery before the industrial revolution and con-tinued to be so for many years afterwards. An analysis of tanners' inventories in the sixteenth and seventeenth centuries suggests that less than 3 per cent of their capital was tied up in plant and the rest in stocks of hides and skins in the process of tanning, bark, and finished leather awaiting sale. The main outlay facing textile manu-facturers was the purchase of wool: one Wiltshire manufacturer in the 1690s spent £1,400 a year on wool. In metal-working the biggest expenditure was on stocks of bar iron. Even in relatively capital-intensive industries costs of raw materials outweighed fixed capital charges; 70 per cent of all production costs in iron smelting, for example, was incurred in obtaining the charcoal used in the furnaces.

The importance of working capital compared with fixed capital in pre-industrial England arose for a number of reasons. In most industries production processes were long, depending either on the slow operation of little-understood chemical reactions – as in tanning – or on the laborious pace of human muscle, perhaps assisted by wind and water power, both ponderous and subject to interruption by the elements. Putting-out, whatever its other virtues, lengthened the manufacturing period because of the time spent in distributing and collecting materials. Poor transport and defective market mechanisms obliged manufacturers to hold stocks of raw materials and finished products. Tanners, for example, were compelled to hold expensive stocks of bark since oaks could be barked only in the spring. Woollen manufacturers, brewers, and other craftsmen whose raw materials were produced annually faced the same prob-lem. And once goods were ready for the market it was not always possible to sell them straight away. The delay could be as little as a week until market day came round again, or it could be several months if output was intended for foreign markets and had to wait on the availability of shipping space or favourable trading conditions abroad. Within England trade could easily be interrupted by bad weather, an outbreak of plague, or even, in local markets, by a shortage of customers or an absence of coin.

For many manufacturers labour was the largest single cost of production. In spinning and weaving labour accounted for roughly half the final costs of production. The proportion was possibly even higher in the metal-working and leather-using crafts. Labour costs were relatively low in industries using large quantities of fixed and circulating capital. One Sussex ironmaster reckoned his labour in 1746 as less than 18 per cent of the costs of smelting and casting. Labour was, in fact, probably more important in smelting than this figure suggests for the production of charcoal, which accounted for so much of the costs of smelting, was itself a labour-intensive operation.

Urban craftsmen often employed no more than a single journeyman and an apprentice or two, for markets were limited and kept the unit of production small. Frequently no labour was employed at all beyond members of the immediate family. Larger-scale employment did exist. Paper mills employed up to a dozen workers in the seventeenth century. Iron works, brass and battery works, sugar and alum houses sometimes employed dozens of workers although the general run of labour requirements was more modest. At the end of the seventeenth century thirty or forty collieries in England each provided work for between thirty and forty men although many more managed with a mere handful of labourers. The naval dockyards were among the largest employers of labour in the country. The Chatham yard employed about forty men in the early seventeenth century and 800 in the 1660s. But the more typical shipyard was manned by a carpenter and his mate. The largest employers of labour were manufacturers who put work out to employees in their own homes. Clothiers in the West Riding of Yorkshire often employed up to fifteen persons, including members of their own families, producing a broad cloth a week or a couple of kersies; larger West Riding clothiers kept up to forty carders, spinners, weavers, and shearers at work. The scale of operations was generally bigger in the west of England and East Anglia where large clothiers sometimes employed several hundred people. One Wiltshire clothier engaged an extra five hundred workers in the early seventeenth century in order to increase production by 400 cloths a year. A century later a clothier in Essex had around five hundred workers on his books although not all worked at the same time. It is impossible to say with certainty how many were employed in putting-out industry since the essence of the system was that workers were taken on and laid off according to the state of demand.

Frequently out-workers were not, strictly, employees but independent producers working on contract for bigger manufacturers on whom they relied for raw materials and the sale of their output. In practice, however, small producers were often so indebted to their suppliers that they became to all intents and purposes employees.

Putting-out was a feature of a wide range of industry in pre-industrial England, especially the woollen industry and many branches of metal-working. Much of the production of gloves and other light leather goods was organized in the same way, as well as the extensive hand and framework-knitting industries in northern and Midland England. In the early eighteenth century the system spread into the manufacture of footwear. The prevalence of putting-out underlines the importance of labour in so many branches of manufacturing. It enabled employers to tap supplies of cheap under-employed labour in rural areas and reduced the need for fixed capital. Employees usually owned their own tools, although in a few occupations where machinery was expensive – Dutch looms, for example, used in the manufacture of ribbons, and knitting frames cost up to £80 apiece at the end of the seventeenth century – employees rented machines from their employers. There are even occasional references in nailers' probate inventories to 'bellows rent' suggesting that even cheap equipment was occasionally rented. Putting-out facilitated the division of labour. In the manufacture of cloth, for example, the various processes of sorting the wool, carding or combing, spinning, weaving and shearing and fulling were usually distinct occupations carried out by different workers. It was also possible for producers who supplied large markets to concentrate some workers on particular lines of specialization in a way that was impossible for small producers. Thus in the early eighteenth century some clothiers concentrated on the semi-luxury trade in 'french fashions' while others, like Thomas Briggs of Ballingdon in Essex supplied the mundane market for bunting and crepes. In shoemaking, some London manufacturers employing labour in Northamptonshire villages specialized in men's, women's, or children's footwear and, in one case, in orthopaedic shoes for the London hospitals.

Putting-out had its limitations. It could not be used in industries requiring bulky plant and power-driven machinery. Neither was it suitable for crafts demanding a high degree of skill or which needed close supervision; nor where production processes had to flow without interruption from one stage to another. Even when technical conditions were favourable to the use of out-workers, high costs of distribution and losses arising from pilfering and fraud by the workers were serious weaknesses. These problems became increasingly apparent during the late seventeenth and the eighteenth centuries as the putting-out system was stretched to meet the demands of expanding markets for manufactured goods. Manufacturers found themselves competing in a tight labour market, bidding up wage rates, and casting their net for employees over wider and wider areas. In these circumstances market pressures to change production functions by introducing machinery became very great. But until the technical problems of mechanization were solved, putting-out remained the most economic way of organizing production in many branches of English industry.

Four aspects of putting-out are worth stressing. First, it was a form of organization that developed in industries where labour costs were a high proportion of total costs and where technical processes could be performed by unskilled, unsupervised labour. Second, putting-out expanded with the growth of demand for industrial goods : manufacturers supplying a small local demand had little need to employ labour beyond the family workshop. Third, although not an exclusively rural phenomenon, many outworkers lived in parts of the countryside where population expansion had outstripped the ability of agriculture to provide a living. Fourthly, in its most developed form, putting-out led to a separation of the functions of trading and manufacturing and to a growing social distinction between employer and employee. Coupled with the fact that putting-out usually took industry beyond the boundaries of corporate towns, this differentiation of function greatly weakened the authority of the craft gilds that for centuries had been a feature of industry in England.

Craft gilds had grown up in the Middle Ages and by 1500 every borough in the land possessed at least one and sometimes a dozen or more. Gilds drew their authority from charters of incorporation granted by the town or obtained direct from the monarch. In the larger towns most crafts had their own gilds but in smaller places kindred occupations often shared a common organization; and sometimes, when the total number of craftsmen was very small, completely different crafts combined together into a single gild. The function of gilds was to regulate all activities related to their craft or crafts in their particular town, including supervision of standards of workmanship, control of admissions of freemen to the gild, conditions of apprenticeship, and regulation of the trade in raw materials and manufactured products. Gilds were strongly monopolistic, preserving trade for themselves, slow to admit new members and quick to harry non-members who tried to trade in areas or goods regarded by gilds as their own preserve.

Much of the strength of gilds sprang from their close identity with municipal government. They were usually controlled by their wealthier members who were also the notables on the city councils. Gilds were useful instruments of city administration. From their ranks were appointed municipal officers who regulated trading in the local market place, and to them was given the task of enforcing local regulations which were found in many towns controlling the conduct of particular occupations. Additional power was given to gilds by the central government which sometimes used them to enforce economic statutes. The most notable case was that of the leather act of 1563 which required that searchers and sealers of leather should be appointed from the members of the leather gilds in municipal areas. The enforcement of the Statute of Artificers, however, which regulated wages and apprenticeships, was put in the hands of local justices and municipal officers and not, directly, into the hands of the gilds.

The functions of craft gilds were being undermined even as early as 1500 and their history during the sixteenth and seventeenth centuries is one of continuous decline. As manufacturing spread into the suburbs of towns and into rural areas, gild authority was weakened. Within the towns themselves gilds were eroded by economic expansion. As trade increased, urban craftsmen drew their raw materials from farther and farther afield and found customers in distant parts of the country. Gilds thus found it increasingly difficult to regulate marketing on a local basis; while their membership tended to split into two groups, one composed of craftsmen who concentrated on manufacturing for local markets, the other specializing in trade and often with little interest in the problems of manufacturers. The trading group was usually wealthier than the working manufacturers and so came to control gild organization. An extreme example of this development occurred in the London Company of Leathersellers. The company had been formed at the end of the fifteenth century by an amalgamation of various crafts using light leather, '. . . Micanicks Glouers, Pursers, and Longe Cutters [who made leather laces] And for unityes sake called Leather Sellers'. Within a century the company had become completely dominated by leather dealers who:

> in process of time wormed [leather-using craftsmen] out of their freedome allowing none of the breede and posteritye of those workmen to be free . . . there not being this daye a leatherdressor free of the Leathersellors company.[1]

The whole process was made easier for the dealers because the manufacturing craftsmen lived in the suburbs beyond the jurisdiction

[1] B. M. *Additional Ms.* 12504, p. 112.

of the company, although they sold their wares in the City itself.

The decline of the gilds was a slow process. It was probably quicker in London than elsewhere where it was hastened by the custom that permitted a member of a company to follow any occupation in the City with the result that the names of the companies often bore little relation to the activities of their members. However neither the London companies nor the provincial gilds willingly surrendered their authority and, before the Civil War, they received a good deal of government support. Both James I and Charles I granted charters to new organizations and renewed the charters of existing ones, partly from a genuine belief in the usefulness of gilds in controlling industrial activity; but partly, also, because recipients of charters paid for their privileges and the ever impecunious Stuarts rarely passed over an opportunity to raise money. Some of these new incorporations, such as the Company of Clothworkers in Bury St Edmunds in Suffolk established in 1610, claimed jurisdiction over workers in the countryside as well as in the towns. But the growth of industrial employment outside the corporate towns posed the city-based gilds with an insoluble problem, while the emergence of new industries such as papermaking and sugar refining which had never been organized in gilds further weakened their prestige. By the end of the seventeenth century, although many gilds remained in London and the provinces, they were no longer very important in the economic life of the country.

The Expansion of Industry

During the two and a half centuries after 1500 market developments continually presented manufacturers with new opportunities and challenged them with new problems. The growth of population increased the demand for essential consumer goods such as clothing, houses, household equipment, food and drink. The long inflation during the sixteenth and early seventeenth centuries brought rising incomes to some sections of the population which generated greater demand for industrial products; and in the late

seventeenth and early eighteenth centuries the demand for industrial goods among all classes widened and deepened as food prices
fell. Overseas markets presented their own opportunities. Western
Europe was a valuable though highly competitive market for
English textiles and during the course of the seventeenth century
the establishment of colonies in the New World provided additional
markets for producers in many branches of industry.

The first response by manufacturers to increasing demand was to
increase production using existing techniques and forms of
organization. Where it was technically feasible the putting-out
system was extended as a means of employing additional labour;
and even when putting-out was unsuitable production was most
readily increased by employing more hands or compelling the existing workforce to work harder. Before the mid-seventeenth century
the increased demand for labour caused little upward movement
of wages because the growth of population enlarged the supply of
labour. In the second half of the seventeenth century, however,
when population grew sluggishly, wages rose; and it is in this
period that economic writings stress the economic advantages of low
wages. As wages continued to rise in the early eighteenth century,
manufacturers turned their thoughts to alternative ways of cutting costs.

Technical developments as a means of increasing output and
lowering unit costs of production were not common in pre-
industrial England. With minor exceptions basic techniques in the
textile industry remained unaltered. In the 1660s the so-called
Dutch loom was introduced into ribbon manufacture and in the
fourth decade of the eighteenth century John Kay and Lewis Paul
developed new methods of weaving and spinning that foreshadowed
the technical advances of the industrial revolution; but these had
little relevance to industrial development in the period under discussion. The leather industry was totally devoid of technical advance before the end of the eighteenth century save for one or two
impractical curiosities. In the clothing trades there had been one
important technical advance as early as 1589 when the Rev William
Lee of Calverton in Nottinghamshire invented the knitting frame,

but it was little used before the late seventeenth century. Production in the metal-working crafts was facilitated by the introduction of slitting mills in the early seventeenth century which cut iron into conveniently sized bars and rods and enabled entrepreneurs to obtain the raw material for metal-working in a form suitable for putting-out. In food processing, porter, a stable beer that could be brewed in large quantities for a mass consumption market, was developed by the London brewers in the 1720s, but it was not important in the provinces for another half century.

Technical advance was more important in some of the lesser industries in pre-industrial England such as mining and metallurgy which were unable to increase output simply by employing labour. During the sixteenth and seventeenth centuries coal output in Britain increased from a little over 200,000 tons a year in the mid-sixteenth century to just under 3 million tons a century and a half later. Increased production was achieved not merely by multiplying the number of small pits in operation, but by sinking deeper shafts and searching for new seams, thereby raising new technical problems. Boring rods to test deep seams were introduced from Germany in the early seventeenth century. Deep mining required improved haulage, ventilation and drainage methods. These were tackled, none too successfully, by a variety of devices including horse- or man-powered winches that lowered and raised men and coal, or drove an endless chain of buckets which ladled water to the surface. Mines were pioneers of pumping machinery. In 1698 Thomas Savery patented his somewhat dangerous 'miner's friend' which was superseded a few years later by Newcomen's atmospheric engine. Many techniques introduced into mining during the sixteenth and seventeenth centuries came from Germany and it is significant that Sir Francis Willoughby, who mined extensively in Nottinghamshire in the late sixteenth century, possessed a translation of the standard German treatise on mining, *De Re Metallica*. Much of the increase in coal production supplied the urban poor in London and other towns, but some was used in industry. It was not normally possible to use coal in place of wood as an industrial fuel without modifying production techniques. This was not successfully achieved in the iron industry until Abraham Darby used coke in his blast furnaces in or about 1709, but a few industries, such as brick and glass manufacture switched to coal much earlier. The production of coke itself had been developed in the mid-seventeenth century and used for drying malt.

The most important innovation in metallurgy occurred in 1496 with the introduction of the blast furnace into iron smelting. Its use spread steadily in the Weald, replacing the bloomeries which had produced small amounts of wrought iron direct from the ore. The pace of innovation was determined by availability of markets and raw materials. Furnace capacity was several times greater than that of the bloomeries and an assured market for iron was necessary which was provided by the growth of London and the demand for ordnance for the south coast defences and navy. Iron masters frequently operated forges as well as furnaces so as to provide an outlet for their pig-iron. The increased capacity of the furnaces also increased the demand for ore and charcoal, and there was a tendency to vertical integration in the industry whereby producers controlled all operations from the digging of ore and charing of wood to the production of articles from the forges.

The blast furnace illustrates several conditions necessary for technical advance in pre-industrial England. Apart from acquiring the necessary technical knowledge – the blast furnace was a continental technique – its introduction required complex forms of industrial organization embracing a chain of processes and demanding considerable technical and managerial expertise. To be economically worthwhile there had to be sufficiently large markets to take the increased production. Capital was needed to erect the furnaces and ancillary equipment, to install forges, to buy or produce raw materials and to finance the marketing of the final product. New methods of production, therefore, were not undertaken lightly and it is not surprising that industrial producers faced with expanding markets were generally content to increase output by existing methods if they could.

Technical developments occurred in the production of brass and copper. Copper production was virtually a new industry introduced by German technicians working for the Company of Mines Royal, a Crown monopoly incorporated in 1568. Together with the Mineral and Battery Company, established three years earlier to manufacture brass sheet and wire, it was a deliberate attempt by the government to establish import-saving industries in England. Other new industries grew up in England without government assistance as rising imports demonstrated to English producers the existence of potentially profitable markets. A paper mill, for example, apparently operated in Hertfordshire in 1495, but it failed and the industry was not successfully established in England for almost another century. By the end of the sixteenth century industries for the production of alum and gun powder had been established, the first sugar refineries had been built and the first copperas works set up.

Economically these industries were not very important. More significant was the development of new products in existing industries, particularly the textile industry. The export market for textiles was intensively competitive and there was little scope for meeting competition by technical cost-reducing innovations. Manufacturers therefore responded to market changes by varying the nature of their product. The growth of production of 'new draperies' for the market was the most important development in the English textile industry in the late sixteenth century. Most woollen cloth traditionally produced for export was of medium to high quality, made with short-stapled wool and fulled after weaving. The new draperies, on the other hand, were made from combed long-staple wool, of a kind traditionally used to manufacture worsteds, and the cloth was not fulled. Although there were many varieties of new draperies, they all differed from the old draperies in that they were of lower quality and less durable, lighter in texture and cheaper to make. They thus appealed to poorer consumers who could not afford the more expensive cloths, while the variety of their finish and their less durable nature captured a fashion market for fabrics that could be worn for a while and then replaced without great expense. They were also more suited to the warmer markets of southern Europe than the heavier woollen cloths.

On the supply side, the development of new draperies was aided by the growing supply of long-staple combing wool which came from the heavier sheep introduced on enclosed pastures. Perhaps an even more important reason, however, was that the manufacture of cheap, coarse cloths had long been traditional in the countryside, supplying household and local needs. These skills were already incorporated into overseas trade in the sixteenth century with worsted manufacture in East Anglia and kersey production (a low quality 'old drapery') in Devonshire. The new draperies were a further stage in the 'commercialization of peasant techniques'.[1] During the early sixteenth century the Flemish textile industry had begun to produce new draperies in order to exploit the markets of southern Europe opened up by the decline of the Italian textile industry. The new fabrics were already spreading to other centres when the religious upheavals in the Spanish Netherlands forced many Flemish weavers to flee to England and elsewhere. Large numbers of refugees were persuaded to settle in Norwich by the city authorities – nearly 4,000 of them by 1571 – where they helped to revive the flagging worsted industry with their 'outlandish commodities' which, in their production methods, were not dissimilar to worsteds. Others settled in Colchester and Coggeshall in Essex where they encouraged the manufacture of the new draperies. In Devonshire the direct influence of foreigners was negligible, but the new cloths grew naturally enough from the established manufacture of kersies.

Another kind of product differentiation occurred in the west of England. Instead of seeking to exploit the market for cheap cloths the west of England producers aimed at the demand for high-quality coloured cloths and in the early seventeenth century commenced the production of coloured 'Spanish cloths', so-called because they were originally made from imported Spanish wool. No doubt the ease with which fine wool from Spain could be imported from Southern Europe into the ports of south-west England played a part in this development; but something must also be attributed

[1] D. C. Coleman, 'An Innovation and its Diffusion: The "New Draperies"', *Econ. Hist. Rev.* 2nd ser., vol. XXII, no. 3, 1969, p. 421.

to the enterprise of clothiers like Benedict Webb who initiated the manufacture of Spanish cloth – or so he claimed – and who spent a good deal of money in attempting to cultivate rape-seed needed for the oil necessary in dressing cloth. The success of Webb and his fellow clothiers is suggested by the fact that 22 per cent of all old drapery exports from London to Germany and the United Provinces in 1640 were Spanish cloths compared with less than 4 per cent in 1628.

New draperies and Spanish cloths were particular instances of a more general process of adjustment taking place in the textile industry during the seventeenth century. In 1600 the main export-producing regions were the west of England and East Anglia, particularly the southern region along the Suffolk-Essex border. The coarse cloth district of the West Riding was a long way behind and possibly exported even less than the several scattered textile regions in southern England. By the end of the century the west of England had successfully switched to Spanish and other col-oured cloths. The neighbouring county of Devonshire had risen rapidly in importance by grafting the new draperies onto the older kersey industry and by developing the manufacture of serges, a mixed cloth using both long-staple wool imported from Ireland and short-staple wool imported from southern Europe. In the east, the Norwich industry went from strength to strength on the basis of new draperies, but the Suffolk-Essex producers fared less well in the face of competition from their neighbours in Norfolk and the mixed cloths of the west of England. The West Riding of Yorkshire had become one of the most bustling centres of textile manufacture by 1700, having turned to new draperies, including worsteds, in the second half of the century. Meanwhile, a minor but potentially significant development had occurred in south Lancashire in the early seventeenth century – the manufacture of fustian, a mixed cloth of linen and cotton. Originally Levant cotton was used, but later on supplies came from the West Indies through the port of Liverpool. The growth of plantation colonies in the Caribbean and the American tobacco colonies provided a market for cheap light textiles, while the growth of demand in England was stimulated by the importation of calicoes from India which whetted the appetites of Englishmen – and women – for these new kinds of textiles.

Pervading the whole of the textile industry was the growth of the finishing and dyeing industries. In the early seventeenth century the standard of English finishing was not adequate for the demands of the quality markets overseas and about three quarters of cloth was exported undyed and undressed. By the end of the century virtually all cloth sold abroad was dyed and finished. The growth of the dyeing industry is one of the minor mysteries of the seventeenth century. On the side of production it may have been connected with the increased production of woad, madder, saffron, weld and other materials that was a feature of English agriculture in the period. On the demand side it was no less a case of product differentiation in response to changes in the consumer market than the new draperies and Spanish cloths.

Whether industries reacted to changing demands by exploiting the existing means of production, by introducing new techniques, or by product variation, capital and enterprise was needed. Neither was lacking. In most branches of industry capital requirements were rarely beyond the resources of individual entrepreneurs and their partners or friends and working capital was usually available in the form of extended credit from suppliers. In iron working and coal-mining enterprise and capital were both supplied by landowners with estates containing mineral deposits and abundant timber. Occasionally the crown took a hand by granting monopolies to entrepreneurs. The Mineral and Battery Company and the Company of Mines Royal, for example, possessed royal charters which combined English capital with German technical skills. In both cases they were new industries requiring large amounts of development capital, lacking assured markets and needing the privileges of monopoly. Other monopolies were established by James I for the manufacture of glass, soap, alum and other commodities, but they did more to stifle enterprise than to encourage it by interfering with already existing industries.

Industrial development in pre-industrial England owed much to foreign influences. The list of industries which imported European technology is impressive: iron smelting, copper mining and smelting, the manufacture of brass sheet and wire, metal working, glass manufacture, paper, alum, sugar refining, tin-plating, new draperies, silk production, and many others. The knowledge of foreign techniques was obtained in several ways. Two waves of alien immigrants settled in pre-industrial England. In the 1560s Flemish, Walloon and Dutch protestants fleeing from Spanish persecution brought with them various skills, notably in spinning and weaving new draperies. Following the revocation of the Edict of Nantes in 1685 between 40,000 and 50,000 French Huguenots settled in England, many of them skilled in the manufacture of textiles, paper, glass, metals and other goods. Other foreigners arrived individually or were invited to England. Englishmen sometimes journeyed abroad in search of new methods of production. In 1665, for example, Andrew Yarranton was sent to Saxony by a group of Midlands iron masters to discover the techniques of tin-plate manufacture. More surreptitiously, John Lombe, a Norwich silk weaver, smuggled details of Italian silk-throwing machinery into England and established the first silk factory in England at Derby in 1718.

Aliens attracted attention because they were foreign and it is possible that their contribution to the advance of industrial technology obscures the achievements of anonymous Englishmen. Their role was in disseminating technical knowledge which already existed elsewhere in Europe but which was not used in England until market conditions made it worthwhile. Technical advance in pre-industrial England, that is, took the form of applying known but previously unused techniques to production rather than of developing completely new techniques. This process was greatly facilitated by foreigners.

The Achievement

Measurement of the growth of output in the most important English industries between 1500 and 1750 is impossible. The lesser industries have left statistical evidence of a kind. Coal production increased fourteen-fold from the middle of the sixteenth to the end of the seventeenth centuries. Glass production rose even more. The output of salt trebled between 1540 and 1640. The production of bar-iron rose from negligible proportions in 1500 to 10,000 tons a year a century later; output faltered in the middle years of the century but then rose again very slowly to roughly 30,000 tons a year by 1760. But the rates of increase of production in these industries mean very little since the base figures were so low. As far as total industrial output is concerned, it undoubtedly increased throughout the pre-industrial period. Whether it consistently ran ahead of the growth of population is another matter.

More significant than statistical or impressionistic evidence of growth, are the signs of increasing diversity in the industrial sector; for economic growth implies not only greater output but also a widening range of consumers' choice. The clearest evidence is provided by the composition of English manufactured exports. In the early sixteenth century the only important export commodity was woollen cloth, most of which was semi-finished. Two centuries later exports included fully-finished woollens of all kinds, new draperies, fustians, linens, silks, iron-ware, copper and brass, tin, glass and pottery, leather goods, coal and many other products. For none of these industries, except woollen textiles, were overseas markets of great importance, and the bulk of industrial output supplied a rising home market.

'... we may take notice that as Trades and Curious Arts increase; so that the Trade of Husbandry will decrease ...', remarked Sir William Petty in 1691.[1] To the perceptive observer the increasing importance of non-agricultural employments was apparent even before the end of the seventeenth century. The signs that caught his eye must have included urbanization: the continued growth of London and the other ports, and the expansion of 'mere villages' such as Manchester and Birmingham. In a few areas industrial employment had become so important that agriculture had been

[1] Quoted by Colin Clark, *The Conditions of Economic Progress,* 2nd ed. 1951, p. 395.

reduced to a minor role in the local economy. When Defoe visited the West Riding in the early eighteenth century he was impressed by its wealth and the variety of its manufactures. Doncaster was 'a great manufacturing town' with knitting as its main industry. Sheffield was 'very populous and large, the streets narrow, and the houses dark and black, occasioned by the continued smoke of the forges, which are always at work'. 'Black Barnsley was eminent still for the working in iron and steel.' Wakefield and Leeds were prosperous and busy cloth towns, and between Leeds and Halifax the countryside was full of large villages devoted to the manufacture of cloth, 'diligent, and even in a hurry of work'. Halifax itself was only a village, but the most populous in the country. Yet there were few people to be seen. 'But if we knock'd at the door of any of the master manufacturers, we presently saw a house full of lusty fellows, some at the dye-fat, some dressing the cloths, some in the loom, some one thing, some another, all hard at work...'[1] In other parts of the country there were large-scale industrial establishments such as the naval dockyards, the great London breweries, Ambrose Crowley's metal-working factory and large collieries, all employing large numbers of workers.

According to Professor J. U. Nef these developments amounted to an early industrial revolution 'no less important than that of the eighteenth century'.[2] His argument rests on undoubted increases in industrial production, the development of new industries and new technical methods, and a growth in the scale of enterprise in many industries. But it is clear that Professor Nef claims too much by concentrating on industries which were of minor importance in the economy. Neither textiles, clothing, leather, nor any of the half dozen consumer-goods industries that formed the bulk of the industrial sector, experienced any important change in their production methods or the scale of their operations. Large aggregations of fixed capital were untypical even in the industries that figure so prominently in Professor Nef's account of industrial

[1] D. Defoe, *A Tour Through England and Wales*, Everyman ed. 1928, vol. II, p. 180 *et seq.*
[2] J. U. Nef, *War and Human Progress*, 1950, p. 13.

development. The employment of large numbers of workers by a single entrepreneur was unusual before 1750, except when it took the form of the extensive use of outworkers within the putting-out system. Finally we must ask ourselves: what is an industrial revolution? If it means merely mechanical change or increased output, then pre-industrial England saw not one but several revolutions. But the concept of the industrial revolution as normally found in economic history means more than this. It means a change in the structure of the economy, a change from an economy characterized by stagnation to one with high and sustained rates of economic growth stemming from the development of industry. None of these things happened in England before 1750. There was a greater volume of industrial production in 1750 than there had been in 1500 and a wider range of goods being manufactured. Almost certainly a larger proportion of the population was employed in industry, and probably, if it could be measured, we would find that industry was generating a greater proportion of the national income in the early eighteenth century than it had done two centuries earlier. But this is a long way from a transformation of an economy through industrialization. Before 1750 the economy remained basically agricultural.

5

Commerce and Communications

The expansion of agricultural and industrial activity described in the previous chapters required and was made possible by improvements in commercial institutions and transport. These improvements are the subject of the present chapter. We shall trace first the geographical pattern of trade and then consider developments in the means of distribution, the financial arrangements necessary for trade, and the growth of transport.

Internal Trade

Accounts of English trade before the industrial revolution inevitably focus on national and – even more – on international trade for which documentary evidence is relatively abundant and it is easy to forget that the bulk of trade was local, involving the movement of goods over a few miles at most. Even as late as 1841 more than 40 per cent of industrial craftsmen in England were supplying exclusively local markets: before 1750 the proportion must have been a good deal higher.[1] A few enterprising spirits were attracted by the opportunities offered by London or some other distant town and fewer still by overseas markets. These few, however, grew more numerous in the course of the sixteenth, seventeenth and early eighteenth centuries.

[1] C. Day, 'Distribution of Industrial Occupations in England 1841–1861', *Trans. Connecticut Academy of Arts and Science*, vol. 28, 1926–7, pp. 94–5.

Many reasons combined to confine trade to local regions. Often it was the simple lack of knowledge of markets farther afield; at other times the dangers and expense of travel and the risk of dealing with strangers many miles away deterred the extension of trade. Poor transport was a major restraint and, not surprisingly, distant trades flourished best where trading areas were served by good water transport. The extent of trade was also affected by the nature of the product. Corn and coal, for example, were bulky products of relatively low value and it was not economical to carry them long distances unless transport costs were low. Wool, on the other hand, was highly valued in relation to bulk and a national and international wool trade developed long before the sixteenth century. The trade in livestock was generally more extensive than the trade in grain or livestock products, for animals possessed the great virtue of being able to walk to market thus keeping transport costs down. Perishable goods such as milk or eggs were scarcely sold at all over long distances, although salted butter and cheese were distributed more widely. Manufactured goods were probably traded more extensively than agricultural produce because of their greater value added in manufacture; but in some cases this advantage was offset by increased bulk.

During the sixteenth and seventeenth centuries there was a steady expansion of internal trade made possible by improvements in transport and the means of distribution. Transport improvements, however, were as much the result of growing trade as its cause and the underlying reasons for the expansion of trade were the growth of population and incomes. As numbers increased in the less fertile regions of the country it became necessary for those areas to import food from other regions. Often population in predominately pastoral districts grew faster than the population in arable regions and grain had to be bought from areas with corn surpluses. Population in the pastoral districts found their livelihoods, not only in the production of stock and livestock products, but also in growing labour-intensive crops such as flax and hemp and by concentrating on various kinds of industrial production, the markets for which were situated in other parts of the country or overseas. The expansion of inland trade, therefore, was a necessary accompaniment of the growing regional specialization occurring in agriculture and industry.

Increasing population in pre-industrial England also led to urbanization which gave a powerful stimulus to internal trade. As we have seen, urban dwellers were mainly consumers and processers of food and raw materials, supplies of which were obtained from the surrounding countryside. Towns themselves were manufacturing and processing centres and there was a return flow of manufactured goods to the countryside. The larger towns were also ports and centres for the distribution of imported goods such as canvas, silks, calicoes, metal wares, glass, groceries, wines, sugar and tobacco. Urban expansion affected the development of trade in more ways than by merely generating a greater volume of demand. To argue that in 1640 the population of London 'was probably more than equalled by that of the two counties of Kent and Suffolk', and that therefore, 'the proportion of the agricultural output of England consumed by Londoners can never have been more than a small fraction of the whole',[1] obscures important qualitative differences between large, urban markets and scattered, rural markets. The greater demands of the former required highly developed market institutions. London, for example, possessed specialized and general markets open for business every weekday. Permanent shops became a feature of London streets early in the seventeenth century and the metropolis was supplied by a complicated network of wholesalers and retailers. Financial institutions evolved earlier in London than elsewhere to facilitate trade, long- or short-term credit was available, and if traders wanted ready cash, it could be obtained more readily in London than anywhere else.[2] The nature of urban demand was also different. The level

[1] A. Everitt, 'The Marketing of Agricultural Produce', *The Agrarian History of England and Wales*, vol. IV, ed. J. Thirsk, 1967, p. 514.

[2] When discussions took place in 1785 on liberalizing restrictions on Irish trade with England, it was said that Irish leather manufacturers would be able to obtain working capital by selling leather in London for cash, which they were not able to do in the poor Irish markets (*Parliamentary Papers*, 1785, vol. VIII, p. 113).

of incomes was higher in towns than in the countryside, for the upper-income groups such as merchants, lawyers, administrators and the more elevated clergy lived in towns and landowners frequently maintained town houses in London or provincial capitals. Urban wage rates also were probably higher than rural wages. Townsmen therefore could afford to be more particular in their demands, and buy high quality and unusual products. Only a market such as London could support a trade in salmon and carp which were packed in barrels of wet straw and sent by horse and wagon from Sussex and the Lake District. Consumption habits changed more rapidly in cities than in country areas, stimulating new trades; and the price-elasticity of demand was probably greater in towns because of the presence of a larger number of customers. Thus farmers or manufacturers were more likely to increase sales of a commodity by lowering its price if they supplied large urban markets than if they sold their output in small market towns or villages.

Internal trade crosses no national boundaries and so escapes the detailed attention of bureaucrats whose records are so valuable in assessing the volume and direction of overseas trade. It is therefore very difficult to discern the major flows of internal trade. Nevertheless from the whirls and eddies of local trade it is possible to map the national currents of trade in a few major commodities. Many of these currents flowed to London. An extensive corn trade, centred on London, developed in the sixteenth and seventeenth centuries. The Home Counties and East Anglia provided the bulk of supplies in the late sixteenth century and by the early seventeenth century grain was also being drawn from the market towns of the upper Thames valley and the south Midlands, as well as from the coastal districts of Yorkshire and the north-east. Before 1640 some sixty towns in eastern England, virtually every one of them by a river, specialized in the marketing of grain. By the early eighteenth century virtually the whole of England south of a line from the Humber to the upper Severn was a granary for London.

A national trade in wool developed earlier than the trade in corn to meet the needs of wool exporters in the late Middle Ages and to supply the expanding cloth industry. The leading cloth producing districts all supplemented local wool supplies with wool obtained elsewhere. In the late sixteenth century manufacturers in the high quality cloth district of the west of England bought short-staple wool from Herefordshire, Shropshire, Staffordshire and the Midlands. The centre of the trade was Cirencester which was visited by wool dealers from the Midlands and elsewhere and by clothiers from the textile districts. By the early seventeenth century west of England producers were also turning to South Wales and the south of England, possibly because of the growing coarseness of wool obtained from the Midlands. East Anglian manufacturers bought much of their wool locally, but they also obtained supplies from Lincolnshire, the Midlands and London. The coarse woollen industry of the West Riding was supplied with local wool, but wool was bought from Scotland, Lincolnshire, Leicestershire and North-amptonshire. By the early eighteenth century Yorkshire manu-facturers were also being supplied from London. London wool dealers sold fleece wool grown in the Home Counties, fell wool taken from carcasses of sheep slaughtered for mutton, and yarn imported from Ireland. But the greatest 'magazine' for wool in the late seventeenth century was the east Midlands which had swung from arable to pasture farming during the previous century. Pos-sessing little textile manufacture themselves, counties such as Leicestershire and Northamptonshire supplied raw wool to virtually every textile manufacturing region in the country.

London was 'the place of greatest concourse for tradesmen deal-ing in leather'.[1] The capital was a large consumer of leather and leather goods, and a major producer of hides and skins so there was a two-way trade, with hides moving out to the provinces where bark was available, and leather moving into the consumers. In the early sixteenth century tanners in Hertfordshire regularly con-tracted with London butchers to be supplied with hides. A century later the trading area had widened so much that provincial tanners asked the City authorities to alter the market day for leather and hides at Leadenhall from Monday to Tuesday or Wednesday so

---

[1] *Minute Book of the Company of Curriers*, 1628–56 (Gild Hall Ms. 6112/1), p. 77.

that they would not have to travel on the sabbath and endanger their immortal souls. By the 1680s leather manufacturers throughout the Home Counties and the south Midlands regularly travelled overland to London to buy hides and sell leather. Almost every year in the seventeenth century tanners from south Yorkshire came to London to buy hides which they shipped to Hull and 'vpp Humber and the fresh waters there to Turnbridge and Bawtrey and hence by land to our seuerall dwellings within the said West Riding of Yorkshire'.[1] Nearly as regularly raw hides were sent to Faversham and other north Kent ports, for use by local tanners who obtained bark from the woods around Canterbury. In return, finished leather was sent back to London. Farther afield large quantities of light leather and gloves were made in western England for the London market.

Turning to coal, practically half of all English production was sent to market by coastal and river shipping. London alone consumed one-sixth of all coal production in the early eighteenth century but counties from Oxfordshire in the west to Essex and Kent in the east were supplied with water-borne coal from Tyneside. Some coal was traded overland, especially from the Warwickshire fields situated near the Fosse Way which supplied markets in Leicestershire, Northamptonshire, Worcestershire, and as far south as Oxfordshire.

A national trade in butter, cheese and meat revolved around London. Essex and Suffolk were regular suppliers of cheese and butter and additional supplies were sometimes obtained from farther afield. The trade in meat was extensive for animals were delivered to butchers on the hoof. Throughout the period there was a well-established pattern of trade. Lean animals were sold by breeders from the pastoral north, and west, and Wales to graziers in the Midlands and Home Counties who fattened the beasts for the market. Farmers in the south Midlands, Lincolnshire, East Anglia and as far away as Wiltshire found it worthwhile to raise poultry, pigs and rabbits for the London market.

It would be a mistake to regard London as the only focus of

[1] P.R.O. S.P. 16/65, no. 45.

inland trade in pre-industrial England, although it was certainly the most important. During the seventeenth and early eighteenth centuries ports and industrializing centres such as Bristol, Liverpool, Manchester and Birmingham stimulated inland trade and acted as lesser Londons in offering new opportunities to producers and widening consumers' choice. Every expanding market town in the country stood at the centre of an enlarging circle of commerce. But it would be equally a mistake to think that, even by 1750, England was a truly national market. Ignorance, conservatism and inadequate communications still contrived to fragment the country into a number of only loosely integrated regional economies. Some progress had been made towards the development of a national economy. But for producers in, say, Kent or Essex, customers in Cumberland or Cornwall were less accessible than those in France or Flanders. And all were more remote than customers found in nearby towns and villages.

Overseas Trade

In spite of the 'richness and quantity of our native commodities to make trade withal, which far exceeds any one kingdom in Christendom or in the known world',[1] the English economy was not self-sufficient. The Mediterranean lands supplied wool, wines, vegetable oils, skins, dyestuffs, sumac, alum and salt; the Baltic fish and furs, timber and iron and grain; while from outside Europe came drugs and groceries, silks and cottons, precious metals and stones. England itself was part of the relatively industrialized zone of western Europe and most of her overseas trade was, in fact, with countries within this area.

Pre-industrial England produced one commodity above all others that was in demand in overseas markets – woollen textiles. Most were sold to the countries of western Europe which possessed important textile regions of their own and which also exported cloth, and the international trade in textiles rested on a delicate balance of com-

[1] Sir John Watts, *A Discourse upon Trade* (1625?), quoted by R. H. Tawney in *Business and Politics under James I*, 1958, p. 33.

parative advantages whereby English producers specialized in certain kinds of fabrics and European manufacturers in other varieties. International markets for cloth were very competitive and the history of the English export trade in the sixteenth and seventeenth centuries is characterized by the inability of producers to expand sales in established markets for any length of time. Technical innovations designed to reduce production costs – and hence increase sales – were notably absent and so trade expansion instead took the form of product differentiation and diversification of markets.

Until the mid-fourteenth century England's principal export had been raw wool, but an export trade in woollen cloth grew up after 1350, largely at the expense of Flemish manufactures. During the fifteenth century the wool and cloth export trades existed side by side but neither showed much sign of expansion. Opportunities for expansion were limited by the stagnation of population growth in Europe and the low income-elasticity of demand for cloth. However, some increases in cloth exports occurred at the end of the fifteenth century and continued intermittently until about 1550. In all, English cloth exports may have risen as much as one-third in volume in the first half of the sixteenth century. London's exports, indeed, rose from roughly 50,000 to over 110,000 short-cloths a year but this was offset by a fall in the export of woollen cloth from the outports and also by a decline in worsted exports.

The main explanation of the expansion of the cloth trade was probably the supply conditions in the English industry. English pastures yielded an abundance of short-staple carding wool of high quality, much in demand in Europe as well as by English manufacturers. However a heavy customs duty was charged on raw wool when it was exported, equivalent in 1500 to almost one-third of its value. Thus English clothiers enjoyed a considerable advantage, particularly as the export duty on manufactured cloth was very low. Labour costs may also have been lower in England than on the Continent because of the greater use of country labour by English manufacturers. On the other hand materials for dyeing and dressing cloth were generally more expensive in England than in Europe since many were imported. Possibly, too, the standard of workmanship was lower in England and three-quarters or more of cloth was exported undyed and undressed. On the demand side, European markets were enlarged by a growing population. Political conditions were relatively stable and excellent commercial facilities existed in Antwerp which received the bulk of English cloth. In the 1540s trade was further encouraged by good harvests and a high level of military demand in Europe; and in the last two years of the decade exports were probably stimulated by the debasement of the English coinage which lowered the price of cloth in terms of foreign currencies.

Modest as the expansion was between 1500 and 1550, it did not continue into the second half of the sixteenth century. The 1550s and 1560s were years of great instability in the cloth trade, with export volumes fluctuating violently as a result of monetary disturbances, plague, bad harvests, and political turmoil in Europe leading to the eventual closure of Antwerp to English merchants. By the 1570s the level of cloth exports settled down perhaps 20 per cent lower than the level reached in the early 1550s. Any competitive edge that cheap wool and cheap labour had given English manufacturers earlier in the century was now blunted. Indeed, as far as wool was concerned, by the end of the sixteenth century English clothiers were looking to southern Europe for fine wool as the nature of English wool gradually changed towards coarser varieties. There was some expansion in the cloth trade in the early seventeenth century with the restoration of peace in Western Europe, but basically the Low Countries and Germany – England's most important customers – were not expansive markets. Exports were seriously disrupted between 1614 and 1617 by William Cockayne's abortive attempts to replace white cloth, which composed most of the export trade, by coloured cloths. The scheme failed because continental manufacturers had a comparative advantage in cloth finishing. A few years later, between 1620 and 1624, trade was again interrupted by currency debasements in Europe that raised the price of English textiles in terms of local currencies and made them uncompetitive. These two incidents underlined the fact that demand for woollen cloth was inelastic. There was some revival of exports in the later 1620s but generally the 1630s and 1640s were years of stagnation.

The difficulties outlined above affected the trade in old draperies – heavy, fulled cloth made from short-stapled, carded wool. While this branch of trade languished in the late sixteenth and early seventeenth centuries, the export of the cheaper, lighter, new draperies increased rapidly. As we saw in the previous chapter, their manufacture in England had been stimulated by the influx of Flemish weavers and by the increasing supplies of long-staple wool becoming available in England. In 1601 the value of new draperies exported from London was possibly about 20 per cent of the value of old draperies and by 1640 the two branches of the trade were roughly of equal value. The combined value of trade in old and new draperies from London rose by about 75 per cent in the first forty years of the seventeenth century. The light fabrics sold particularly well in the warm, less competitive markets of southern Europe and north Africa which took about 65 per cent of London's exports of new draperies in 1640.

During the second half of the seventeenth century the volume and value of textile exports continued to grow but there were frequent interruptions caused by wars with Holland, Spain and France. The available statistics do not permit a reliable estimate of the extent of the growth; and much more significant was the increasing diversity of the textile trade as new draperies, mixed fabrics and coloured cloths displaced the old draperies from their supremacy. The markets, too, continued to change, those of southern Europe growing more rapidly than those in western Europe. By 1700 the Mediterranean countries were taking 40 per cent of all textile exports to Europe. The story in the eighteenth century is much the same: woollen exports to western and northern Europe actually declined in value between 1700 and 1750 whereas exports to the south rose by more than 60 per cent.

The chronic stagnation of the textile markets in western Europe largely explains why woollens became a smaller proportion of total exports after 1640. Table 3 summarizes the position.

TABLE 3   *The Composition of England's export trade (per cent)*

	1640	1700	1750
Woollen manufactures	80–90	48	33
Other manufactures	—	8	20
Foodstuffs	—	8	12
Raw materials	—	6	5
Re-exports	3–4	31	29

Woollen textiles remained the largest single category of exports but their rate of growth was far exceeded by the growth of re-exports and miscellaneous manufactured goods. The former came from the American and West Indian colonies and the territories of the East India Company, chiefly tobacco, sugar and calicoes. Sales expanded quickly in England and Europe as prices fell and fashions changed. English commercial policy ensured that trade in these commodities was channelled through English ports, and the incomes they earned for the producing countries enabled those countries to buy English manufactured goods such as metalwares, clothing, leather and textiles. By 1750, 73 per cent of miscellaneous manufactures and 17 per cent of woollen textiles were exported to markets outside continental Europe.

The remaining items in the export trade were rarely important. Exports of raw wool dwindled away after 1520 and virtually disappeared by 1600. Corn exports, never large, likewise vanished by 1600. In both cases growing internal demand prevented any substantial surplus being available for export. However, corn became important for a while in the early eighteenth century when rising agricultural productivity, coupled with a policy of paying bounties to exporters, enabled English merchants to take advantage of the disruption of the Baltic grain trade. Apart from corn, there was a small but regular export of fish to southern Europe. Tin and lead regularly comprised 5 or 6 per cent of exports between the sixteenth and eighteenth centuries. Coal exports grew after 1700 and reached almost 1.5 per cent of total exports by 1750. Turning to imports, the position is summarized in Table 4.

TABLE 4   *The Composition of England's import trade (per cent)*

	c 1600	1660s (London only)	1700	1750
Manufactured goods	40	37	32	22
Food, drink, tobacco		27	34	41
Raw materials — semi manufactured	60			
goods		36	35	36

Manufactured imports declined in relative importance throughout the period. In the late sixteenth century England imported textiles – chiefly linens, mixed fabrics and silks – and other goods. By the end of the seventeenth century the main manufactured goods imported were still textiles such as linens, silks and calicoes, many of which were re-exported. The most important food imports in the sixteenth century were wines, fruit, hops and spices. During the seventeenth century imports of sugar and tobacco increased rapidly as did tea, coffee and rice in the eighteenth century. It was primarily these colonial groceries, large proportions of which were re-exported, that accounted for the importance of food imports in the late seventeenth and early eighteenth centuries. The third category of imports, raw materials, comprised a little over one-third of total exports throughout the period. The bulk of them were textile fibres, including wool, flax, hemp and – increasingly – silk and cotton – as well as dye-stuffs and finishing materials. Other items included skins and furs, timber, iron and steel – growing in importance in the eighteenth century as domestic production fell below demand.

In sum, the composition of English foreign trade changed very gradually between the sixteenth and eighteenth centuries, the most significant shifts occurring after 1660 as the re-export trade developed. The growth of the re-export trade distracts attention from how slowly the composition of the *domestic* export trade altered. In 1700, for example, woollens still comprised around 70 per cent of exports of English goods (i.e. excluding re-exports) compared with 80 or 90 per cent half a century before. Similarly, on the import side, the remarkable feature of trade was its stability – again except for the growth of the import of goods intended for re-export.

The same feature can also be seen in the direction of trade. As late as 1700 Europe took 85 per cent of English exports. Europe contained the nearest, richest and most populous markets although they were also the most competitive. Within Europe the Low Countries, Germany, France and the Baltic were the most important markets although they declined relatively as English merchants turned their attentions to the less competitive markets in Spain, Portugal and the Mediterranean. Taking Europe as a whole, it remained important to English merchants during the seventeenth and eighteenth centuries, in spite of competition from European manufacturers and tariffs placed on English goods, for four reasons. The first was the growth of the re-export trade, most of which was with Europe. Secondly, virtually all grain and fish exports from England went to Europe. Thirdly, Spain and Portugal bought English manufactures, not only for their own use, but to re-export to their own South-American possessions. Finally, as a result of commercial policy, Anglo-Irish trade grew vigorously in the early eighteenth century. Nevertheless, Asian, African and American markets grew more rapidly than European markets after 1700 as their incomes rose from the export of goods to England and Europe; and by 1750 non-European territories absorbed roughly 20 per cent of English exports.

Imports also came mainly from Europe, although the net was spread a little more widely than for exports and, by 1700 32 per cent came from non-European sources. By 1750 the proportion had risen to 45 per cent; the figure might have been lower but for colonial groceries and East Indian textiles and spices imported into England for re-export to Europe. Manufactured imports from Europe declined in relative importance as English industry expanded and as import duties were raised in the late seventeenth and early eighteenth centuries.

Overseas Trade and the Home Economy

At the end of the seventeenth century the value of English goods exported was about £4.4 millions compared with a gross national product estimated at roughly £50 millions. Taking into account invisible exports English exports were equivalent to about 10 per cent of gross national product. The proportion of manufacturing production exported was higher, but only the woollen industry exported as much as a third of the value of its output. Perhaps about 8 per cent of iron output was exported in one form or another at the beginning of the eighteenth century, and about 10 per cent of leather production. Grain exports in 1700 were probably between 1 and 2 per cent of total production, rising to 7 per cent by 1750. The majority of farmers and manufacturers in England had little interest in foreign or colonial markets. Yet to regard overseas trade in this narrow way is to understate its role in English economic life. Although small in itself, overseas demand extended the market and thus encouraged the growth of production which led ultimately to improved organization and new technical methods. It was no accident, for example, that the textile industry was the first to exploit the advantages of cheap country labour by use of the putting-out system, and among the first in the eighteenth century to develop new inventions. Quantitatively overseas markets were small; qualitatively they had a considerable influence on the organization of production and distribution.

Contemporaries were under no illusions that the state of overseas trade influenced the health of the home economy. As cloth production for export expanded during the first half of the sixteenth century, men began to wonder about the wisdom of becoming dependent – as they thought – on foreign markets and the disruption of trade in the 1550s brought these doubts to a head. In

1564 we find William Cecil speculating ruefully on reasons why 'the deminution of clothyng in this realme wer proffitable to the same . . .'

> first, for that therby the tilladg of the realm is notoriously decayed, . . . Secondly, for that the people that depend upon the makyng of cloth of worss condition to be quyetly governed than the husband man. Thyrdly, by convertyng of so manny people to clothyng, the realme lacketh not only artificers, which wer wont to inhabitt all corporat townes, but also laborers for all comen workes.[1]

These fears were undoubtedly exaggerated. Tillage was not 'notoriously decayed' throughout the realm, nor even in the cloth producing districts. On the contrary, the growth of trade between 1500 and 1550 created new incomes in the textile regions at a time when population was increasing and agriculture offered little hope of a comfortable life. It was true, however, that a depression of exports created unemployment since workers employed on a putting-out basis were quickly laid off as orders ceased to arrive.

The distrust of overseas trade expressed by Cecil was common in the sixteenth century, but it did not last. When the cloth trade was again seriously depressed in the 1620s, the reaction was different: 'The cloth trade is . . . the axis of the commonwealth, whereon all other trades . . . do seem to turn and have their revolution', wrote Edward Misselden in 1623,[2] and the government explored several ways of reviving trade. Misselden overstated the importance of the cloth trade no less than Cecil – not even taking into account its multiplier effect did it determine the level of activity throughout the whole economy. But there is no doubt that the expansion of overseas commerce was increasingly seen as a dynamic force, particularly after 1660 with the development of the colonial, East Indian and re-export trades. Overseas commerce stimulated investment in docks, harbours and shipping and a complex of financial

[1] *Tudor Economic Documents*, ed. R. H. Tawney and E. Power, 1924, II, p. 45.
[2] Quoted by B. E. Supple, *Commercial Crisis and Change in England, 1600–1642*, 1959, p. 6.

and commercial services. The amount of shipping, for example, employed in the American, West Indian and East Indian trades practically doubled between the 1660s and 1680s. Economic writers and policy-makers alike in the later seventeenth century thought that foreign trade was the only sure route to economic growth.

Foreign trade brought in imports which contributed to English economic development in various ways. Imported raw materials aided the growth of several branches of the textile industry, particularly the production of linens, canvases, silks and fine woollen cloths. Other industries depending at least partly on imports included shipbuilding, metal and light leather production, dyeing and cloth finishing. The import trade in tobacco, sugar and groceries stimulated a range of ancillary industries including tobacco processing, sugar refining, confectionery and glass manufacture. Imports of manufactured goods, too, had an important, if indirect, effect in changing consumption habits and demonstrating the existence of a demand for goods that might be produced at home by the establishment of import-replacement industries.

To many observers in the sixteenth and seventeenth centuries, however, the import trade appeared merely as a threat to England's supplies of gold and silver. A belief that the balance of trade was adverse was widespread in the sixteenth and seventeenth centuries, made all the more enduring since there was no certain way before the reform of the customs' administration in the 1690s of knowing whether imports exceeded exports or *vice versa*. An inquiry by the Privy Council in 1563–4, when exports were depressed, revealed a small deficit on commodity trade. When cloth exports were higher there may have been a surplus, no one could be sure, although it was clear that the balance depended on the health of the cloth trade. Some branches of trade were always in deficit. In the sixteenth and early seventeenth centuries the value of imports of canvas, linen and wines from France exceeded the value of English exports to France, but this deficit was covered by surpluses earned in the trades to Spain and the Low Countries. The Baltic which provided naval stores, raw materials and grain, was a deficit trade but was tolerated because of its strategic value. The value of East Indian goods imported to England always exceeded the value of exports to the East Indies, but many of these goods earned specie when re-exported to Europe. By the end of the seventeenth century, indeed, the balance of trade was favourable, largely because of the earnings of the re-export trade.

Concern with the balance of payments is familiar enough today. During the sixteenth and seventeenth centuries it arose less because of the need to pay for imports required to maintain the standard of living than because an export surplus was the only way that England could obtain supplies of gold and silver which were the basis of the money supply. Before the end of the seventeenth century very little paper money circulated in England and the conduct of trade depended on the supply of gold or silver coin. When the balance of payments was adverse specie flowed out, causing a dearth of coin and a contraction of trade. Not only was coin needed as a means of exchange but producers required cash to buy raw materials and pay their employees. With fixed capital unimportant in all but a few occupations and with credit facilities poorly developed, the supply of working capital – cash – was vital and hence a favourable balance of trade was of paramount importance.

A further reason for the importance of overseas trade in the eyes of contemporaries was that it was a major source of revenue for the government. Customs duties were the most important and convenient form of taxation before the development of income tax. They were easier to raise than taxes on property and possessed the added advantage to a government composed largely of landowners that they were paid ultimately by consumers. Overseas merchants were among the richest men in England and had readier access to liquid funds than landowners whose wealth was tied up in property. Merchants were therefore a convenient source of loans to the crown whose income continually fell short of expenditure. In the early sixteenth century the crown was forced to borrow from foreign merchants but it gradually turned to Englishmen as their wealth increased. Since the collective wealth of merchants was greater than that of individuals, the crown preferred to borrow from groups of merchants such as the Company of Merchant Adventurers or from the City of London which, in turn, raised money from the merchant community. By the end of the seventeenth century government credit was re-organized and there was less direct dependence on the resources of merchants in overseas trade. Nevertheless mercantile wealth was deeply involved in projects like the Bank of England which took over the role of lending to the government.[1]

Commercial Institutions – Markets, Middlemen and Merchants

'The evolution of the institutions of the Mercantile Economy is largely a matter of finding ways of diminishing risks.'[2] Any trade involving more than an exchange between neighbours de-manded a knowledge of market opportunities and involved risks. Hundreds of market towns had grown up during the Middle Ages for the conduct of local trade, many of them very small, and in Tudor and early Stuart England roughly 800 towns possessed public markets, that is a market town for approximately every 4,000 or 5,000 people in the country. Every week, or two or three times weekly in the bigger towns, the market place was opened for trade. Urban producers displayed their goods on stalls and farmers brought in raw materials from the surrounding countryside. Trading conditions were regulated by the town authorities who charged tolls and restricted the dealings of stran-gers. 'Foreign' craftsmen were frequently excluded altogether in order to preserve the monopolies of local craftsmen, but dealers in raw materials were not severely constrained since their goods were needed by the urban population. Indeed market officials often tried to see that raw materials were delivered to the market and not sold beforehand. Thus butchers trading in Liverpool market in 1541/2 'that doyth bryng eny oxe cowe or other beffe to the

[1] For a discussion of public finance see p. 183–91.
[2] Sir John Hicks, *A Theory of Economic History*, 1969, p. 48.

towne shall bring the hydes thereof to the market with the hornes and ears attached'.[1] Similar regulations existed in many other towns.

Much of the trade in local market towns was between men known to one another who would allow credit for short periods with little risk of loss. A centralized market place was obviously an advantage since it increased knowledge of market opportunities and made the supervision of trade easier. Some market towns also developed a more specialized trade in corn, cattle or some other commodity. Roughly two-fifths of English market towns in the sixteenth century specialized in this way, although they continued to act as general centres of trade as well. Market towns in eastern England tended to concentrate on corn, the Midland towns on livestock and leather goods, and the west on livestock, dairy products, gloves, wool and cloth.

Local market towns, nevertheless, were not ideal institutions for the conduct of an expanding national trade. They were often physically confined and became congested as the volume of trade increased. Even more important, the discrimination practised in most of them against dealers living outside the towns was incompatible with a widespread network of trade. It was to escape municipal controls on long-distance trade that annual fairs, altogether freer than the local weekly markets, developed during the Middle Ages. Some market towns possessed the right to hold fairs as well but most fairs were held in the countryside away from the towns. They dealt mainly in cattle, sheep and horses, although the famous Stourbridge Fair held every September in the fields outside Cambridge, sold wool, hops, manufactured goods and imported commodities of many kinds. But essentially fairs handled agricultural goods and their timing reflected the farming cycle. They enabled cattle breeders to sell off their leanstock and sheep farmers their wool after shearing. Such annual events were important enough to be celebrated by drinking and entertainment and fairs took on the one character that remains with them today.

In distant trade middlemen were necessary to link producers and

[1] J. A. Twemlow (ed.), *Liverpool Town Books*, vol. 1, 1918, pp. 20–1.

consumers. In the early sixteenth century their activities were viewed with suspicion and provided ample subjects for Sunday sermons. To the Rev Thomas Lever, for instance, preaching at St Paul's Cross in 1550, middlemen were 'Marchantes of Myschyefe that goe betwixt the barke and the tree: Betwixt the Husband man that getteth the corne, and the householder and occupyeth Corne ...'[1] Lever was preaching to the converted and in the sixteenth century middlemen were usually prohibited altogether or strictly controlled by government. The hostility shown towards middlemen was itself an index of their increasing importance. As long as trade was purely local, dealers were unnecessary and when they interposed themselves between producers and consumers they possibly did, in Lever's words, 'make all thinges dere to the byers: and yet wonderfull vyle and of small pryce to many, that must nedes sett or sell that whyche is their owne honestlye come bye'. Yet Lever himself recognized that to 'take awaye all merchauntmen from anye town or cytye, and ye shall leave almost no prouyson of thinges that be necessarye'. More than a century after he wrestled with these problems, the London Company of Curriers, seeking the repeal of obsolete legislation restricting the leather trade, argued 'the more buyers and sellers the better for the public'.[2] Such a justification a century earlier would have courted failure, but the expansion of internal trade during the sixteenth and seventeenth centuries brought about a change in attitudes towards middlemen.

For producers middlemen reduced the risks and inconveniences of distant trade; for consumers they smoothed out price fluctuations over time and distance. In an agrarian-based economy most production was seasonal, whereas demands arose regularly throughout the year. Middlemen bought at harvest time, or in anticipation of the harvest, and sold produce gradually during the year. Farmers were thus assured of a predictable price and were saved the risks of price fluctuations and costs of storing goods. Consumers were

[1] *Tudor Economic Documents*, III, p. 49.
[2] *Hist. Mss. Comm., Report 12, Appendix 6,* 'House of Lords Mss, 1689–90', pp. 111–4.

supplied regularly at more stable prices – and possibly, on average, lower prices – than they would otherwise have paid. It was this aspect of their business that aroused most suspicion of middlemen and provoked a fury of condemnation against the sins of regrating (buying cheap and selling dear) forestalling (buying up supplies before they reached public markets) and engrossing (cornering supplies). Middlemen were no more endowed with altruism in an economy motivated by profit maximization than other sections of the community. Their knowledge of the market gave them opportunities for exploiting their customers and their alleged sins were not entirely the figments of censorious clerics. But without middlemen inland trade on an extensive scale would have been impossible.

Another important function of middlemen was that of buying in bulk and selling in small quantities. Legislation curbing the activities of middlemen frequently fell down at this point. Thus the weavers of Halifax complained of an act of 1555 that 'taketh awaye the Wooldryver, so that they cannot nowe have theyr wooll by such small pocions as they were wont to have', and in 1675 leather dealers defended their trade by pointing out that a dealer 'in leather as well as one of cloth and other commodities is necessary, especially for supplying the poor traders and artificers, by furnishing them with leather curried and dressed and proper for their use, who could not provide for supplies to last till the return of the market'.[1] Middlemen also performed the reverse function of buying small quantities of materials from many sources and bulking them into large consignments for substantial customers. In the sixteenth century, for example, woolmen bought wool in small lots which they made up into consignments worth hundreds or even thousands of pounds. This function led to another: that of sorting raw materials into different qualities and types suitable for different purposes. Sorting developed in the wool trade from about 1570 as manufacturers produced textiles of an increasing range of quality and type which demand different kinds of wool. The leather trade was another in which sorting was an important

[1] *Tudor Economic Documents*, I, pp. 187–8; *Cal. S. P. D.*, 1675, p. 88.

task. Dealers cut leather into 'such Pieces and Parcels as are most fit for the respective Uses of the various Artificers dealing with them for the same ... the different parts of One Hide and Skin being useful for distinct and different Purposes, and seldom worked up by any one Artificer'.[1]

Middlemen made possible the development of retail shops. Workshops where artisans sold goods they manufactured themselves had long been a feature of English provincial towns. Retail shops, supplied with goods by wholesalers, appeared in the larger towns in the early seventeenth century, dealing in tobacco, spices and imported groceries. These were commodities of high value which could be broken down into small quantities and transported easily from the point of import to shopkeepers in various parts of the country. There were, for example, seventy-two licensed retailers of tobacco in Wiltshire in 1637. Retail shops trading in English goods were also found in London in the early seventeenth century. Among the earliest were corn chandlers selling meal and corn, and haberdashers who sold gloves and other goods. Saddlers, too, developed a retail side to their business quite early. By the early eighteenth century retail shops displaying haberdashery, groceries, leather goods, ironmongery, pottery, earthenware, and many other things behind glass windows were a familiar sight in London and the provinces.

Middlemen developed earlier in the wool trade than in most other branches of commerce. At the bottom end of the business broggers bought and sold wool in small quantities, probably combining wool dealing with agriculture or manufacture. Their customers were poor clothiers and most of their trade was local. Socially and economically they were inferior to the woolmen who supplied exporters in the early sixteenth century, and the specialist wool dealers whose customers were large-scale clothiers producing for overseas markets. Many large dealers lived in London and employed factors who travelled around the countryside buying wool from farmers. Many of the substantial wool dealers in the early sixteenth century had been Merchants of the Staple who

[1] *House of Commons Journals,* vol. 23, p. 35.

turned to the inland trade as the export trade in wool declined. They were joined in the later sixteenth century by fellmongers who bought sheepskins from farmers and butchers and sold wool to clothiers and skins to leatherdressers; according to the latter in the early seventeenth century fellmongers knew nothing about skins and 'if they durst would cast the pelt vpon the dung hill hauing before suckt out theire proffit by pulling of, sorting, and selling the wooll'.[1]

Other specialized dealers were found in the leather and corn trades. The main dealers in tanned leather were curriers who, by virtue of their position in the manufacturing process between tanners and the leather-using craftsmen, were well placed to act as cutters and wholesalers of leather. Leathersellers were middlemen in the light leather trade dealing in uncut leather, which they supplied to small working craftsmen, and in gloves and other leather goods which they sold from their own shops or supplied to haberdashers and other retailers. Corn dealers supplied London with grain even before the sixteenth century and were found in all expanding communities. Some concentrated on buying unground corn for delivery to town millers while others sold meal and flour. They were closely supervised by municipal authorities who feared that middlemen would exploit urban consumers, but without them towns could not have been fed.

Some traders engaged both in internal and overseas commerce, but the latter tended to be in the hands of merchants who concentrated on foreign markets. There were several reasons for this. Overseas trade was riskier than inland dealings. It usually required bigger capital outlays and returns on investments were slower. If losses were to be avoided overseas merchants needed a detailed knowledge of their markets and the workings of the foreign exchanges. They needed to know about ships and insurance and required at least a rudimentary knowledge of foreign languages, laws and customs, particularly when trading with distant parts of the world lying, as Professor Willan has put it, 'outside the range of the Ten Commandments'.

[1] B. M. *Add. Ms.* 12504, fo. 112.

In the early sixteenth century a considerable proportion of the export trade and even more of the import trade was in the hands of foreign merchants. In the 1540s, about 55 per cent of woollen exports were shipped by the English Company of Merchant Adventurers and the remainder was shared more or less equally by the merchants of the Hanseatic League and other aliens. The Hanse merchants had enjoyed privileges in England since the thirteenth century in return for loans made to the crown but in the second half of the sixteenth century their position was threatened by the rising wealth of English merchants. From about 1550 a series of bitter quarrels with foreigners, occurring against a background of stagnant trade and recurrent disruptions of European commerce by political events on the Continent, culminated in the eviction of the Hanseatic merchants from England in 1598. Most Englishmen traded as members of one of the regulated companies incorporated by the crown giving them a monopoly of a particular branch of trade. Merchants were assured of protection from their companies which were in a stronger position to negotiate trading privileges with foreign rulers than merchants trading individually. To the government, trading companies offered a means of disciplining individual merchants whose behaviour in foreign countries might provoke an international incident. Of more practical importance, they were convenient sources of loans, and a nursery of ships and sailors.

The most important organization in the sixteenth century was the Company of Merchant Adventurers which by 1600 was responsible for roughly three-quarters of the cloth-export trade from London. No other company matched it in importance: neither the Eastland Company nor the Levant Company, the two next most important companies, handled more than 10 per cent of the cloth trade. The Company of Merchant Adventurers had grown from informal groups of merchants in the cloth trade operating from various English ports in the fourteenth and fifteenth centuries. The London group was the most important and was recognized as a distinct body by the City authorities in 1486. During the first half of the sixteenth century the Adventurers exported cloth to Antwerp where they had established their headquarters in the previous century. Although the Adventurers were mainly Londoners, entry to the company was not strictly controlled in the first half of the century, but later the company became a tight monopoly. As the volume of trade declined in the 1550s and '60s exporting merchants closed ranks and tried to prevent newcomers from entering the trade. The company was aided in its monopolistic aims by the crown. On several occasions in the 1550s and 1560s the government used the Merchant Adventurers to pay off its debts to Antwerp financiers. In return the Adventurers received a royal charter in 1564 granting them a monopoly of the cloth trade to Germany and the Low Countries, 'in consideration of the faithful and acceptible service at sundrie tymes done by the said Merchant Adventurers unto us sithence we came to our crown ...' At the beginning of the seventeenth century membership of the company numbered perhaps 3,500, but only about 200 members were active in trade and fewer than thirty merchants handled almost half the company's trade.

The second half of the sixteenth century was the heyday of trading companies. Several were established to extend trade to new areas including the Russia Company founded in 1555, the East-land Company in 1579, the Levant, Barbary and Africa companies established during the 1580s and the East India Company in 1601. Some, like the Merchant Adventurers, were regulated companies whose members traded with their own capital within the rules set by the company, but others including those trading with Russia, the Levant and East India adopted a form of joint-stock. A common stock was raised to finance a single voyage and was wound up when the venture was completed. In their early days the only real difference between joint-stock companies and regulated companies was that the former were financed by capital contributed jointly by their members and the profits or losses were shared. But gradually the stock became permanent and shareholders were able to pull out of the enterprise by selling their shares. Joint-stock was almost invariably adopted in the distant trades where the risks were high and the capital outlay necessary too great for individual merchants to undertake.

Trading companies were continually challenged by those who did not share their privileges. Individual merchants – 'interlopers' – infringed their trades, particularly when the companies attempted to be excessively exclusive. In the early seventeenth century the Company of Merchant Adventurers had trouble from interlopers in the German branch of their trade; and had to endure constant sniping from outport merchants who agitated in parliament for free trade, by which they meant an end to the monopolies of the London-based companies. During the Cockayne project in 1614–17 the charter of the Company of Merchant Adventurers was temporarily suspended and in the depression of the 1620s it was forced by parliament to open up some branches of its trade to non-members in an attempt to revive sagging cloth sales. The company was restored to its full privileges by Charles I but its days were numbered since the whole notion of monopolies established by the royal prerogative was under attack by parliament. The husk of the old company survived into the Restoration years but its importance faded as trade passed into the hands of individual merchants and partnerships. A similar fate befell the other regulated companies. Like the craft gilds they had outlived their usefulness by the late seventeenth century. On the other hand, joint-stock companies such as the East India Company, the Levant Company, the Royal Africa Company or the Hudson's Bay Company survived trading to distant regions where corporate enterprise and capital were valuable assets in combating the hazards of commerce.

By the end of the seventeenth century many merchants traded individually or in partnerships. Some merchants shipped anything that came their way; others concentrated on particular markets or goods. Merchants sometimes accompanied goods on board ship, but since this required long absences abroad it was more usual to appoint a supercargo – very likely the ship's captain – who travelled with the goods, arranged their sale, and brought home the receipts or a cargo of imported goods. The bigger merchants employed factors overseas to look after their affairs, just as in earlier years the Merchant Adventurers had their apprentices resident in Antwerp or one of the other staple towns. A refinement of the factor system was to assign goods to an overseas commission house which acted on the merchant's behalf. If merchants did not own ships or belong to a ship-owning syndicate, they had to hire cargo space. Since few merchants could fill a ship completely with their own cargoes, there was considerable scope for the services of shipping agents. Cargoes and ships had to be insured and by the beginning of the eighteenth century underwriters specializing in insuring ships and their contents existed in London. Meeting at Lloyd's coffee house, they were part of the complex of commercial institutions that developed to reduce the risks of overseas trade.

Commercial Institutions – Currency and Credit.

A market economy needs money as a means of exchange, whether in the form of cows, cowrie shells, or, as in the case of pre-industrial England, gold and silver coins. A bullion coinage was in use in England long before 1500. Gold and silver were universally prized, and from this function as a 'store of value' precious metals came to be used as a means of exchange. The crown early assumed the responsibility of minting gold and silver into coin, partly because it could be profitable to do so and partly in order to regulate the quantity and quality of the money supply. In the sixteenth and seventeenth centuries English prices were generally quoted in pounds, shillings and pence but coins bearing these names were not necessarily in circulation. In the sixteenth century the coins in greatest use were silver, the chief ones being the penny, the groat and the teston (or shilling). There were no coins called a pound, but golden sovereigns, that usually circulated at a value of one pound, were minted. Other gold coins issued from time to time included ryals (or nobles), angels and crowns. All these coins were rated against the money of account (pounds, shillings and pence) according to their weight and fineness. Since gold coins were more highly rated than silver they were not much used for the common run of trade in the sixteenth century. However, for reasons to be explained later, gold gradually came to displace silver as the main monetary metal by the end of the seventeenth century.

Domestic production of gold and silver was negligible and England therefore relied on imports of bullion which, in the long run, depended on the existence of a favourable balance of commodity trade. For many years in the late sixteenth and early seventeenth centuries there seems, in fact, to have been a trade deficit, although there may well have been compensating inflows on capital account. Bullion movements were also influenced by the activities of speculators who could make gains by shipping bullion from one international centre to another to take advantage of variations in exchange rates. In theory, exchange rates were identical in the various European capitals, but inadequate communications created imperfections in the foreign exchange markets that were exploited by speculators. More important, however, in influencing bullion flows were international differences in silver/gold ratios that arose when a bimetallic coinage was in use. The relationship between the two monetary metals in England was established by the ratings of silver in coin and gold in coin at the mint to the imaginary money of pounds, shillings and pence. As a result of the debasement of the coinage between 1542 and 1551 the amount of silver in coin was reduced by much more than the amount of gold in coin. But the ratings of silver and gold coins remained unchanged with the result that the silver/gold ratio fell. Under these circumstances it paid merchants to ship gold overseas where it was worth more in terms of silver, and to import silver into England. Although the silver/gold ratio at the mint was raised in 1551 it continued to be unfavourable compared with the ratios on the continent and remained so for the rest of the century. In the seventeenth century the position was reversed. The mint price of gold was raised in 1604 and it became profitable to import gold from abroad. In 1611 gold coins were enhanced by 10 per cent (that is their rating in terms of £ s. d. were increased) thereby raising the silver/gold ratio still further. It continued to be profitable to import gold and export silver until, by the late seventeenth century, there was a serious shortage of silver coin in the country and gold gradually became the main monetary metal.

We still have to establish how the government actually obtained supplies of gold and silver for minting into coin. The first source was the government itself which received coin and bullion from overseas as payments or as gifts from foreigners; and also coin or bullion paid by Englishmen as taxes. As far as bullion or coin in private hands was concerned, the government could either coerce or attract. Bullion and most foreign coins were not legal tender in England and their owners were supposed to deliver them to the mint to be coined. From time to time the government also declared that certain old, worn coins should no longer circulate. Bullion or worn coins could be attracted to the mint by the price the government was prepared to offer. But here it was in a difficulty. Until 1666 the mint was meant to be a profitable institution and a charge (seignorage) was made for coining. An individual, therefore, would only deliver bullion or coin to the mint if the price he received, less seignorage, was higher than the market price. But if the mint offered higher than market prices it ceased to be profitable. A way out of the difficulty was to combine raising the mint price with reducing the weight and/or fineness of coins, as was done during the Great Debasement between 1544 and 1551 which profited the government by nearly £1.3 million. However debasement had undesirable social consequences and conflicted with another of the mint's functions, which was to guarantee the quality of the coinage. It was in fact impossible to reconcile the profit-making function of the mint with its monetary function of maintaining the quality and quantity of the coinage. For long periods, particularly in the seventeenth century, mint output of silver coins was very small, despite the abolition of seignorage in 1666. By the end of the century the existing silver coinage was so worn and badly depreciated that the government was forced in 1696 to accept the costs of a major recoinage. The recoinage was not well managed and its result was to reduce the supply of silver coins in circulation still further thereby helping to establish gold as the major monetary metal.

That a 'scarcity of money' was a recurring theme in the economic literature of the seventeenth century is not surprising. The outflow of silver coupled with a semi-permanent deficit on the balance of trade until the 1660s left an inadequate supply of depreciated clipped and worn silver coin in circulation which was not being replaced in sufficient quantities by new issues from the mint. The increasing issue of gold coin only partly eased the situation since it had a lower velocity of circulation than silver (it was prized as a 'store of value') and was not suitable for the mass of small transactions that comprised much of English internal trade. The need for coins of small denominations is clearly realized when it is remembered that in the early eighteenth century skilled artisans rarely earned more than about £14 a year: a golden guinea was almost a twelfth of their total annual income. As Ralph Vaughan wrote in a work published in 1675, 'the greatest part of the commerce of the kingdom, and almost all the inland commerce, is made in silver, the want whereof doth very greatly prejudice the same.'[1]

Deficiencies in the supply of gold and silver coins were not made good by the use of paper money. The development of paper money was very slow in the seventeenth century and hardly occurred at all outside London. This was partly because the acceptability of token money depended on a sophistication in money matters that was slow to evolve but also because acceptability depended upon confidence which was frequently undermined by the poor state of private and public credit. The first steps towards the use of paper money were made about the 1630s or '40s when the London goldsmiths began to develop banking functions. The first of these was as a place of deposit. Goldsmiths accepted coin and other valuables belonging to merchants and landowners for safekeeping. The second function, that of making loans, grew naturally from the first. Experience showed that deposits were not all claimed simultaneously and, provided a sufficient reserve was kept, they could be lent or used to discount bills of exchange. The third

[1] Quoted by B. E. Supple, 'Currency and Commerce in the Early Seventeenth Century', *Econ. Hist. Rev.*, 2nd ser., vol. x, no. 2, 1957, p. 244, n. 6.

function of banks, that of note issue, developed from the other two. Receipts were issued by goldsmiths when valuables were deposited with them and which were, in effect, promissory notes redeemable on presentation to the bank. Instead of making loans in coin a goldsmith might issue notes promising payment of a specified sum and such notes became assignable to third parties. The use of cheques grew from the practice of depositors writing instructions to goldsmith-bankers ordering payments to third parties from their deposits.

London was the natural place for banking to develop in the second half of the seventeenth century for it was a rich community of businessmen requiring banking facilities. Provincial landowners who spent the winter in London needed a means whereby their rent receipts accruing in the countryside could be remitted to the capital to finance the good life; and the whole business community demanded currency and loans. Dozens of banks mushroomed to fill these needs only to be plucked at the first dawn of a liquidity crisis. By the 1720s there were roughly two dozen banks in London, divided into two groups, one in Westminster specializing in the affairs of the landed aristocracy and the other in the City of London closely linked with merchant dealings. Outside London there was hardly a bank in 1700 and barely a dozen in 1750. The Bank of England was established in London in 1694 as part of the reorganization of public finance which will be considered in the next chapter. It was formed to lend money to the government and immediately advanced £600,000 in the form of notes drawn on itself which were used by the government to settle their own accounts. Bank of England notes thus entered into circulation in the London region and, indeed, largely replaced notes issued by the London banks. The smallest denomination was £10 and the notes did not circulate extensively outside the capital where there was still a scarcity of money of small denominations. This shortage was inadequately plugged by private tokens that circulated over limited areas, discounted bills of exchange, and other credit instruments.

Credit dealings were a common feature of life in pre-industrial

England. They were necessary for three reasons. In the first place the shortage of coin often compelled sellers to grant credit to their customers. Secondly, the use of credit grew from the absolute poverty of much of the population which relied on loans to make ends meet. Thirdly, credit was used because commercially minded men, then as now, saw a gain to be made by borrowing money and investing it in some profitable enterprise.

Although the demand for credit was great, the market for credit was disorganized, particularly for long-term loans. Lenders were a motley collection, frequently indistinguishable as a group, for money-lending was a spare-time occupation for most people. Practically anybody with a little cash to spare was tempted to lend it to persons known to them and probate inventories provide eloquent evidence of the extensive network of credit enmeshing society in the sixteenth and seventeenth centuries. Farmers, shopkeepers and petty traders advanced credit to their customers almost as a matter of course. As a group, merchants were prominent as creditors, but they were hardly more numerous than widows. Probate inventories suggest that widows lent money extensively, their advances often amounting to a considerable proportion of their estates. In Devonshire during the sixteenth and seventeenth centuries, for example, debts averaged 30 per cent of the total value of widows' estates worth more than £75. Many widows, evidently, found it difficult to follow the trade or craft or their dead husbands and invested their capital instead and lived on the interest. This fact was not lost on those who defended usury in the heated debates on the subject in the sixteenth century, when 'widows and orphans are marshalled, a tearful orchestra, by the capitalist baton.'[1]

London was the greatest credit pool in the country enlarged by

---

[1] R. H. Tawney, introduction to T. Wilson, *A Discourse upon Usury* (1572), 1925, p. 121. I am grateful to Mr Malcolm Thick for pointing out to me the frequency with which widows appear as creditors in collections of probate inventories and for his calculations based upon M. Cash (ed.), *Devon Inventories of the Sixteenth and Seventeenth Centuries*, Devon and Cornwall R. S., n.s., vol. II, Torquay, 1966.

inland traders and overseas merchants lending money as a natural offshoot of their commodity trade. In the late sixteenth and early seventeenth centuries, for example, merchants, mostly from London, supplied three-quarters of the funds invested in overseas trading and colonizing companies. Later in the century substantial city business men invested their wealth in the Royal Africa, East India, or other joint-stock companies. Throughout the seventeenth century London merchants lent money to the government although it was less risky to stick to the private market. Little credit, even in London, came from specialized sources until the development of banks from the middle of the sevententh century injected an element of professionalism into the money market.

Borrowers were an even more heterogeneous collection than creditors. Small farmers and artisans relied on credit to keep in business. Frequently they were financed by middlemen who advanced cash on crops unharvested and goods unfinished, or who supplied raw materials on credit. Middlemen themselves took credit as well as giving it; wool growers, for instance, often granted credit to dealers who bought their wool. Large-scale producers also conducted their business on credit. The great clothiers, allowed credit to exporting merchants and if the merchants were slow to pay, the clothiers themselves delayed paying their wool suppliers. On the other hand, when wool sales were brisk clothiers paid up promptly and even bought wool for cash. Most of the demand was for short-term working capital, but as distant trades developed and opportunities slowly opened up for large-scale investment there was a growing demand for long-term development capital.

At the local level many loans were made by verbal agreements, but these were treacherous arrangements which often brought the parties into dispute. Frequently, loans were given, not in the form of cash, but as book credits for goods supplied. If the debt remained unpaid, the supplier would simply refuse to grant further credit. When cash was lent bills obligatory might be drawn up. These were enforceable at law, but were not legally assignable to a third party. More substantial loans were made on bond, by which debtors agreed to pay a sum greater than the principal and accrued interest in event of default on the original bargain. To make bonds more attractive to lenders sureties were normally found to guarantee the loan. In this way bonds became safe instruments which would be used for longer-term lending than bills obligatory, say for six months or a year. Bonds issued by joint-stock companies in the later seventeenth century were technically short term credit instruments repayable on call or at three months; but they were renewable and became, in effect, long term loans, which their holders could sell to other investors if they wanted cash. More secure still were mortgages or pledges by which land or goods were given in security for loans and during the seventeenth century landowners gradually came to make extensive use of mortgages to raise money for agricultural improvements.

In the sixteenth century the best organized section of the credit market was connected with the finance of foreign trade where bills of exchange were used. At any one time there were English merchants abroad in possession of foreign currency earned from the sale of goods overseas which they wished to send to England in the form of sterling. At the same time there were foreign merchants in England with English currency which they wished to deliver home. It was costly and inconvenient to remit coin and bills of exchange offered a way of avoiding the necessity. Englishmen abroad used their foreign earnings to buy bills of exchange from foreign merchants. These were sent to London where they were sold to foreign merchants with sterling to dispose of. In a similar manner, foreign merchants in England holding sterling funds bought bills from Englishmen that were delivered abroad and sold for local currency. The price of bills was set according to the rate of exchange which was determined by the gold or silver content of sterling and the foreign currency concerned, and by the demand for and supply of sterling and foreign currencies. The exchange rate was also influenced by the prevailing rate of interest since selling a bill was tantamount to receiving a short-term loan repayable at some later date, perhaps thirty days, albeit in a different currency.

The loan element in bills of exchange resulted in their also being used within England to make loans at interest, which was either illegal or strictly circumscribed by the sixteenth century usury laws. Two devices were used: in the case of 'dry exchange' there was an actual transfer of bills, one outward to, say, Antwerp, and one back to London; in the case of 'fictitious exchange', there was no transfer of bills but merely a loan at interest disguised as an exchange dealing. These practices were denounced by moralists who regarded them as sinful; and their strictures have obscured the fact that the more normal and more valuable function of bills of exchange was to finance foreign trade. Similarly, the existence of individuals who specialized in buying and selling bills – they were to all intents and purposes bankers – in the sixteenth century has overshadowed the many more numerous dealings in bills by merchants whose main business was shipping goods.

The legalization of interest in 1571 resulted in the practices of dry and fictitious exchange gradually dying out and straightforward bills of exchange were adapted to internal trade. They were particularly valuable in remitting money from one part of the country to another. Landowners, wishing to transfer rents to London would buy bills from persons wishing to borrow money, repayment being made by the borrowers' agent or bank in London. The involvement of an agent or bank accounts for the importance that inland bills acquired in the seventeenth century money market. A lender might well be reluctant to advance money to a potential borrower if he were uncertain about the latter's credit; but if repayment were assured by somebody known to be credit-worthy, perhaps a well-known London merchant or bank, then he was much more forthcoming. One thing more was needed to extend the use of bills: assignability. As long as the law enforced the payment of bills only to the person named as the creditor, it was difficult to assign the bill to somebody else. From about the middle of the seventeenth century it became general practice, which was recognized by the common law at the end of the seventeenth century, for bills to be made payable to the bearer. It was thus possible for holders of bills to sell them for cash before they matured. The London bankers became important purchasers of bills at a discount. To banks bills were a useful source of investment, combining profitability – the difference between the face value of the bill and its discounted price – with liquidity, for bills normally matured in three months at the longest.

By 1700 London possessed a credit system that eased the liquidity problem caused by the deficiencies of the currency and which enabled short-term loans to be raised without much difficulty. The system was less well adapted to long-term investment, although the bonds of the joint-stock companies were, in practice, instruments for long-term borrowing. The provinces were not so adequately provided for, although provincial merchants could probably raise money in London as long as London connections would vouch for their credit. The development of bonds, banks and bills reduced the risks of lending and this was reflected by a steady fall in the rate of interest during the seventeenth and early eighteenth centuries.

The Means of Transport

Roads, rivers and the sea were the three complementary means of transport in pre-industrial England. There is a widespread belief that before the transport system was revolutionized in the late eighteenth century roads in England were, in the words of an eighteenth-century pamphleter, 'what God left after the Flood.' Certainly they were not good, but neither were they uniformly bad. As Defoe observed in the early eighteenth century, they were worst when crossing the claylands of England. Travelling north from London he found that for thirty miles there were:

> tolerable good ways and hard ground, 'till you reach Royston . . .'
> Then 'you enter the deep clays, which are so surprisingly soft, that it is perfectly frightful to travellers, and it has been the wonder of foreigners, how, considering the great number of

carriages which are continually passing with heavy loads, those ways have been made practicable'. . . .

Defore explained that his reason:

'for taking notice of this badness of the roads through all the midland counties is this; that as these are counties which drive a very great trade with the city of London, and with one another, perhaps the greatest of any counties in England; and that, by consequence, the carriage is exceeding great, and also that all the land carriage of the northern counties necessarily goes through these counties. . . .'[1]

Defoe's remarks are testimony both to the deplorable state of some of the English roads, and also to the immense volume of traffic they carried. Much of the traffic was local, but there was a national road network, based on the Roman roads, radiating from London and carrying a large amount of inter-regional trade. The Midlands were possibly more dependent on road transport than most parts of the country, for they lacked good water ways and were far from the sea. The north, likewise, relied on roads a good deal. Towns such as Kendal and Carlisle were supplied with groceries sent from London either directly by road, or by sea to Newcastle and then across country by road; and in the reverse direction knitted hosiery from the northern dales were sent by carriage from Kirkby Stephen to London in the early eighteenth century. Goods of high value were best suited to road transport for they were able to bear the high costs, but bulky commodities such as grain and coal were also transported over considerable distances by wagon or packhorse. Horses were quicker than wagons and better at navigating steep, rocky tracks and miry clays, but in the south and east of England, particularly, wheeled traffic was widely used for moving heavy loads.

Two problems, one technical the other administrative, bedevilled road transport and both were worsened by the extra demands put upon roads as trade expanded. Techniques of road

[1] D. Defoe, *A Tour Through England and Wales*, Everyman ed. 1928, vol. II, pp. 118–9.

building were not always understood and in some areas there was a shortage of stony material for providing hard surfaces. Whether road construction would have been tackled more effectively had the system of administration been different is difficult to decide. The common law placed the responsibility of maintaining roads on local communities and under a statute of 1555 – the first dealing with roads – parishes were obliged to look after the roads passing through them. Surveyors were to be appointed, rates levied to raise money and labour and materials found to repair roads. This arrangement placed the burden of road maintenance on those least able to afford it and in a great many parishes nothing effective was done. Evidence of a growing concern with the state of the roads is provided by the appointment by James I of a Surveyor of the King's Highways, an office that appears to have been filled for the rest of the century without bringing in any improvements in road conditions. More practical steps were taken by local quarter sessions and the central government in restricting the size of wagons using public roads. In 1663 local justices obtained a private act of parliament turning part of the Great North Road running through Hertfordshire, Cambridgeshire and Huntingdonshire, into a toll road thus placing the cost of maintenance on the users of the road. By the end of the century this device was being used in half a dozen other places, and in 1706 the first turnpike to be administered by private enterprise rather than local JPS was established. Thereafter turnpikes were created fairly frequently, at the rate of about eight a year by the 1720s. The acts establishing turnpike companies gave them power to levy tolls and borrow capital for road improvements. Their success in improving road conditions varied very much from place to place; but 'several of these turnpikes had been set up of late years,' wrote Defoe, 'and great progress had been made in mending the most difficult ways ...'[1]

Although roads often carried long-distance traffic, their more important function in pre-industrial England was to transport goods over short distances to navigable rivers or the coast. In the early eighteenth century, for example, London tanners collected their

[1] *ibid.*, II, p. 119.

bark in the woodlands of Surrey, Sussex and Hampshire; it was taken in carts to Guildford and loaded into barges on the river Wey and so carried to the Thames and London. The rivers and the sea were the main arteries of English trade and the country was fortunate in possessing nearly 700 miles of navigable rivers in the early seventeenth century. This figure was increased to 1,100 miles a century later by improvements made to rivers. The backbone of the inland waterway system was formed by the four major river networks: the Thames and its tributaries which tapped the traffic of the Home Counties, the south, and the south Midlands; the river Severn which, with the Wye and Avon, served the west of England; the Humber and the major rivers flowing into it – Trent, Idle, Aire and Ouse – covering the east and north Midlands and south and west Yorkshire; and the smaller network of the Dee, Mersey and Weaver in the north-west. By the end of the seventeenth century few places in England were more than about fifteen miles from the sea, natural river, or improved waterway.

Efforts to improve inland waterways were not unknown in the sixteenth century and included the cutting of the first canal in England in 1564–6 linking Exeter with its port of Topsham. But more schemes existed on paper and in the heads of impractical projectors than on the ground. The early seventeenth century was even fuller of paper proposals, including more than one to link the Thames and Severn river systems by canal. More substantial achievements were made in the later seventeenth century when projectors used private acts of parliament to undertake river improvements. The first important burst of activity was in the early 1660s, with another in the late 1690s and a third in 1719–21. The timing was determined by the relative cheapness of interest rates in those years; and in general the financing of river improvements was made possible only by the growing wealth of the trading communities in London and the provinces. The majority of investors in improvement schemes were local people interested less in the direct returns on their capital than the external economies of cheap transport. These they certainly gained: a horse pulling a barge could move perhaps twelve times as much freight as a packhorse at less than half the cost of land carriage. Many schemes for river improvement were intended to assist the transport of agricultural goods and coal to the growing urban markets, but they proved invaluable also for supplying manufacturers with raw materials.

The inland rivers led to the great 'river round England'. The sea carried much of the home trade of pre-industrial England and was the only highway to foreign and colonial markets. England's long, deeply indented coastline opened up large areas of the country to sea-borne trade and provided a multitude of good harbours. The North Sea was the busiest sea lane carrying the important bread-and-butter commerce with western Europe and the Baltic and serving as the main means of communications between northern and southern England. The coastal trade of eastern England consisted of the movement of agricultural produce, raw materials, manufactured goods and imported commodities to and from London. From about 1550 shipments of coal from Newcastle to London grew rapidly and came to dominate the traffic. Another bustling route was along the south coast where a string of ports from Kent to Cornwall handled the products of a populous and relatively well industrialized hinterland. In the west, Bristol was the centre of an important trade linking south-west England and South Wales.

To handle the increasing volumes of goods entering the coastal and overseas, trade, there was an expansion of ports, shipping and ancillary services. London was the most important port in pre-industrial England, whether measured by the volume or value of its trade or the tonnage of shipping passing through it, but during the seventeenth century the western ports grew more quickly with the expansion of the Atlantic trades. We have already noted the increased investment in ports and harbours in the late seventeenth and early eighteenth centuries. These included major developments such as the construction of wet docks in London, Bristol and Liverpool, and also dozens of relatively small-scale works including the building of piers, quays and harbour walls in places such as Margate, Bridlington, Whitby, Paignton and many other small harbours. There was also a growth of merchant shipping. From an estimated 50,000 tons in 1572, the tonnage of English-owned ships rose to 115,000 tons in 1629 and doubled again by 1686. By 1751 it was about 420,000 tons. However statistics do not reveal important changes occurring in the size and design of ships. Until the third quarter of the sixteenth century most English merchant ships were small – barely a dozen were bigger than 200 tons – but as trade increased to the Mediterranean and more distant lands, English yards began building larger ocean-going vessels. These were not well suited to the short-haul trades across the North Sea since they carried large crews and were more expensive to operate than Dutch-built ships, but from about the middle of the seventeenth century English shipbuilders also constructed bulk-carrying vessels along Dutch lines. Some of these were used in the North Sea trades to carry cloth, grain, timber and other bulky goods. Others were employed in the coastal trade; by the end of the seventeenth century there were about 1400 colliers plying along the east coast. The great East Indiamen were the pride of the merchant fleet, but they represented only a fraction of the tonnage of English shipping.

The Achievement

By 1750 the market exercised a more powerful stimulus on economic development than it had done two centuries before. There had developed a network of wholesale and retail institutions facilitating the growth of national and international trade; financial arrangements had evolved to meet the needs of producers and merchants; and the system of transport had undergone considerable improvement. These advances in commercial institutions made possible the expansion of internal trade that was a major feature of the economic life of England between 1500 and 1750. They also assisted the growth and diversification of England's overseas trade. Even in 1500 England had not been a self-sufficient country; by 1750 her commercial connections embraced most of Europe and reached eastwards to Africa and Asia and westwards to America and the West Indies.

The real measure of commercial development in pre-industrial England is to be found in the agricultural and industrial expansion outlined in the earlier chapters. Merchants, money and credit, and transport were the means whereby the needs of a growing population were translated into actual demands which stimulated farming and manufacturing. As commercial institutions became more efficient production was further stimulated, calling forth even greater improvements to the mechanisms of the market. These improvements must rank with agricultural advances as the most significant changes in the pre-industrial economy. The latter permitted the growth of incomes and the release of resources for non-agricultural production; the former provided the mechanisms by which the market economy operated more effectively. Yet, just as agricultural improvements did not create the conditions for an economic transformation before 1750, neither did the growth of the tertiary sector of the economy. Although the market was a more powerful engine of growth in the eighteenth century than it had been in earlier centuries it was still far from being an efficient engine.

6

The Government and the Economy

The pre-industrial economy was closely regulated by the government – a feature it shared with many underdeveloped countries of
the world in the twentieth century. But the role of the government
in the English economy before 1750 differed from the usual function of governments in underdeveloped countries today. Nowadays
governments act as producers, entrepreneurs and providers of
capital in order to promote high rates of economic growth. In pre-
industrial England the self-appointed task of successive governments was to regulate a private enterprise economy organized
around the market.

The nature and origins of economic policy in the sixteenth,
seventeenth and early eighteenth centuries have been hotly de-
bated. It has even been questioned whether there was any such
thing as economic policy during the period, or whether 'policy, as
actually found in history, is a set of devices into which government
drifts under the pressure of practical problems.'[1] The effectiveness of government regulation is likewise questioned. Did the government guide the economy in certain, predetermined directions; or
did it hamper economic enterprise and frustrate economic man?
Over the whole debate hovers the notion of mercantilism, a
chameleon-like creature able to change its colour to match the
hue of any argument. The immediate purpose of this chapter is not

[1] G. Unwin, *Studies in Economic History: The Collected Papers of George Unwin*,
ed. R. H. Tawney, 1927, p. 184.

to pursue the mythical beast of mercantilism through the thickets of argument and counter-argument, but to survey the extent of government activity. This done, we shall be in a better position to assess the nature and effectiveness of the government's role in the economic life of pre-industrial England.

The Government as Producer and Consumer

The government rarely adopted the direct role of producer in the pre-industrial economy. In the early sixteenth century the crown supported one or two iron works in the Sussex Weald for the production of ordnance, but mostly it relied upon private producers for iron. More important were the naval dockyards at Chatham, Woolwich, Portsmouth and Plymouth which the government were obliged to maintain because most private yards were too small to build the large vessels required by the navy. In most cases, however, direct production was too complicated for the crown to undertake and inevitably put it at the mercy of courtiers and officials more concerned with their own pockets than the interests of the government. This was the lesson of the Royal Alum Company which between 1613 and 1647 was not so much a means of producing alum as a way of parting the king from his money. Alum was an important raw material used by cloth finishers and leather manufacturers and supplies were imported from Italy in the sixteenth century. In 1607 the crown granted a patent to a group of projectors to develop native deposits of alum discovered in Yorkshire, and in 1613 the business was taken over by the crown and farmed out to contractors. Imports of alum were prohibited and the exploitation of other deposits prevented. But the alum project was badly run, the crown and private investors lost heavily, while users of alum were obliged to buy an inferior product at high cost. The only gainers were one or two corrupt entrepreneurs.

The alum patent was part of a wider policy of granting industrial monopolies in the late sixteenth and early seventeenth century, although it was unusual for the crown to become closely involved in their operation. Industrial patents were a convenient device for governments wishing to develop the manufacturing potential of the country 'but without command of resources sufficient to involve the state in public enterprise on its own account.'[1] During Elizabeth's reign they were granted to foster the manufacture of soap, saltpetre, alum, glass, paper, brass and copper and other enterprises. Several Elizabethan grants were intended to establish new import-saving industries such as brass and copper but others merely placed existing trades into the hands of monopolists. For example, in 1592 Edward Darcy, a minor official of the royal household, was given the exclusive privilege of controlling the manufacture of all light leather in England. This grant was bitterly opposed by the London Company of Leathersellers and the City authorities, since it infringed the interests of established manufacturers and eventually the government withdrew the patent on payment of £4,000 by the company and the City of London. Elizabeth was wise enough not to push monopolies too hard and revoked more than a dozen of them in 1601 to placate parliamentary opposition. But the precarious finances of the first two Stuarts made them less cautious and patents of monopoly became a minor, though significant, grievance which merged with larger issues to bring about the Civil War.

By contrast with its limited role as producer, the government was the greatest consumer in the country. In the late sixteenth century total expenditure by the crown was probably between £500,000 and £600,000 a year. By the first decade of the eighteenth century government spending averaged £6 millions a year, of which two-thirds was military expenditure. The rest went on the upkeep of central government, the Court, administration and justice. Local government spending was very small.

Before the Civil War the royal household was supplied with food by a system of purveyance. In its simplest form, royal purveyors commandeered goods or bought them in the markets at reduced prices, but in the late sixteenth century counties were permitted to compound with purveyors by the payment of taxes which were

[1] W. H. Price, *The English Patents of Monopoly*, 1913, p. 7.

used by local justices or the royal purveyors to purchase supplies at market prices. Purveyance expenditure amounted to more than £20,000 a year for the household of Henry VIII and double that amount for Queen Elizabeth. Nationally it was not very important, but suppliers in the Home Counties were stimulated by the demand for food and drink. In 1660 purveyance was replaced by a regular parliamentary income granted to the crown and raised from the excise duties. Henceforth purchases were made by the Lord Steward and Lord Chamberlain who dealt with appointed suppliers and private tradesmen on contract. These contracts could be lucrative, but any businessman supplying the Court had to resign himself to the hazards of irregular payment.

Throughout the pre-industrial period the government made large but intermittent purchases of food and equipment for the army and navy. In the earlier part of the period victualling was organized in a similar manner to purveyance, but after the Restoration the task of obtaining supplies passed to permanent officials who either let out contracts to private producers or engaged agents to supply goods on commission. The quantities of food and equipment required for the army and navy were large enough to have considerable economic repercussions in certain regions. During the sixteenth century the military garrisons at Berwick and Calais were supplied with grain from East Anglia and livestock from Kent and the Midland counties. The leather and metallurgical industries both benefited from military demands. The development of shoemaking in Northamptonshire was stimulated in the second half of the seventeenth century by military orders, the first of which were placed when Northampton was a garrison town for the parliamentary armies during the Civil War. The naval demand for ironware encouraged Ambrose Crowley to centralize production in a factory in north-eastern England from which he sent goods coastwise to his warehouses by the Thames. In order to obtain contracts he kept an office at Greenwich close to the naval dockyards at Woolwich and Deptford. As with suppliers to the royal household, suppliers to the army and navy had to suffer fluctuating demand and be prepared to grant long credit. Relatively few producers were involved in meeting government orders, but they were necessarily large-scale operators and government contracts were a forcing-house of entrepreneurship.

The Government as Regulator – Control of The Factor Markets

The direct intrusion of the central government into the market as producer and consumer was limited and irregular: its indirect role as regulator of the market economy was pervasive and enduring. It controlled – or attempted to control – the use of land, capital and labour, and the production and sale of goods and services. These two aspects of regulation will be considered separately even though in practice there was no dichotomy between the regulation of the factor and the product markets and we must be wary of imputing to government regulation a tidiness it did not possess.

In the sixteenth century a central issue in economic policy was the use of land. The growth of population was straining food supplies and adding to the number of landless labourers, some of whom wandered the countryside begging, stealing and constituting a threat to national security. To the government – and public opinion at large insofar as it was expressed in petitions and sermons – the main problems were enclosing and engrossing when accompanied by the conversion of tillage land to permanent pasture. From the end of the fifteenth century there was a stream of legislation against enclosers and engrossers. An act in 1515 tried to prevent conversion of tillage land to pasture and compel the re-conversion of recently enclosed land. Two years later the government established a commission to discover the extent of depopulation caused by enclosing and engrossing, and in 1533 there was a new approach to the problem of enclosure when the number of sheep that individuals could keep was restricted by law. In 1549 – after another commission – a short-lived tax was imposed on sheep numbers. Further enactments restricting enclosing and engrossing in the 1550s caused the statute book to be cluttered with legislation and it became necessary to tidy up the law in 1563.

Up to this point the government directed its efforts primarily at wool growers who were thought to be responsible for enclosure. However the search for pasture was a much more complex issue in the mixed farming districts and this was gradually recognized in legislation. In 1556 an act tried to ensure that graziers kept adequate numbers of store cattle which were necessary if meat and dairy production was to keep pace with the growing demand for food. Further legislation in 1589 recognized the existence of landless labourers by insisting that every cottage built should have four acres of ground attached. Good harvests and low corn prices in 1593 encouraged the House of Commons to repeal all legislation relating to land use; and although measures against enclosing and engrossing in the mixed farming regions of England were hastily re-imposed when grain prices soared in 1597, they specifically recognized the need of enclosure for convertible husbandry. Indeed after the anti-enclosure riots in the Midlands in 1607, enclosure ceased to be a matter of serious concern to the government. Existing laws continued to be enforced sporadically, especially in the 1630s, but they gradually fell into disuse.

The timing of legislation against enclosing and engrossing was determined by high corn prices, the content by the aims of the government and the interests of landowners who were able to influence policy in parliament. The motives of the government were clearly stated in the preamble of the 'Acte for the maintenance of husbandrie and tillage' passed in 1597 which stated that the 'Strengthe and florishinge Estate of this Kingdome hath bene allwayes and is greatly upheld and advaunced by the maintenance of the Ploughe and Tillage ...' Arable farming was thought to create employment and prevent 'Ydlenesse, Drunkenesse, unlawfull Games and all other lewde Practises and Condicions of Life', and 'a cause that the Realme doth more stande upon itselfe, withowt depending upon forraigne Cuntries either for bringinge in of Corne in tyme of scarcetye, or of vente and utterance of our owne Commodities beinge in over great Abundance.' As long as the crown believed that enclosures caused social disturbances, unemployment and food shortages, they were prohibited. But members of parliament were able to bring a practical realism to bear on legislation and modify the more extreme efforts to prevent enclosure and conversion. By the end of the sixteenth century informed opinion recognized various reasons for enclosure: for cattle as well as for sheep; to rest land exhausted through over-cropping; or to introduce convertible husbandry systems. It also became realized that enclosure did not necessarily result in depopulation and so by the early seventeenth century opposition softened.

There was in any case another aspect of the enclosure problem to be considered. A policy of preventing the movement of land out of tillage would, if successful, depress grain prices, but 'if corn is too cheap, the husbandman is undone, whom we must provide for, for he is the staple man of the kingdom.'[1] Grain farmers – the great majority – wanted high prices, whereas consumers desired low prices. In a century of generally rising prices legislation was normally concerned with keeping land in tillage, but in some years good harvests caused the price of grain to fall and then policy shifted towards propping up grain prices. Little could be done to stimulate home demand when prices were low, but the exports provided a safety valve for over-production. A series of acts during the sixteenth and first half of the seventeenth centuries permitted the export of corn when domestic prices fell below certain levels. Market prices, however, were usually above these levels, but exports were still permitted from certain regions from time to time under special licence. After 1660 policy shifted much more decisively in favour of producers. In 1662 high duties were placed on imported grain – before there had been no effective restriction on grain imports – and the price ceiling above which exports were prohibited was raised. In 1670 all restrictions on exports were removed and three years later bounties were introduced, payable to corn exporters, which remained in operation for about five years. They were re-introduced in 1689 when export duties on corn were also removed. Meanwhile even stiffer duties had been imposed on imports. The act of 1689 remained the basis of policy until 1815

[1] Quoted by J. Thirsk, *The Agrarian History of England and Wales*, vol. IV, *1500–1640*, 1967, p. 321.

although its operation was suspended from time to time when corn prices in England rose to high levels.

This new legislation reflected changing supply conditions in agriculture. Whereas the long-term movement of corn prices had been upwards during the sixteenth and early seventeenth centuries, the trend was in the reverse direction after 1660 and the government, sensitive to the interests of landowners, reacted by opening up foreign markets. Whether the payment of bounties actually kept land under the plough is difficult to say: probably their effects were slight. Corn production was already expanding on the light soils in the late seventeenth century as the result of technical developments, while high production costs were compelling some farmers on the heavy clay soils to move into pasture production in spite of the existence of bounties.

If enclosure provided the chief topic of economic discussion in the sixteenth century, usury provided the second. In both instances debate was freely spiced with moral considerations that added to the interest without clarifying the economic problems involved. In both cases, too, public debate – and government policy – waned during the seventeenth century as the economic aspects became divorced from the moral. With enclosure, the issue was whether men should use their land as they pleased or whether they should consider their tenants as well as their profits. With usury, the question was whether owners of money-capital should charge other people for using it or whether, as good Christians, they should lend it for nothing.

Loans were as much a feature of pre-industrial society as poverty. However it had long been an offence under canon law to charge interest on money lent and it became an offence under secular law in 1487 and 1495. At this time credit was probably becoming even more widespread – or at any rate more obvious – and the state took over the traditional Christian position which condemned usury as exploitation of the needy. The church, however, had always accepted the case for charging interest on loans made to finance enterprises that were expected to yield a profit. An absolute prohibition on usury was obviously impractical, although popular among debtors, and in 1545 the law was modified to permit interest up to a limit of 10 per cent. Moralists were outraged that parliament 'should be so voyde of God's Holy Spirit, that thei should allow for lawfull any thynge that God's worde forbideth,'[1] and in 1552 usury was again completely forbidden. This act came after a decade of sharp inflation and it was probably a deflationary measure intended to reduce prices by curbing the flow of credit. Far from putting an end to usury, however, the statute of 1552 sent it underground and stimulated a widespread discussion of the subject in which participants began to distinguish between usury and interest, the one an unchristian and unjustifiable oppression and the other a reasonable charge for borrowing money for commercial undertakings. This distinction underlay the act of 1571 permitting interest rates below 10 per cent, although creditors were given no legal redress against defaulters.

The moral objections to usury did not evaporate with the act of 1571, but by the beginning of the seventeenth century most discussions of interest assumed that it was the price of capital and not the mark of man's fall from grace; and the focus of debate became the economic consequences of high or low rates of interest. This question was given point by the evident economic superiority of the Dutch in the seventeenth century, which Englishmen often attributed to the lower rates of interest prevalent in Holland. There was a gradual decline in the legal maximum rate of interest: to 8 per cent in 1625, to 6 per cent in 1651 and 5 per cent in 1714. The fall in the legal rate probably followed a reduction in the market rates for commercial loans which reflected, in turn, the growing confidence of investors and possibly also the increased supply of investible funds.

In the sixteenth century the question of usury was frequently linked in the public mind with that of the foreign exchanges, a natural enough association since transactions using bills of exchange were a form of short-term loan. In addition, exchange fluctuations were regarded as a major factor determining bullion flows to and

[1] Quoted in T. Wilson, *A Discourse upon Usury*, ed. R. H. Tawney, 1925, introduction, p. 131.

from England. This was to put the cart before the horse since a fall in the exchange rate was a consequence of a deficit on overseas trade, leading to an outflow of bullion, and not a cause. Nevertheless, 'the demand for exchange control appeared in every slump with the automatic regularity of a reflex action.'[1] A long series of acts and proclamations in the late sixteenth and early seventeenth centuries attempted to control private exchange dealings and five royal commissions investigated the operation of the foreign exchanges between 1564 and 1621, every one set up in a period of slack trade. But it was impossible to supervise the whole network of English and foreign merchants involved in exchange dealings, and in the second quarter of the seventeenth century the attempts petered out. By then the view was gaining ground that the exchanges reflected the state of trade and it was irrelevant as well as impractical to control exchange transactions.

Discussions of the use of land and capital captured public attention in the sixteenth century because they were important issues in which economic and religious considerations merged, and they tended to overshadow more enduring problems connected with the employment of labour. However, labour was the subject of the Statute of Artificers in 1563, the most famous of all Tudor economic statutes. The act was concerned with three related topics, the level of wages, conditions of employment, and the mobility of labour. Under the act local justices were to meet annually to 'yelde unto the hyred persone bothe in the tyme of scarcitie and in the tyme of plentie a convenient proporcion of wages.' The rates assessed were maximum ones, and it was an offence either to offer or accept higher wages. Sporadic attempts at wage fixing dated back to the Black Death and the revived attempt in 1563 was probably prompted by a temporary shortage of labour following high mortality in the late 1550s. More generally, the growing prevalence of wage labour in the economy raised the question of its regulation and remuneration and it is noticeable that whereas land-

[1] F. J. Fisher, 'Commercial Trends and Policy in the Sixteenth Century', *Econ. Hist. Rev.*, vol. v, 1940, reprinted in *Essays in Economic History,*' vol. i, ed. E. M. Carus-Wilson, 1954, p. 161.

use and usury gradually waned as topics of economic discussion, wages and unemployment became more important. When the act was re-issued in 1603 an important amendment made wage rates assessed for the textile crafts minimum and not maximum payments. This was done in response to complaints of hardship from workers in the cloth manufacturing districts, many of whom were becoming almost completely dependent on industrial wages. Workers in other occupations continued to be subject to maximum wage legislation, for, although numerous, they were less concentrated geographically than textile workers and therefore constituted a less serious danger to social and political stability. Assessments of wages remained the responsibility of justices of the peace. Justices in many parts of the country continued to assess wages until well into the eighteenth century, although existing assessments were often re-issued without revision and, where new rates were struck, the criterion adopted was the state of the labour market and not the cost of living as the original act required. Furthermore, wages actually paid parted company from the assessed rates to an increasing extent in the second half of the seventeenth century.

Under the terms of the Statute of Artificers employees in stated occupations had to be hired by the year. More important, the act provided for compulsory apprenticeships of seven years' duration in agriculture and other occupations and restricted the social classes from which apprentices for certain occupations could be drawn. The apprenticeship regulations were adapted from the widespread gild practice of seven year periods of service, but their purpose is not entirely clear. They were not part of the original bill introduced into the House of Commons but were added by members of parliament during its passage through the House. No doubt MPS were concerned to maintain standards of workmanship, but other motives were also present. A later discussion of the statute argued that a master 'should have the longer service of his prentice which must needes turne to his great proffitte, for one yeares service at the latter ende is more worthe than ffower at the begynnynge.'[1]

---

[1] *Tudor Economic Documents*, ed. R. H. Tawney and E. Power, 1924, I, p. 356.

Long apprenticeships assured employers of a supply of cheap, tied labour and the fact that they were made compulsory may be seen as a further reaction to the labour scarcity existing in the late 1550s and early 1560s.

In certain circumstances men or women could be obliged by the Statute of Artificers to work in agriculture, domestic service or in any other occupation. The intention of the government was to secure an adequate supply of labour for agriculture, but when the clause was discussed in the House of Commons it was extended in such a way that labour could be directed into any occupation, a change that obviously undermined the original intention. This was typical of much of the statute which was far from being a well thought out piece of economic policy. What started out as an attempt to stop wages from rising became as a result of additions to the original bill by MPs a rather muddled act which, if effective, would have seriously restricted the workings of the labour market. In fact the apprenticeship and employment clauses of the statute were never very effective. Enforcement of apprenticeship was left to the gilds whose powers were declining and to private informers whose activities were erratic. In the early seventeenth century the courts interpreted the statute as applying only to the occupations named in the act and an increasing range of employment fell beyond its scope. No serious effort ever seems to have been made to draft labour into agriculture or other occupations.

The Statute of Artificers dealt only with the employed: the unemployed fell within the scope of the poor laws. Pauperism was increasing during the sixteenth century as population rose faster than employment opportunities, creating unemployment and underemployment. Large towns such as London and Norwich struggled with increasing numbers of poor people, devising means of punishing the idle, employing the unemployed, and relieving the destitute. The central government followed the lead of municipalities with the usual mixture of motives. A genuine Christian solicitude for the destitute was combined with a fear of possible political disturbances arising from social distress; while the notion that unemployed labour was a wasting economic asset was gradually grasped. The first important national legislation dealing with pauperism came in 1536 and made the poor the responsibility of local parishes, which were empowered to collect alms and receive the genuinely unemployed. The economically disturbed decades of the mid-sixteenth century intensified poverty and produced additional legislation. A short-lived act in 1547 made vagrancy an offence punishable by slavery; and a more important statute in 1572 established the principle of compulsory assessments of parish poor rates for the relief of the genuinely impoverished, while maintaining severe punishments for the persistently idle. High corn prices and population growth brought a new urgency to the problem of pauperism at the end of the sixteenth century. In 1597 the House of Commons considered thirteen bills on pauperism and unemployment which resulted in two acts of Parliament. One authorized the erection of houses of correction for the punishment of idle rogues, vagabonds and beggars; the other reaffirmed the responsibility of parishes for their poor, who were to be put to work with money raised by compulsory assessments. The impotent were to be cared for in hospitals and pauper children apprenticed. A codifying act in 1601 remained the basis of poor law administration until 1834. Several other acts of parliament in the seventeenth and eighteenth centuries added to the main corpus of legislation but most of them dealt with local issues and the history of poor relief during these centuries is the story of administration in 15,000 parishes.

The economic effects of the poor law were probably slight. Although many parishes kept stocks of raw materials for the use of the unemployed, the law was inadequate to deal with underemployment endemic in a pre-industrial economy. Before 1750, periodic high mortality, and after 1750, industrialization, solved this problem more effectively than any government. Neither did the poor law prevent poverty. At best it relieved it and insofar as it involved transfer payments from the rich with a high propensity to save or hoard to the poor with a high propensity to consume, it may have raised effective demand in the economy. But the fundamental causes of poverty in pre-industrial England lay in the low level of productivity of all factors of production which no form of government regulation could remedy.

The Government as Regulator – Control of the Product Markets

The main period for the formulation of legislation controlling the factor markets was the second half of the sixteenth century when pressing economic problems provided a strong incentive for regulation. Much the same pattern emerges from a study of regulations affecting the product markets, at least as far as internal trade is concerned. The chronology of the regulation of overseas trade is rather different and will be considered separately.

Control of product markets took three forms: price control, the setting of manufacturing standards, and the regulation of marketing. Price control was the most difficult – it still is – and the least common in pre-industrial England, although it was attempted in the case of labour under the Statute of Artificers. Apart from labour, bread was the one commodity consistently subject to this form of control and many acts and proclamations between the thirteenth and eighteenth centuries attempted to regulate its price and weight according to price of flour. Bread was the staple diet of the masses and this no doubt accounts for the persistence with which the central and local governments regulated its price.

An alternative method of regulating the production of essential consumer goods was by controlling the mode of manufacture, which was done, for example, with tanned leather, footwear and cloth. 'Everie sort of people of necessitye must use and have leather,'[1] and its manufacture was therefore supervised by municipal and central governments. The most important act was passed in 1563 establishing a complicated set of regulations for tanning, currying and shoemaking. The act pulled together regulations in earlier statutes dating back to the fourteenth century. Its timing, as with so much economic legislation in this period, was determined by acute economic distress. However the detailed provisions of the act were not the work of government ministers, but members of parliament

[1] 2 and 3 Edw. VI, cap. 9, preamble.

who grafted them onto a bill that originally had been intended to deal only with the sale of leather. The tanning regulations were taken from earlier legislation and re-arranged into a set of completely unworkable clauses. The government kept the clauses in operation for forty years, in spite of widespread complaints from tanners, for it derived an income from prosecuting manufacturers who broke the law: any social concern behind the original act quickly gave way to blatant fiscalism. The tanning regulations were eventually modified in 1604 and remained on the statute book until 1808; but they fell into disuse during the seventeenth century. The industry was not keenly interested in enforcing them and parliament was too occupied with other matters to be concerned with what went on in the tanyards of England.

The technical control of cloth-making, by contrast, remained a live interest into the eighteenth century. Woollen textiles attracted the attention of legislators because, like leather, they were widely used by poor consumers. More important, woollen cloth was a major export commodity and the duty on exports an important source of government revenue. It followed, therefore, that the manufacture of cloth should be supervised to maintain the quality of exports and so that the product could be standardized for taxation purposes. During the Middle Ages the gilds had regulated technical standards, but with the migration of the textile industry into the countryside the task passed to the state 'and the Yorkist and Tudor Parliaments evolved some measures which in complexity and intricacy rivalled a modern Insurance Act.'[1] The strands of earlier legislation were gathered together in the great cloth act of 1552. Twenty-two varieties of woollen cloth were recognized and their weight and dimensions stipulated. The act was passed in the wake of depression in the export trade. But it did little to prevent manufacturers from skimping on quality in order to keep down costs, particularly in country areas where it was difficult to enforce technical standards, and complaints of bad workmanship continued to be frequent. A further act, in 1597, tried to stop the practice of tentering, or stretching, cloth, but it

[1] H. Heaton, *The Yorkshire Woollen and Worsted Industries*, 2nd ed., 1965, p. 130.

was a necessary part of the manufacture of coarse cloths and the act was opposed by manufacturers, ignored and finally repealed in 1623. A new act established a fresh set of rules for the length, breadth and weights of various types of woollen cloth – once again a depression in the export trade was the occasion of legislation. Manufacturing standards continued to be set in the later seventeenth century and a series of acts, in 1708, 1725, 1738 and 1765 attempted to impose regulations on Yorkshire manufacturers of woollens and worsteds, possibly the most vigorous branch of the traditional woollen industry with important markets in Europe. The last act remained in force until 1821 when a committee decided it was not fulfilling its purpose and recommended its repeal.

Statutes were not the only weapons in the armoury of economic policy with which manufacturers could be attacked. A much more flexible means of control was to grant licences for the regulation of particular industries. In 1575, for instance, a minor poet and courtier, Sir Edward Dyer, was granted a patent for twenty-one years to enforce the unworkable tanning regulations contained in the act of 1563. In 1630, to take a later example from a different industry, a commission was granted to Anthony Wither and Samuel Lively to supervise the operation of the cloth acts in the important textile counties of Oxfordshire, Gloucestershire, Wiltshire and Somerset. Grants were also made to extend the authority of gilds to rural areas. A commission of enquiry into the trade depression in 1622 suggested that corporations should be established in every county to regulate the manufacture of cloth. Only one county incorporation was set up, but several were created in towns including Leeds, Bury St Edmunds, Ipswich and Colchester. Other grants were made in the sixteenth and early seventeenth centuries for the regulation of industries not subject to statutory control such as leather dressing and the manufacture of new draperies. They were rarely successful for any length of time.

More common than either the direct control of prices or the imposition of technical standards was the regulation of trade in agricultural and industrial produce. In one trade after another

Tudor governments imposed restrictions on middlemen, sometimes absolute prohibitions, sometimes a system of licensing, in the fond belief that by curbing middlemen prices would be kept down. But in every trade the realities of the market made rents in the mesh of regulations so that shoals of middlemen were able to swim through with immunity. During the seventeenth century the government abandoned its attempts to regulate the internal market even though legislation often remained, unenforced, on the statute book.

The difficulties facing governments in trying to control middlemen are clearly illustrated in the leather trade. The government's interest in the industry, as we have noted, arose from the importance of leather to consumers. Rising prices of footwear in the 1540s and '50s were the spur to action. It was generally assumed that middlemen were the cause of increasing prices, but the government was ignorant of the structure of the leather industry, even to the point of knowing whether curriers, who processed leather after tanning, were actually leather workers or merely dealers in leather. Between 1548 and 1563 six acts alternately allowed curriers to and prevented them from buying and selling leather. These rapid reversals of policy were the outcome of intensive lobbying by the two London companies of curriers and cordwainers (shoemakers), each trying to obtain exclusive control of the leather trade and both arguing that their particular proposals would achieve the government's aim of keeping prices down. Although the leather act of 1563 made the purchase of leather for resale illegal it did not prevent the trade and the act was largely ignored throughout the next century and a quarter. When restrictions on the leather trade were eventually abolished in 1689, the law merely came into line with widespread practice.

Similar difficulties faced the government in regulating the wool trade. Many small clothiers relied on middlemen for wool supplies, whereas large-scale clothiers often bought direct from the growers and resented the competition of dealers. Not surprisingly, when prices were rising wealthy clothiers were able to persuade the government to clamp down on dealers, ostensibly to prevent the evils commonly attributed to middlemen, but in practice to restrict competition among buyers in the wool market. In 1552 all wool dealers were forbidden by statute except in Norfolk, an exception extended to Halifax and surrounding parishes three years later. The act remained in force for seventy years; but from about 1570 it became riddled with exceptions as the crown granted licences allowing the purchase of wool for resale in various parts of the country. Large clothiers, however, were able to prevent a complete reversal of policy until the depression of the 1620s. But in 1624, with wool sales depressed and prices falling, the government repealed the act of 1552 and the wool trade was henceforth open to anyone even though large manufacturers continued to attack the activities of middlemen for several decades.

No government located in London could be unaware of the need for middlemen to supply the metropolis with corn. The government itself was familiar with the nature of the grain trade since it was frequently in the market buying corn for the army and navy. As a result, Tudor policy controlling the grain trade showed a good deal more realism than its policies for wool and leather. At no time were corn dealers prohibited; instead the government accepted the mechanisms of the private market but tried to regulate them in the interests of the population of London, military requirements, and the poor generally. As with the other major trades, the 1550s and 1560s were the formative years of policy when local urban regulations were embodied into national acts. In 1552 corn dealers were permitted to operate as long as they were licensed by three justices of the peace. Forestalling was prohibited but licensed dealers could buy corn in the open market for re-sale at a high price in a different place. Eleven years later the licence system was tightened up: only married men over the age of thirty and householders might obtain licences. Respectability thus assured, they could trade as before and it was even permissible to purchase corn outside the markets if a special licence was obtained. These two acts remained in force until 1772 although they were modified from time to time; but they largely ceased to be enforced in the later seventeenth century.

The privy council also took a close interest in the corn market in the sixteenth century, concerning itself with the operation of the law regulating exports, the licensing of dealers and the purchase of grain for the army and navy. A stream of correspondence flowed between the privy council, local justices and municipal officers inquiring into the state of the grain trade, permitting exports here, prohibiting them there, as local gluts or shortages became apparent. The climax of this detailed regulation was the issue in 1587 – a year of high prices – of the *Book of Orders* instructing local officials to make detailed investigations into the supply of grain. Subsequent re-issues of the *Book of Orders* in 1594, 1608, 1622 and 1630 all occurred in years of high prices. The privy council retained its interest in the grain trade until 1640. Later in the century, however, as grain prices declined in the long term, government interest waned.

A survey of regulations governing the internal trade in wool, leather and corn does not exhaust the extent of governmental control of the product markets. We must remember, too, that statutes and proclamations emanating from the central government imposed regulations on, but did not replace regulations made by local authorities. The two sets of controls complemented one another and the administration of statutory regulation depended on the co-operation of local justices and market officials. National legislation was usually little more than municipal regulations writ large which perhaps explains why so much of it ceased to be effective as trade expanded. Municipal regulations were made in the interests of local producers and local consumers and assumed that middlemen were unnecessary or wicked. They were not likely to succeed for any length of time in the face of economic development, even when supported by the government or powerful interests such as large-scale clothiers or London gilds. These economic groups appreciated better than the government the importance of dealers and when they mouthed well-worn condemnations of middlemen it was for reducing competition among buyers, not for protecting the interests of consumers. The control of the product markets by the government was rarely based on adequate knowledge of the markets and was never able to restrict the relentless enterprise of entrepreneurs.

The Government as Regulator – the Control of Overseas Trade

No aspect of governmental control of economic life in pre-industrial England has received more attention that the regulation of overseas trade. According to Adam Smith, 'the encouragement of exportation and the discouragement of importation are the two great engines by which the mercantile system proposes to enrich every country . . . its ultimate object is . . . to enrich the country by an advantageous balance of trade.'[1] Whatever the truth of this view in 1776, it is not an adequate description of commercial policy in the sixteenth and much of the seventeenth centuries. In the first place, the government regulated overseas trade in order to raise revenue and not to 'enrich the country'. Duties were charged on both imports and exports and the former were normally not raised to levels that would discourage imports. The situation was changed in the 1690s when customs duties were raised in order to meet the increasing costs of war. However in response to requests from manufacturers, rates were kept low on imported raw materials and exports; and by 1722 the latter duties were abolished. It was only then that the tariff became a discriminatory weapon.

In the second place, there were no systematic attempts to prohibit the export of raw materials or the import of manufactured goods before the late seventeenth century. By the early sixteenth century the export duty on wool had been raised so high as a fiscal device that it effectively restricted the export of raw wool. In the early seventeenth century, however, wool prices began to fall in the long term, encouraging the belief among clothiers that continental manufacturers would buy English wool if they could. A series of proclamations in the first half of the seventeenth century prohibited wool exports, and the ban was continued by statute in

[1] Adam Smith, *An Inquiry into the Nature and Causes of the Wealth of Nations*, 1776, Everyman ed., 1910, vol. II, p. 137.

1662. But the prohibition of wool export cannot be interpreted as a straightforward case of 'mercantilist' policy. Clothiers certainly favoured the ban but landowners favoured a policy of export. The views of the former won the day on the grounds that if exports were permitted wool sales – and prices – would be even further depressed, not encouraged, because home sales would fall as English textile manufacturers would be adversely affected by competition from continental manufacturers using English wool. The argument was probably spurious – European textile producers had been managing without significant supplies of English wool since the 1520s – but it was adequate to convince a government of landowners naturally concerned about the price of an agricultural product.

Turning to the regulation of the trade in hides and leather, it is clear that the only principle governing policy was expediency. Before the Restoration neither hides nor leather could be legally exported, although considerable quantities of calf skins were allowed to be exported from pastoral districts under licence. There was an adequate enough market for hides at home and few farmers could see a profit in being free to ship them overseas. But the situation changed in the later seventeenth century. Agricultural prices were falling so the trade in calf skins was thrown open in 1662 and the export of leather permitted in 1668 for seven years as a way of stimulating the demand for hides. Leather users complained that they would be subjected to competition from foreign craftsmen using English leather and for ten years, between 1675 and 1685, the London Company of Cordwainers supported by other leather users were able to prevent parliament from renewing the act permitting the export of leather. Eventually, however, the pro-export lobby of tanners, landowners, and merchants, were able to open up the export trade once again. But though tanners won this particular battle, they were unsuccessful in the early eighteenth century in stopping the export of oak bark, one of their major raw materials, to Ireland.

These examples should warn us against assuming that commercial policy was intended to foster English industry in the sixteenth and seventeenth centuries. If we turn to imports, there is likewise little reason for believing that policy was intended to encourage industrial growth in England. From time to time restrictions were placed on imports of manufactures, mostly of the kind that contemporaries regarded as luxuries. In 1563, for example, a year in which the balance of payments was causing concern, the importation of girdles, rapiers, daggers, knives, saddles, stirrups, gloves, leather, laces and pins was banned. At other times imports of hats and caps, wool-cards, silks, buttons, and gold and silver thread were prohibited. More important were the restrictions imposed on the import and use of calicoes in the early eighteenth century which served inadvertently to encourage the growth of an English cotton industry.

In the sixteenth and early seventeenth centuries one of the most important ways of controlling overseas trade was to establish trading companies. The companies were a source of revenue, a means of generating employment at home, a nursery of shipping, and an instrument of foreign policy. If we keep these functions in mind, we can understand why regulated companies became less important as a means of organizing overseas trade in the second half of the seventeenth century. First, as government finance was gradually reorganized after 1660, the crown became less dependent on merchant loans, and merchants therefore were in a weaker position to demand monopolistic privileges. Second, the belief that trading companies created employment had taken some hard knocks in the first half of the seventeenth century when the cloth-export trade to western Europe was chronically depressed. During the crisis of 1620–24, indeed, the attitude to companies had vacillated considerably. In 1622 and again in 1624 the Company of Merchant Adventurers was forced to liberalize its monopoly and allow non-members to export cloths to its privileged areas. At the same time the monopoly of the Eastland Company was strengthened in the belief that it was the best means of increasing exports and shipping to the Baltic. The different treatments meted out to the two companies reflected differences in their trades. Most of the Eastland trade was in coloured and finished cloths which gave employment to more occupations than the Merchant Adventurers' trade in white cloth. Furthermore, the Eastland trade required bigger ships than the short hauls across the North Sea. The attack on the Merchant Adventurers was also part of the growing parliamentary opposition to privileges granted by the crown, an opposition that grew stronger as the constitutional struggle developed and inevitably focused on the most powerful trading monopoly of all.

The argument between trading monopolies and their opponents was also relevant to the third function of companies as instruments of foreign policy. An effective foreign policy required a strong navy which, in turn, depended on a good supply of substantially-built merchant ships to supplement specialist men-of-war. Any trade, therefore, that promoted the growth of English shipping was favourably viewed by the government. The Eastland Company seemed particularly attractive for it used largish ships and it competed directly with Dutch ships carrying imports from the Baltic. However merchants outside the regulated companies took a different view. Those engaged in the small but growing trade to Asia, Africa and America, for example, also experienced Dutch competition and to them the answer to competition seemed to be a general prohibition on foreigners shipping goods to England. As the geographical pattern of English overseas commerce became more diverse and Anglo-Dutch trading rivalry grew stronger, so this view became more influential. It is against this background that we must see the emergence of the navigation system in the second half of the seventeenth century.

Navigation acts, intended to reserve English trade for English ships, were not new in the seventeenth century. Concern at the dependence on foreign shipping, coupled with growing nationalism had produced several such acts in the sixteenth century but it had been impractical and impolitic to push a navigation policy too hard. A navigation bill had been introduced into Parliament in 1621, proposing that imports should be brought to England only in English ships or ships of the country of origin of the goods, but it was unacceptable to the government as the Dutch were political allies at the time. In any case there were not enough suitable

English ships available to make the act operative. Another depression of trade in 1649 focused the attention of merchants and government alike on measures to assist English trade. As Dr Hinton has written,

> the features of this crisis were ... a decline of exports and a decline of shipping. Nothing is to be found that indicates a decline in the quantity of imports ... The crisis of 1649 looks strikingly similar to the crisis of 1620, though without the monetary disturbance. The main factor was probably freight rates. The English revolution doubtless made freight rates inordinately high, but even had they been normal they would have been higher than Dutch freight rates when the United Provinces were not at war.[1]

At this time political relationships with the Dutch were strained and the Council of Trade – a body established by parliament in 1650 with strong links with merchants outside the regulated companies – proposed a navigation act. The act, passed in 1651, required that imports were to be carried in English ships or ships belonging to the country of origin of the goods, and direct from that country or the port of first shipment. Thus a blow was struck both at the Dutch carrying and the Dutch entrepôt trade.

The act of 1651 did not work satisfactorily for it was practically impossible to determine whether a ship was English-owned or not. When the law came under review at the Restoration there had been nine years of administrative experience on which to base modifications. A new act in 1660, reinforced by additional legislation in 1662, provided for the registration of foreign built ships in English ownership. A further modification was that the obligation in the earlier act to bring all European goods into England in English ships or ships of the country of origin was altered so that the restrictions applied only to enumerated commodities – mostly bulky goods from regions where shipping was most likely to be encouraged; important trades in manufactures from the Low Coun-

[1] R. W. K. Hinton, *The Eastland Trade and the Common Weal in the Seventeenth Century,* 1959, p. 85.

tries, France and Germany were virtually unaffected by the new act. Colonial goods such as sugar, tobacco, cotton and dyestuffs had still to be carried to England in English ships.

The navigation laws were modified by subsequent legislation and supplemented by measures reserving colonial markets for English producers. Thus strengthened, the navigation system became the centre piece of national economic policy. Taken in conjunction with the gradual evolution of a protectionist tariff from the 1690s we can see the government groping to a conscious control of commercial relationships. However the navigation code did not attempt to disrupt or deflect the existing flow of English commerce into entirely new directions, but to direct it along channels through which it was already running.

Public Finance

No consideration of the government's involvement in the economic life of pre-industrial England is complete without an account of public finance. The government's need for money was a major factor in determining economic policy, while the methods it adopted to raise money by taxation and loans had important economic repercussions. In brief, public finance in pre-industrial England is the story of the attempt to adjust inadequate revenues to rising expenditure in a manner that did not impose insupportable burdens on economic activity in the country.

The Tudor and early Stuart view of public finance was that 'the king should live of his own'. The realm was an estate – often described as the 'manor of England' – and like other land-owners the king had to match his expenditure to his income. The major sources of revenue were rents, feudal dues, including purveyance and wardship, and customs duties which were traditionally regarded as the crown's prerogative. In the later years of Elizabeth the ordinary revenue of the crown amounted to roughly £300,000 a year just over half of which came from rents and feudal revenues. In the early seventeenth century, when the annual ordinary revenue was approaching £500,000, the importance of land and feudal dues fell a little in relation to income arising from the customs duties. The economic burden of feudal obligations was not very great but they were troublesome. Wardship in particular was a grievance. In certain circumstances landed estates inherited by minors could be administered by the Court of Wards until their owners came of age. The crown, or its officials, enjoyed the income of the land during its trusteeship and it was sometimes difficult for heirs to regain their property when they came of age. Wardship, in fact, was a capricious kind of land tax, the value of which may be judged from the unsuccessful proposal made by the Lord Treasurer in 1610 to exchange it for an annual parliamentary grant of £200,000. Wardship was eventually abolished in 1646.

Far more people were affected by customs duties than feudal charges, for duties raised the cost of commodities to consumers. Three groups of commodities paid specific duties. Imported wines paid a complicated schedule of high duties. In the case of French wines in the 1550s and '6os, for example, the duty was equivalent to about 80 per cent of the value. There were also heavy specific duties on exported wool, amounting to 40 shillings a sack for native merchants in 1558 and rising steadily later in the century. Exported cloth also paid a specific duty: 1s. 8d. for a notional shortcloth before 1558 and 6s. 8d. thereafter. Even allowing for the cost of the licence that was needed before white cloth could be legally exported, duties did not amount to more than about 8 or 9 per cent of the value of cloth exported in the late sixteenth century. Other commodities paid duties calculated on their value. The rates were low – a shilling in the pound – although they were supplemented from time to time, particularly by James I and Charles I, by additional impositions. For customs purposes commodities were valued according to an official Book of Rates. The origins of such books are obscure. One was in use in 1507 and was re-issued periodically when the rates were adjusted according to changes in market prices. Major revisions were made in 1558, 1604 and at various times in the seventeenth century; even so, official values were usually lower than market values, so that the effective level of *ad valorum* duties was less than 5 per cent.

The major disadvantage of customs duties as a source of revenue was that their yield was not dependable but varied according to the state of trade. In 1560–3, for example, it was 40 per cent lower than in 1558–60. The customs also required a large administrative machine for their collection and evasion was easy. Such considerations encouraged the crown to farm out the customs to private individuals who paid an annual rent and administered the duties in the expectation of making a profit. The customs were farmed on several occasions in the 1560s and '70s, and although Lord Burghley brought their administration back to the direct control of the crown, the first two Stuarts made extensive use of farming. The Great Farm was first let in 1604 for an annual rent of £112,000 and by the 1630s was run by a syndicate of businessmen who paid a rent of £150,000 a year. The petty customs – on wines, sweet wines and currants – was originally let separately, but by the 1630s was in the hands of the same syndicate for a yearly rent of £60,000.

From its ordinary revenues, the crown was expected to meet the normal expenses of the court and running the country. Any surplus income was set aside to meet extraordinary expenditures, of which the most important were wars and interest changes on loans raised to cover expenditure in excess of income. Extraordinary income was obtained from sales of crown land, parliamentary taxation, loans, and revenue earned from the enforcement of economic controls or other state intervention in economic life. Throughout the Tudor and Stuart period ordinary expenses almost invariably exceeded ordinary income and the crown was constantly seeking for additional sources of money.

The crown raised considerable amounts of money by selling land, particularly in the 1540s and 1590s, but the disposal of capital merely made it more important to find other sources of revenue. Parliamentary taxation provided an irregular income in the sixteenth and seventeenth centuries but was small in yield. Direct taxes were the traditional tenths and fifteenths charged on movable property, and the Tudor subsidy assessed on movables and land. These assessments bore little relationship to the actual wealth of the community and the parliaments of Elizabeth and the early Stuarts were most reluctant to raise them to more realistic levels. Thus although direct taxation was a grievance leading to the Civil War, its burden was light. Resentment arose from the manner of levying taxation, not its incidence. As Bacon noted, 'although the same *Tribute* and *Tax*, laid by Consent or Imposing, be all one to the Purse, it workes diuersly vpon the Courage.'

Despite land sales and notwithstanding taxes so reluctantly granted by parliament there remained an uncomfortable gap between income and expenditure in the sixteenth century which widened to a yawning chasm after 1600. Edward VI left debts of £200,000 which increased to nearly a quarter of a million pounds by the beginning of Elizabeth's reign. At the end of the reign this had been reduced to £100,000 but by 1608 it had risen to almost £1 million. The royal demand for loans could be met only by men of wealth and liquidity, which meant in practice merchants and financiers in overseas trade. Until the late sixteenth century the wealth of English merchants was rarely adequate to meet all needs and the government had to borrow on the European money market. Henry VIII raised nearly £1 million at Antwerp in three years of which £75,000 was still outstanding at his death. Elizabeth borrowed £500,000 from Antwerp bankers between 1558 and 1574, and in a single year, 1560, more than a quarter of a million pounds was outstanding. However foreign loans were short-term and unlike domestic creditors, European bankers insisted on charging interest, sometimes as high as 18 per cent. Repayment of the loans depressed the exchange rates just at the time when the government desired high rates of exchange, so after 1574 foreign borrowing ceased. Although the crown needed to raise a total of £461,000 in loans between 1575 and 1603 all was borrowed in England, mostly in London, and interest was paid on only £85,000.

The first two Stuarts were caught on an ascending escalator of war finance, inflation and extravagance, forcing them deeply into debt. Increasingly the crown relied on the City of London for financial assistance. The City spread the requests for money among the livery companies, but its willingness to help was in inverse proportion to the crown's requirements and declined further with every default or deferment of repayment. By the end of 1627 £230,000 was owed to the City in principal and accrued interest on loans raised in 1617 and 1625, and the crown sought another £120,000. In order to induce the City to lend the money the crown was compelled to make over large amounts of land to the City which was then sold to repay outstanding creditors. However many were still waiting for their money in the 1630s and it is hardly surprising that the crown was unable to raise any new loans in the City during the decade.

Lacking credit in London, Charles 1 was reduced to exploiting the financial possibilities of patents of monopolies, incorporations, licences and similar devices. There was a rush of grants in the 1630s. In 1637 and 1638, for instance, several grants were made for the enforcement of manufacturing and marketing regulations in the leather industry. There was an increase in the number of patents of monopolies granted to individuals for the production of particular commodities and several charters of incorporations given – or rather sold – for the establishment of gilds of master craftsmen. The royal prerogative was occasionally used to remedy a genuine grievance or plug an obvious legal loophole, but most grants were hopeful attempts at raising money. 'Projects of all kinds,' wrote a contemporary, 'many ridiculous, many scandalous, all very grievous, were set on foot; the envy and reproach of which came to the king, the profit to other men, insomuch as of £200,000 drawn from the subject by these ways in a year, scarce £1,500 came to the king's use and account.'[1]

Even without the upheavals of the Civil War and Interregnum, a reorganization of public finance was inevitable. The notion that the 'king should live of his own' was eroded in every year in which revenue exceeded expenditure and government credit became more incredulous with every new default. The government urgently needed an adequate and regular revenue and a soundly based system of credit. This came about gradually after the Restoration.

[1] Quoted by W. H. Price, *English Patents of Monopoly*, p. 42.

In 1660 the Restoration parliament voted customs duties calculated to yield £400,000 a year based on a new book of rates. By the end of the 1680s, when trade was at its peak, the income from customs duties had risen to £640,000 and in the early eighteenth century they yielded between £1 million and £1.5 million a year, depending on the state of trade. Until 1671 the customs were farmed as they had been earlier in the century, but thereafter they were administered by commissioners. Parliament also voted excise duties on beer, ale, cider, aqua vita, coffee, tea, chocolate and sherbet to replace the income the crown had once received from the Court of Wards. Additional duties were placed on a wide range of consumption goods during the next forty years and by the early eighteenth century excise duties were more valuable than the customs, bringing in between £1.5 million and £2 millions a year in the early part of the century, and over £3 millions a year by 1750. Customs and excise duties together accounted for between two-thirds and three-quarters of government revenue after 1700.

A third stream of public revenue consisted of various taxes voted by parliament. By 1700 the most important was the land tax charged on the assessed value of land. Direct taxes of all kinds were worth just under £2 million a year in the early eighteenth century. At their peak they brought in about a third of total public revenue but their share declined as the value of customs and excise increased. The land tax added to the costs of landownership and caused difficulties for some small owners. It was also the only major form of taxation to be charged on the country's productive assets; but its incidence was not heavy and it did not check the growth of savings and capital accumulation.

In the first decade of the eighteenth century government income averaged about £5 millions a year, almost ten times greater than it had been a century earlier. However expenditure had risen much more, mainly as a result of the wars of the late seventeenth century, and the gap was covered by borrowing. In 1700, the government's indebtedness was four times bigger than its annual income. The scale of the debt is a tribute to the reforms that had occurred in government credit since the 1630s. In the early years of the

Restoration it looked as though Charles II intended to continue where his father had left off. Money was borrowed from creditors rash enough or bold enough to lend to the king and spent without check, while unpaid tradesmen's bills piled up. However the Treasury, and particularly Sir George Downing, its energetic secretary between 1667 and 1672, gradually gained control over government borrowing. An early innovation was the repayment of creditors in rotation. After 1665 taxes were raised for specific purposes and money was borrowed on the security of specific revenues such as the customs and excise duties. Creditors were now much more confident of being repaid and receiving their interest. In 1667 Downing introduced another reform by making exchequer orders assignable. These orders were given to creditors as receipts for loans which they presented to the Treasury for repayment on maturity. By making them assignable it was possible for persons holding orders to sell them for cash to the London merchant banks without waiting for them to mature. These reforms nearly foundered in 1672 when repayment of £1.2 million worth of exchequer orders was stopped by the crown – not by the Treasury – to meet urgent war expenditure. In 1677 the holders were offered 6 per cent a year on the outstanding sum, but payment soon fell into arrears. Eventually the government agreed to fund the remaining debt and interest and after 1705 creditors received an annual income of 3 per cent. The government had thus stumbled on the device of a perpetual debt whereby investors received a guaranteed income on money lent.

With the rehabilitation of short-term government credit after 1660 wealthy London investors were attracted by the opportunities of long-term lending to the government. The Stop of the Exchequer undermined confidence for a time, but it flooded back after 1688 with the accession of a new dynasty whose purse strings were tightly in the hands of parliament. The 1690s were full of projects for lending money to the government. In 1693 there was the 'Million Loan' whereby the government tried to borrow £1 million in return for 14 per cent annuities payable from various excise duties; and in the following year the 'Million Lottery Loan' offered 100,000 tickets for sale at £10 each, yielding between £1 and £1,000 a year for sixteen years. Also in 1694 a group of business men headed by William Patterson established a bank to advance £1.2 million at 8 per cent to the government, payable partly in cash and partly in bank notes. The interest was guaranteed from additional customs and excise duties and the bank was empowered by charter to borrow money on security of parliamentary revenue. Two years later the Bank of England – so it was incorporated – took over many of the government's short-term obligations as well. Thus in a very short space of time the Bank had established itself as the government's bank. Initially it was only one scheme among several and for a while after 1710 the South Sea Company was a serious competitor. However the Bank of England outlasted its rivals, bolstering up public credit and acting as the 'bankers' bank' as the private banks in London used its notes and lodged deposits with it.

By 1700 public finance had been reformed. The government enjoyed a predictable income from taxes voted by parliament, the Treasury controlled income and expenditure, and public borrowing had been placed on a sound basis. The economic consequences of this 'financial revolution' remain to be considered. Government securities widened the range of investment opportunities which in earlier years had been largely confined to land and the bonds of joint-stock companies. They probably also stimulated confidence in the private sector and contributed to the long-term fall in the rate of interest. Those who lent to the government were, on the whole, the wealthier members of the community with a high propensity to save. The interest they received was paid out of taxes levied largely on consumption. These taxes bore particularly heavily on the poor who thus paid a larger share of their income in taxes than the rich. Dividends on government stock, therefore, were transfer payments from the poor with a high propensity to consume to investors with a high propensity to save. Whatever welfare objections there may be to a fiscal system of this kind, it was favourable to economic development. Over the last century governments in Meiji Japan, Tsarist Russia, the Soviet Union, and elsewhere have deliberately held down consumption in order to free resources for investment. The financial revolution in England in the late seventeenth and early eighteenth centuries seems to have had a similar result, although there were important differences. The fiscal system was not planned to promote economic growth in England and the government did not deliberately use money raised by taxes and loans to stimulate the economy. And neither were consumption levels in England depressed as ruthlessly as they were in, for example, late nineteenth century Russia. It was fortunate for post-Restoration politicians struggling to find ways of obtaining simultaneously a Protestant, solvent and frugal monarchy, that prices of basic foodstuffs were falling. The weight of increased taxation on consumption was lightened by rising agricultural productivity which helped to secure not only an industrial, but also a financial and political revolution.

The Aims and Formulation of Economic Policy

There are, broadly, two opposing hypotheses advanced to explain the mass of regulations imposed on the economy between the early sixteenth and early eighteenth centuries. One holds that the government was responsible for economic policy, both in the sense that it was clear about the direction it wished the economy to go and that it was responsible for the measures introduced to achieve its aims. A variant of this view admits that the government sometimes lost control of the details of economic policy in the face of powerful pressure groups or through ignorance, but ultimately it was the government that controlled policy. The opposite hypothesis sees economic regulation as the product of economic crises and vested interests. There were no guiding objectives of economic policy; indeed no policy at all that can be ascribed to government, which was merely a puppet manipulated sometimes in one way and sometimes in another.

Neither formula adequately explains the facts. Implicit in this chapter has been the assumption that economic policy – using the word policy to mean what was done and not why it was done –

must be seen against the economic background of the time. The features of the pre-industrial economy must always be kept in mind when considering the role of the government. Historians of policy who ignore the economic background cannot begin to understand the policy they study. But equally historians who ignore the influence of ideas on economic policy cannot make much sense of economic legislation. One idea that pervaded practically all thinking before 1750 was that the government had the right, even the duty, to regulate the economy in the national interest. This belief was far from providing a blue print for economic planning, however. 'Tudor and Stuart governments,' Professor Supple has observed, 'directed their regulatory efforts to the maintenance of social order, public peace, national security and the achievement of economic prosperity – simply defined.'[1] Everyone shared these aims: the governed as well as the government, poor farmers clamouring for protection from exploitation by avaricious landlords and landlords seeking freedom to use their land as they pleased. All proposals from pressure groups for particular policies emphasized that the suggested course of action would make the realm secure and prosperous.

The difficulty with aims so general that they command general consent is that they do not provide much guidance as to the means of achieving them. It was possible to propose completely conflicting policies and justify them on the ground that they would secure the peace and prosperity of the country. During the 1550s and 1560s, for example, there was a wide measure of agreement that social order and internal peace and prosperity had been undermined by the growth of and subsequent depression in the cloth export trade. The remedy, it seemed, was to discourage any further expansion of the cloth industry. In the 1620s, in a similar situation, the government took a different line, seeking ways of reviving the cloth trade and creating employment. Similar conflicts arose in practically every field of policy. Did middlemen exploit consumers and producers or did they contribute to the prosperity of the realm? Were privileged companies the best way of fostering over-

[1] B. E. Supple, *Commercial Crises and Change in England, 1600–1642*, 1959, p. 226.

seas trade, or was trade best left to individual merchants? Above all, how was economic prosperity to be achieved? Not through agriculture, presumably. In the sixteenth century Tudor legislators regarded agriculture as the basis of political and social stability, not as the source of economic growth. In the later sixteenth and early seventeenth centuries the government toyed with the policy of promoting industrial expansion by patents of monopoly, but this policy conflicted with the restrictionist philosophy embodied in, for example, the Statute of Artificers and was, in any case, motivated more by a desire to raise money than to stimulate industrial growth. During the seventeenth century there was a growing belief that economic expansion was most likely to be encouraged by the regulation of overseas trade: the attainment of a favourable balance of trade became, in the words of Professor Wilson 'a sort of short-hand for a dynamic economic model.'[1] Its achievement required stimulating exports as a way of increasing production and employment, and curbing imports in order to reduce competition from foreign goods in the home market. By the end of the century, as we have seen, commercial policy was being shaped towards these ends; not on the theoretical grounds just outlined, but as a by-product of attempts to increase the flow of income to the government from the customs duties.

A major reason for economic policy was the state's need for money. Again, this objective was accepted by the ruled as well as the rulers and petitioners were quick to point out the gains that would accrue to the Treasury if their proposals were accepted. Fiscalism was not necessarily incompatible with the other purposes of economic regulation, for a government that was bankrupt was unable to afford armies to maintain the peace and security of the country. But too often money-grabbing contradicted any desired economic and social motives or ends. For example, Elizabethan government used well-intentioned but defective tanning regulations as a source of profit. The first two Stuarts learnt the sorry lesson

[1] Charles Wilson, 'Government Policy and Private Interest in Modern English History', in *Economic History and the Historian: Collected Essays*, 1969, p. 147.

that the exploitation of the economy for fiscal ends provoked social and political unrest, and throughout the sixteenth and seventeenth centuries the fiscal functions of customs duties prevented them from being used as a protectionist device. Until public finance was established on a sound footing the scope for using policy to direct the economy towards any pre-conceived ends was very circumscribed.

Economic policy, therefore, was the result of dealing with economic problems as they arose in order to secure peace, stability, prosperity and money. But we are still left with the problem of deciding who actually formulated policy. In a strict sense all policy was the crown's. It was the king's parliaments that enacted statutes, the king who issued proclamations, granted charters and patents of monopolies, and the king's ministers who gave advice in the privy council or as individuals. But it is only in this narrow sense that it can be claimed that the crown – or the government – was in control of policy. The king and his parliaments did not always see eye to eye, ministers and the crown sometimes differed on what was to be done. Most important of all, the government frequently lacked relevant information on which action could be based and it was therefore exposed to pressures from vested interests. Thus in the formulation of economic policy it is necessary to consider the roles of the monarch and his advisers, parliament and particular groups within the economy.

The role of the crown was potentially very powerful since it was the monarch that determined the national interest. The king acted as though policies ensuring his own survival and prosperity were also the best policies for the realm at large, but this was not a cynical view in an age that accepted monarchy as part of the natural order of society. By the exercise of the royal prerogative policy could be made and unmade at will. Trading companies such as the Merchant Adventurers owed their existence to charters given by the crown which could be revoked in certain circumstances, as the Merchant Adventurers discovered in 1614. Royal proclamations were used by Tudor and Stuart monarchs to vary the operation of statute law and as means of enforcing policy. Above all, the crown summoned and dismissed parliament at will – at least before the Civil War – and as long as it could control parliament it could control policy.

In practice, however, the king's power was limited. There were many other things to occupy the mind of a monarch than the state of the economy. The vignette of the Lord Treasurer waving the accounts of the Kingdom before an uninterested King in 1665, begging him 'please to cast your eye upon them and to spend upon this subject but one hour'[1] must have been a recurring one in the sixteenth and seventeenth centuries, depending on the character and mood of the monarch. The Cockayne project affords an example of a king personally involved in economic policy and pursuing a line of action in the face of opposition from his advisers. But on most occasions royal power in economic matters was exercised by the king's ministers and from the mid-sixteenth century the Privy Council was a most influential group in the formulation of policy. In the field of economic regulation its function was two-fold: initiation of policy and enforcement. It was able to initiate policy by introducing bills in parliament through Councillors who were also members of parliament, or by the exercise of the royal prerogative. Enforcement was a very time-consuming activity. A stream of correspondence and instructions flowed back and forth between the Council and the various bodies responsible for implementing economic controls in the countryside. The day to day burden of enforcing existing regulations meant that the Privy Council had little time to act as an instrument of long-term economic planning.

The Privy Council did not rely entirely on its own members when dealing with economic affairs but sought advice wherever it could be found. In the 1560s, for example, the opinion of John Mershe a London MP and governor of the Company of Merchant Adventurers, was asked on several matters affecting the interests of the City of London; and the Council frequently approached the Court of Aldermen directly for advice. The London gilds were another source of advice – sometimes given unsolicitously – but

[1] Quoted by H. Roseveare, *The Treasury*, 1969, p. 57.

often information was obtained in informal ways. When, for example, Lord Burghley wished to know something about tanning he asked William Fleetwood, Recorder of London who claimed, in a modest way, to be an authority:

> ... Although my skill in Tanning of Lether be small, yet for these xiii yeares I haue giuen my mynde thate weyes to vnderstand of that facultie, my wifes mother in Buckinghamshire was married into a Tanner ... a man both of great welthe verie wise and most skillfull in his arte, and such a one as made the best lether in this lande ... he tolde me vnto the time of his deathe allwaies that it was impossible to make good leather, according to the worde of the lawe, and wished many times of god that the Law might be reformed ...[1]

By the early seventeenth century the Privy Council had formalized its methods of seeking advice by appointing sub-committees and setting up commissions to investigate various matters. In 1622 a committee was established to enquire into the state of trade which included persons who were not members of the Council. This was followed by a commission of trade which met intermittently in the 1620s and became a more or less permanent body. During the Civil War and Interregnum the functions of the Privy Council passed to parliament and its Council of Trade which in turn established the first Board of Trade in 1650. The Privy Council resumed its role as a policy-making body after the Restoration but many of its administrative functions gradually passed to other bodies such as the Commissioners for the Customs, the Board of Trade, and the Treasury. These institutions relied on semi-professional government officials who gathered information and acted as a barrier between the government and pressure groups.

Apart from the crown and Privy Council, the most important legislative body was parliament and a great deal of economic regulation was embodied in parliamentary statutes. Many statutes were in fact, sponsored by ministers of the crown who sat in the Lords or Commons but as both Elizabeth and the early Stuarts

[1] B.M., *Lans. Ms.* 20, fo. 10.

found, the House of Commons had a mind of its own which it was increasingly willing to voice. Private members of parliament were able to introduce bills into the Commons or Lords independently of the government. To take perhaps the most significant case, Professor Bindoff has shown how the Statute of Artificers, far from being a piece of central government planning, originated, in part, from private members' bills. Parliament also won notable victories in curbing the royal prerogative. Elizabeth was usually able to control parliamentary opposition but in 1601 she was forced to yield to a popular clamour against patents of monopolies and abolish the more obnoxious of them. Several successful onslaughts on the crown's prerogative powers occurred in the 1620s when parliament forced the Merchant Adventurers to surrender some of their privileges. Parliament was also responsible for the Statute of Monopolies in 1624 making illegal 'all monopolies, commissions, grants, licences, charters, and patents for the sole buying, making, working or using of any commodities within the realm.' In the same year parliament prevented informers from laying informations about alleged breaches of economic regulations in the Exchequer court at Westminster thereby ending a long standing grievance.

But the most notable struggle between parliament and the crown was over taxation. Even the Tudors had found it difficult to wring money from the Commons and in the early seventeenth century the quarrels between James I and Charles I and their parliaments over taxation led to a political crisis that was resolved only by civil war. The Restoration settlement seemed at first to be a reversion to old times with the king and Council restored to authority and parliament still granting taxation too little and too late. But there was a fundamental difference in that the king could no longer ignore parliament; and after the Revolution of 1688 its role was unchallenged. By the end of the seventeenth century, composed of representatives of the landed and business classes chosen in frequently contested elections, the House of Commons had become an effective forum for expressing the views of the economic and financial interests of the country.

It remains to examine the role of private interests in the economy in the formulation of policy. There is a danger of creating a false dichotomy between private interests and government, as though the rulers and the ruled had opposing interests. In fact, as we have suggested, all sections of society shared the common beliefs that the realm should be peaceful and prosperous. But disagreements arose on how to achieve these desired ends and vested interests, therefore, were often able to manipulate policy for their own purposes. Pressure groups were sometimes well organized bodies such as the trading companies and London gilds. The gilds were well placed to influence policy. Their proximity to Westminster made it easy to lobby members of parliament and privy councillors, their financial resources permitted them to spend money in furthering their causes, and their membership enabled them to lend a little physical persuasion to proceedings if necessary. When, for example, the claim of the London Company of Cordwainers to levy a quarterly fee on shoemakers living in Westminster was being tested before the Court of the Star Chamber, the solicitor acting for the Westminster craftsmen was attacked in the street and members of the cordwainer's company were 'saieng yt if ... my L. highe Treasourer were a showemaker they wold shutt upp his window vnless yt he wold paye quarteridge vnto them'. On another occasion, a currier abused in 'slanderous and unseemly terms' a member of a House of Commons committee which was considering the marketing regulations for the leather trade contained in the act of 1563.[1] Generally pressure groups did not have to go to violent lengths to get their way. In an age lacking an impartial civil service, trading companies and gilds were the natural source of information on economic affairs and the Privy Council frequently turned to them for advice.

Other pressure groups were less organized. When the bite of regulations became too sharp, injured parties spontaneously complained to parliament or the Privy Council. Particularly hard felt grievances, however, sometimes coalesced to produce concerted action from groups normally lacking formal association. Thus in the

[1] B. M. *Lans. Ms.* 24, fos. 183–184; *House of Commons' Journals*, vol. I, p. 240.

early seventeenth century merchants from the outports maintained a stream of complaints against the privileges enjoyed by the exclusive London-based companies. At the end of the century an excise duty imposed on leather provoked more than one hundred petitions of complaint from manufacturers in many parts of the country, many of them using identical wording. Later, between 1711 and 1717 tanners in various parts of the country organized a national petition protesting against the export of oak bark to Ireland and contributed to a common fund to cover the cost.

Ultimately the most powerful pressure group of all were the common people. In his essay 'of Seditions and Troubles' Francis Bacon, eventually to become Lord Chancellor of England, wrote that 'The *Matter* of *Seditions* is of two kinds; *Much Poverty,* and *Much Discontentment*', and went on to propose a programme for removing the *'material Cause* of *Sedition'*:

> ... the Opening, and well Ballancing of Trade; The Cherishing of Manufacturers; the Banishing of Idleness; the Repressing of waste and Excesse by Sumptuary Lawes; the Improuement and Husbanding of the Soyle; the Regulating of Prices of things vendible; the Moderating of Taxes and Tributes; And the like[1]

Every government in Tudor and Stuart England had to consider how best to secure social order and public peace since none was absolutely sure of its authority; and, in the absence of a police force or standing army, governments did what they could by policy to avoid civil commotion. The alleviation of distress, for example, was one motive lying behind the continual pre-occupation with the poor law in the sixteenth and seventeenth centuries. Similarly fear of potential or actual disturbances arising from agrarian grievances was a significant factor behind the enactment and enforcement of legislation against enclosing and engrossing. The point was not lost on petitioners pleading for particular courses of action, who invariably argued that their proposals could provide employment and relieve poverty. Although the masses were unorganized and

[1]Francis Bacon, *Essays*, World Classics ed. 1937, pp. 59, 60.

inarticulate, Christian charity and public prudence both required that the country's rulers did not ignore them entirely.

There were many channels through which vested interests were able to influence policy. One of the easiest was to elicit the services of sympathetic members of parliament. London companies frequently used MPs to introduce bills into the Commons or to oppose bills contrary to their interests. When the Commons met regularly in the late seventeenth century members of parliament were valuable allies of pressure groups. But in earlier days when the Privy Council was paramount in policy making, a privy councillor was a more formidable ally still. Since the Council itself was an amorphous body, vested interests were able to gain the ear of individual members. Thus when Sir Edward Dyer was seeking a patent for the enforcement of the leather act of 1563, he first submitted his proposals for approval to Sir John Popham, lawyer and privy councillor, before the matter was considered by the whole Council. But even Privy Councillors could be thwarted by the personal actions of the king. In 1613/14 the Privy Council's opposition to the Cockayne scheme was overridden by the king and certain courtiers whom Cockayne had bribed and flattered. A few years later the efforts of Lionel Cranfield, Lord Treasurer and privy councillor, to bring some sort of order to the King's chaotic finances aroused the hostility of the Duke of Buckingham and other court favourites who organized a successful campaign for his impeachment. In doing so they not merely caused the downfall of an efficient minister, but postponed the necessary reform of public finance for half a century.

The precise role of private interests in creating or influencing economic policy can be gauged only by close examination of individual legislation. When the formulation of policy required considerable economic or technical knowledge private interests could be very influential. Alderman Cockayne was able to persuade James I that the export of coloured cloth was preferable to the export of white cloth on the simple argument that it would generate additional employment, ignoring the principle of comparative advantage that underlay the international cloth trade. Similarly the bewildering vacillations in policy relating to middlemen in the leather trade in the 1540s and 1550s occurred because the crown did not know whether middlemen were necessary or not. In the same way pressure groups were responsible for the regulations imposed on middlemen in the wool trade between 1552 and 1624. Later in the century the Irish Woollen Act of 1699 which prohibited the export of Irish woollens to any country except England and Wales, was the product of lobbying by west of England cloth producers and, '... so far from being an example of the way in which the state controlled commerce it showed how commercial interests control state policy', for it was contrary to the political interests of the government.[1]

Yet when the peace and prosperity of the country was clearly at stake, governments attempted to control economic policy. During the 1550s and 1560s the Privy Council sought remedies for the severe economic difficulties besetting the country. More confidently, it handled the trade depression of the 1620s, asking for and receiving advice from interested parties, but ultimately deciding what should be done. Three decades later, the government decided that the interests of overseas commerce were best served by a navigation act and not by perpetuating the privileges of trading companies. The view of the government as a sort of referee choosing its policy from the clamour of advice offered to it has been advanced by Professor Charles Wilson[2] and obviously has much to commend it. When opposing courses of action were suggested somebody had to choose the one to be followed. When the issues involved were important ones, such as how to advance the commercial or political interests of the realm or how to avoid the social and economic dislocations of a trade depression, the government clearly had to make a choice. But issues were often confused and the referee was not always aware of the nature of the game being played. Indeed, who was the referee?: the crown?; the Privy Council? or the House of Commons? All three institutions were at

[1] H. K. Kearney, 'The Political Background to English Mercantilism, 1695–1700', *Econ. Hist. Rev.*, 2nd ser., vol. XI, 1959, p. 495.
[2] Wilson, *op. cit.*, p. 153.

times responsible for economic policy. And they all shared the common belief that the state should regulate the economy in the interests of stability and prosperity. Pressure groups believed in the same objectives and, whether formal organizations or *ad hoc* creations, they played a valid role in the formulation of policy by suggesting the practical steps by which vague aspirations could be achieved.

Enforcement and Effectiveness

Economic policy in pre-industrial England frequently foundered on the means of enforcement and the paper plans produced at the Palace of Westminster appeared a good deal less formidable in the parishes and provincial towns. Thus any assessment of the effectiveness of economic policy must start with a consideration of the ways by which it was implemented. Starting at the top, the key role was played by the Privy Council, buttressed by the prerogative courts such as the Exchequer. The Privy Council had the responsibility for seeing that economic regulations were enforced in the countryside, if necessary instructing justices to pay attention to particular regulations. The Civil War disrupted its authority and after the Restoration – although the matter awaits investigation – the Council seems to have surrendered a good deal of its authority to the newly emerging bureaucracies such as the Treasury. The day to day enforcement of economic regulations in the countryside was the responsibility of several groups: unpaid and overworked justices of the peace; municipal officials, likewise unpaid; public servants such as customs and excise officers, underpaid and frequently corrupt; and private informers, the supreme testimony to the pervasiveness of economic man who made a living out of informing on the misdemeanours of their fellow men.

Justices of the peace were the most important cogs in the machinery of enforcement. Of medieval origin, the office of justice had evolved into an essential part of the fabric of local life by the sixteenth century. By 1580 there were over 1,700 JPs in England, although the number actively involved in the administration of justice was much smaller. The geographical spread was uneven, with some counties possessing a better ratio of justices to population than others. The majority of justices were landowners and often members of well-established county families. Some of them were clothiers or had connection with the cloth trade and many of them possessed a little legal training. Since the office was unpaid only the relatively wealthy could afford to take it on. The duties were heavy and in the early seventeenth century justices were responsible for the administration of more than 300 statutes, including such cumbersome regulations as the wages and apprenticeship laws and the poor law. Their tasks ranged far beyond the implementation of social and economic policy and included the enforcement of the criminal law, the prosecution of fornicators who begat bastard children, and idolaters and recusants who offended against the Reformation settlement. With the best will in the world JPs could not enforce all economic regulations efficiently, for they were too few and the regulations too numerous. Before 1640 the Privy Council tried to control their activities by issuing instructions through the judges of assize and writing direct to JPs. Even so, the activity of justices was sporadic, particularly in the case of legislation concerned with technical standards and apprenticeship. Sometimes the personal interests of JPs conflicted with their duties as magistrates, particularly when enclosure was involved. The justices were perhaps a little more assiduous in assessing wages under the Statute of Artificers; even so the frequency with which new assessments were made, rather than old ones re-issued, declined during the seventeenth century. The longest lasting task of JPs was the administration of the poor law which they shared with village constables and other parish officials – the poor, after all, would not go away. But the standard of administration varied enormously from parish to parish.

In the boroughs the authority of justices was reinforced by municipal officials. City corporations possessed a great deal of authority including the regulation of marketing, the location of crafts and the relief of the poor. Under various statutes municipalities also appointed ulnagers of cloth, searchers and sealers of leather and so on. These unpaid officials were usually nominated by the appropriate urban gilds and they could not be relied on to enforce the law systematically and impartially. Frequently the appointments were sinecures, losing all function and surviving only as honorary municipal offices. Even where the officials took their duties seriously, their authority rarely extended beyond the jurisdiction of the boroughs.

Until the end of the seventeenth century the collection of the customs was in the hands of officers notorious for their corruption, even in an age that accepted corruption as an inevitable part of public service. Frequently customers connived at smuggling, even to the extent of assisting in the loading of contraband cargoes. Considering the occupational hazards, this is perhaps not surprising. Customs officers were often attacked in the course of their duties. One sixteenth century officer at Chester when rowing out to a ship in the harbour to inspect its cargo was greeted with gunfire and he probably did not believe the excuse that the shot was fired 'to intent . . . to scoure the gonne'.[1] When the customs were farmed the life of a customs officer was very frustrating, since the farmers, being merchants themselves, sometimes failed to support prosecutions laid against offending merchants. When excise duties were introduced in the late seventeenth century, excise officers joined customs officials as the most despised figures in public life. After a period of experimentation the collection of excise duties was organized along similar lines to the customs and was controlled by commissioners accountable to the Treasury. Customs and excise officers were paid and responsible to superior officials. Even so some of the collectors were not beyond corruption and evasion of customs and excise duties became a minor national pastime in the eighteenth century. Nevertheless, the customs and excise were much more efficiently administered than other areas of economic regulation.

It was left to private enterprise to plug the gaps left in the official means of implementing economic policy. The crown often granted patents to individuals empowering them to enforce statutes

[1] P. R. O. Exchequer, Special Commissions, E 178/498.

in various parts of the country and most statutes from Henry VIII onwards offered informers a share of the penalties exacted from offenders. Like so many occupations in pre-industrial England, informing was a pursuit often combined with other activities, but it also attracted the professionals possessing sufficient capital enabling them to operate on a large scale. They were often Londoners with a smattering of legal knowledge and an eye for profit, who employed agents in various parts of the country to seek out, or invent, offences. Informations were usually laid in the Court of Exchequer at Westminster. Since defendants frequently could not afford to travel to London to attend the Court, informers were permitted to compound with the offender, collect the penalty and pay the crown's share into the Exchequer. Not surprisingly, informers frequently cut corners by making unauthorized compositions with alleged offenders and pocketing the Exchequer's share of the penalty. Informers were responsible for most presentments for breaches of economic regulations coming before the courts. They were heartily disliked for the activities, all the more so because of their capacity for finding offences where none existed and the extortionate compositions that they claimed. Parliament tried to regulate them on a number of occasions in the late sixteenth century and after 1624 they were forbidden to lay informations in the Westminster courts. Thereafter they had to operate at the local quarter sessions, before magistrates who might be unsympathetic, and with the likelihood of the defendant appearing to contest the charge. By the late seventeenth century, therefore, informers had been reduced to nuisances who occasionally enmeshed traders and manufacturers in half forgotten regulations.

To be at all enforceable economic policy needed to be realistic. We can see this clearly if we look at the Tudor attempts to regulate the foreign exchange business which simply did not work since it was impossible to keep track of dealings in foreign currencies. It was likewise impossible to stamp out usury since creditors were ingenious in disguising it and debtors were usually so desperate for funds that they were prepared to pay it. None of the prohibitions on middlemen were ever effective and it is noticeable that when the government had some knowledge of the state of the market, as it did in the case of corn, it did not try to eliminate middlemen altogether. In fact, the great body of internal economic controls was unenforceable in any consistent manner because it ran counter to the interests of entrepreneurs motivated by profit. Command economies today have found it impossible to eliminate the market as a means of economic organization and the rickety machinery of government available to the Tudors and Stuarts had even less success. When the role of government was purely supervisory, such as licensing corn dealers, policy could be implemented as long as local justices and other officials stirred themselves. But efforts to divert factors of production to uses not indicated by the market were doomed to failure. The regulation of overseas trade was probably easier than controlling economic activity within the country. Imports and exports were funnelled through major ports and it was possible to keep a check on the main trade flows, although remote creeks and havens were the Almighty's gift to the smuggler. Trading companies proved a practical way of encouraging shipping and regulating overseas trade as long as it was conducted overwhelmingly with nearby Europe. But as the pattern of overseas commerce became more complex, companies based on specific geographical regions became less appropriate and policy inclined towards a navigation system. But the navigation system became a practical policy only after the first Dutch War added between 1,000 and 1,700 Dutch built ships to the English merchant fleet. Once ships were available the navigation code was enforceable, more or less, in English waters, but much more difficult to police in colonial seas.

How effective was government policy in securing the general objectives of security and prosperity in pre-industrial England? To answer this question adequately, we need the answer to another: would the economic history of England between 1500 and 1750 have been different had the government made no attempt to control economic life? And to pose such a question brings us close to the mire of counterfactual history, through which there are practically no sign-posts to guide us. Security meant avoiding public disorder at home and defending the realm from foreign enemies. Specific economic measures taken included relief of the poor, price regulation, control of marketing and manufacturing, and measures intended to prevent the shift of land and labour out of arable farming, and industries out of the corporate towns. None of these measures was workable for any length of time, except the first. If serious public disorder was prevented in pre-industrial England – and it was not at all times – the credit cannot be given to the economic and social policies of governments. And it was perhaps as well that some of the government's policies were unsuccessful, for their economic cost was potentially high. The effect of the enclosure acts and the Statute of Artificers, for example, would have been to prevent the most profitable use of factors of production, thus frustrating the growth of wealth and perpetuating economic conditions conducive to poverty. The best guarantee of security was a prosperous economy.

Seventeenth century commercial policy as a means of achieving prosperity has, on the whole, received an approving nod from historians. The navigation acts have been seen as a means of successfully stimulating the English shipbuilding industry and entrepôt trade and the so-called colonial system as a way of extending the markets for English manufactured goods and providing valuable raw materials. As Professor Charles Wilson has written, these were policies 'resting on the assumption that some men should be encouraged to better themselves, and by so doing, better society as a whole';[1] they were, he suggests, reasonable policies for a backward economy to adopt and they were probably effective. Commercial regulations were certainly policies that evolved naturally from the economic and political conditions of the time, but a full investigation of their effectiveness remains to be carried out. The navigation acts, for example, assisted the growth of English shipping, but at a cost. If laws were necessary to compel Englishmen to use English ships instead of Dutch ships, presumably the former were more expensive. Hence merchants were burdened with heavier freight charges than they would have paid had there been

[1] Charles Wilson, *England's Apprenticeship*, 1965, p. 375.

no restrictions. Possibly the penalty of heavy freights lasted for a short period only and disappeared as techniques of building and operating English ships improved under the protection of the navigation acts; but we do not know. Similarly the benefits accruing from the monopoly imposed on colonial trade were gained at a price. Two centuries ago Adam Smith argued that:

> the effect of the monopoly has been, not to augment the quantity, but to alter the quality and shape of a part of the manufactures of Great Britain, and to accommodate to a market, from which the returns are slow and distant, what would otherwise have been accommodated to one from which the returns are frequent and near. Its effect has consequently been to turn a part of the capital of Great Britain from an employment in which it would have maintained a greater quantity of manufacturing industry to one in which it maintains a much smaller, and thereby to diminish, instead of increasing, the whole quantity of manufacturing industry maintained in Great Britain.[1]

If this view is to be refuted it must be shown that colonial markets were a vital and irreplaceable stimulus to English manufacture and trade. They may have been, given the fact that the larger and potentially more lucrative markets of western Europe were highly competitive and protected by tariffs. But the purchasing power of colonial markets was closely linked to the prosperity of the English economy and it was the English market that provided the main incentive for English producers. Yet one of the consequences of the colonial system was to force English consumers to buy goods from English colonies that might have been obtained more cheaply from other sources. For example, it has been suggested that the protection given in English markets to sugar imported from the British West Indies in the eighteenth century resulted in British consumers paying about £446,000 a year more than if they had been permitted to buy foreign sugar.[2] To the

---

[1] Adam Smith, *An Inquiry into the Nature and Causes of the Wealth of Nations,* 1776, Everyman ed., 1910, vol. II, p. 107.

[2] R. P. Thomas, 'The Sugar Colonies of the Old Empire: Profit or Loss for Great Britain?', *Econ. Hist. Rev.,* 2nd ser., vol. XXI, no. 1, 1968, p. 31.

extent that consumers gave up manufactured goods in order to buy sugar, English industry lost a market at home – 'frequent and near' – in return for gaining a market in the British West Indies.

It is not suggested that when the balance sheet is finally drawn up the costs of policies adopted in the later seventeenth and the eighteenth centuries will be found to have outweighed the benefits. But remembering the hidden costs of policies which appear superficially advantageous; remembering too, that many economic regulations were unworkable because they ran counter to market trends; and remembering, finally, that much economic policy was not enforced at all or was enforced only sporadically, it is as well to be cautious in attributing much positive gain to the economy of pre-industrial England from government economic policy. Englishmen in the later seventeenth century were not agreed that policy had much effect. 'I find,' wrote Sir George Downing as a good administrator convinced of his own value 'that a Gardener doth not more contribute to the growing of his herbs and trees than doth the Government of any country to the growth of its trade.'[1] A more sceptical view was taken by Sir Dudley North: 'we may labour to hedge in the Cuckoo, but in vain; for no People ever yet grew rich by Policies, but it is Peace, Industry and Freedom that brings Trade and Wealth, and nothing else.'[2]

[1] Quoted by H. Roseveare, *The Treasury*, p. 60.
[2] Sir Dudley North, *Discourse on Trade*, 1691.

7

Wealth and Poverty
in Pre-industrial England

Poverty was the pervading condition of pre-industrial England. A small minority of the population was very much wealthier than the great majority and rich even by the standards of the twentieth century. Probably Englishmen were no worse off than their contemporaries in Western Europe and they may indeed have been more prosperous than many. But measured against the expectations of populations in modern industrialized economies, Englishmen between 1500 and 1750 were miserably poor and could rarely expect to see any marked improvement in living conditions during their lifetimes.

The Growth of Wealth

It is impossible to measure the growth of wealth in pre-industrial England since the data relating to the increase of output and incomes are so sparse. All that can be done is to project back to earlier periods growth rates for the early part of the eighteenth century for which a few figures are available. Using this method, Professor Simon Kuznets has suggested that the long-term rate of growth of *per capita* production between 1500 and 1750 was not greater than 0.2 per cent per year, a rate that achieves an increase in production per head of 65 per cent in the 250 years. This compares with *per capita* growth rates in modern developed countries of at least 1.5 per cent per year.[1] If we assume that population in England increased by 0.3 per cent per annum in the same period,[2] the growth of aggregate output can have been only about 0.5 per cent per annum. Obviously, these calculations cannot be verified but they do illustrate that the likely growth rates of *per capita* and total production were much lower than are commonly found in developed economies in the nineteenth and twentieth centuries, and they provide a framework in which it is possible to consider the growth of wealth over shorter periods.

During the first half of the sixteenth century it seems unlikely that average *per capita* incomes increased at all. The population increased by roughly 25 per cent which was certainly faster than agricultural production, with the result that food prices rose and the real incomes of wage-earners – a substantial minority of the population – fell. Other sections of the population fared better, particularly farmers with fixed or relatively fixed costs of production and landlords whose estates were let out on flexible leases. Clothiers supplying the expanding export markets and exporting merchants also enjoyed rising prosperity and so too did the handful of people engaged in other growing industries such as iron-smelting. There is evidence that imports of manufactured goods, wines and luxuries increased which suggests that some classes in society were becoming more prosperous; but, overall, the growth in population left little room for any general rise in levels of wealth.

The two decades from the late 1540s to the late 1560s were a period of great economic difficulty. Harvests were poor or bad in 1545, 1549, 1550, 1551, 1555 and 1556. Total agricultural output may have fallen in the first half of the 1550s, food prices rose steeply and there was widespread concern about the adequacy of

---

[1] Simon Kuznets, 'Capital Formation in Modern Economic Growth, and Some Implications for the Past', *Third International Conference of Economic History*, Paris, 1968, pp. 30–1.

[2] i.e. from 2.8 million in 1500 to 6.2 million in 1750. Professor Kuznets' assumed figure of less than 0.2 per cent per annum seems too low for England (*ibid.* p. 30.).

the country's corn supplies. In the late 1540s there was a boom in cloth production to supply export markets, but in the following decade exports fluctuated wildly about a falling trend until, in 1564, they were only half the volume of the early 1550s. However any reduction in average incomes in the economy was arrested by the high mortality of the late 1550s which resulted in fewer people to share the country's wealth. A characteristic feature of pre-industrial England was that economic growth was more often the result of rising mortality than rising production.

The late 1560s, the 1570s and early 1580s appear to have been modestly prosperous years compared with the difficulties of the previous twenty years. There was a sequence of good or adequate harvests and food prices rose less quickly than they had done during the 1540s and 1550s. Exports, too, recovered from the disastrous levels of the early 1560s – although the peaks of the early 1550s were never regained – bringing employment to the manufacturing regions. Even wage earners enjoyed a brief respite from the long decline in real wages that occurred between 1500 and 1650, since the shortage of labour that followed the mortality of the late 1550s caused money wages to rise. Demand at home increased, bringing prosperity to industries supplying consumer goods. But the prosperity did not last. An accelerating rate of population growth from the 1570s again overhauled the growth of production and between 1585 and 1600 grain prices were, on average, nearly 50 per cent higher than they had been in the previous decade. In 1586 crop failure coincided with a depression in trade creating widespread distress, and although good harvests in the early 1590s brought better conditions, bad harvests between 1594 and 1597 caused suffering and depressed purchasing power. The century ended with wage earners worse off than they had been at the beginning of the century.

During the first fifteen or twenty years of the seventeenth century there was possibly a small but widespread improvement in *per capita* incomes. Epidemics in the late 1590s had temporarily checked the growth of population. More important, harvest conditions were generally satisfactory and only 1608 and 1613 stood out as really bad years; possibly agricultural productivity was rising, thus keeping the increase in food supplies somewhere near the increase in demand with the result that grain prices rose relatively slowly. The export sector, too, was prosperous as the trade in old draperies expanded, until disrupted by the Cockayne scheme, and the trade in new draperies increased even more rapidly. But economic growth once again proved a fragile plant in the 1620s when it was stunted by bad harvests and trade depression which depressed the level of effective demand at home. Real wages fell to their lowest point for a century and recovery was slow. Better harvests in the second half of the 1620s helped to raise the level of effective demand; but harvests were generally deficient in the 1630s and the trade in old draperies remained stagnant.

Reviewing the century from 1540 to 1640 as a whole, only the years between the mid-1560s and mid-1580s, and the first two decades of the seventeenth century stand out as periods when the growth of *per capita* incomes could have reached the upper limits of 0.2 per cent per annum suggested by Professor Kuznets. The record of the next century, particularly after 1660, is a little more cheerful, for the growth of population slackened and pressed less hard against resources. However the century started badly. The 1640s and '50s were difficult years economically as war caused physical destruction and disrupted internal and overseas commerce. Five bad seasons in a row from 1646 to 1650 caused the price of food to rise, cutting deeply into margins of subsistence. Hunger and disease took their toll of the population; and not only did mortality rise in the short run but, as we saw in Chapter Two, the middle decades of the seventeenth century commenced a new phase in population history in which mortality rates were generally higher and fertility rates generally lower than in the previous century. For the first time it became possible for agricultural production to increase consistently faster than population.

The early 1660s were the turning point in the history of grain prices. From then on the secular trend was slowly downwards interrupted only by short spells of high prices in the mid-1670s, the mid-1690s, 1708–14, 1728–9 and 1739–40. Economic expansion was hampered in the 1660s by war, plague and the Fire of London, but from the end of the third Dutch war a boom in overseas trade added its impetus to growing effective demand in the home market. Unlike earlier periods, the export trade did not depend heavily on the textile industry and a large number of manufactures benefited from the growth of markets in the colonies, Africa and Asia; while the re-export of colonial and East Indian goods stimulated shipping and ports, and also provided the purchasing power by which colonial territories were able to buy English manufactured goods. Economic growth was checked during the 1690s by war with France which disrupted trade, and poor harvests which caused the price of grain to rise steeply. However the home markets recovered as grain prices fell from 1699. The fall was again interrupted by poor seasons in 1708 and 1709 – corn prices in the latter year were the highest for half a century – but the decline in prices resumed after 1714 and persisted with occasional setbacks practically to the middle of the century. Sagging corn prices were not welcome to grain farmers and landlords whose estates lay in arable regions, but they were an important cause of rising real incomes enjoyed by many sectors of the community. This rise was re-inforced by increasing money wages and the home market became an increasingly powerful stimulus to manufacturers and traders. Overseas trade was less buoyant in the early eighteenth century than it had been in the 1670s and 1680s, even though it recovered after the peace of 1713. Together, the growing strength of the home and overseas markets stretched existing forms of production to their limits before 1750 and created conditions leading to industrialization and sustained economic growth in the late eighteenth century.

The growth of wealth occurred only slowly and intermittently between 1500 and 1750. The reasons for this dismal and erratic performance have been discussed in the previous chapters. The low level of technology, the unskilled nature of the workforce, and, above all, the lack of market opportunities, provided little incentive for private producers to increase output. In addition, the growth of wealth was continually disrupted by bad weather, epidemics and wars, and it was often exceeded by the growth of population. An important cause of the apparently faster rate of growth of *per capita* incomes after 1650, compared with the previous century and a half, was the slowing down in the rate of population growth.

The Distribution of Wealth

The wealth of pre-industrial England was unequally distributed both geographically and socially. The wealthiest counties lay south of a line running from the Wash to the mouth of the Severn and the richest county by far was Middlesex. Even excluding the city of London, its wealth per acre in the early sixteenth century was more than twice as great as the second wealthiest county, Somerset, which was, in turn, slightly wealthier than Essex, Kent and Surrey. According to tax assessments in 1515 the city of London contained almost 9 per cent of the lay wealth of the country. The most prosperous core of the country, therefore was London and the Home Counties. A second wealthy group was Somerset, Gloucestershire and Wiltshire; and a third Suffolk and Norfolk. London's wealth was based on its importance as an administrative, trading and manufacturing centre and its demands for food and raw materials added to the prosperity of the surrounding countryside already endowed by nature with a good climate and terrain for agriculture. The wealth of the western counties owed much to the prosperity of the cloth industry. East Anglian prosperity rested on a good climate for corn-growing and a cloth industry geared to the export markets.

The poorest parts of England in 1515 were the most northerly counties which were very much poorer than the richest; wealth per acre in Lancashire for example was less than 2 per cent of the equivalent figure in Middlesex. The most impoverished counties were situated in the geographically less well endowed part of the country where the land was less fertile, the climate wetter and the summers cooler than the south and east. They were remote from the relatively rich markets of London and the southeast and remote, too, from the markets of western Europe.

Changes occurred in the regional distribution of wealth during the sixteenth and seventeenth centuries but are difficult to chart. London grew rapidly in wealth; according to some commentators its growth was at the expense of other parts of the country: 'it is no good state for a body to have a fat head, thin guts, and lean members'.[1] But other observers realized that London's demands for consumer goods generated wealth in the surrounding countryside. Norden, for instance, noted that farmers in Middlesex 'commonly became very riche' by trading with the capital. The land tax assessments for 1693 reveal the poorest counties were still Cumberland, Westmorland, Northumberland, Durham, Lancashire, Yorkshire, Shropshire and Derbyshire. The region south of the Wash-Severn line remained the richest part of England, but the textile districts of East Anglia and the West of England had become relatively a little less prosperous since the early sixteenth century, while counties such as Bedfordshire, Berkshire, Buckinghamshire and Hertfordshire all advanced in relative wealth as they were pulled increasingly into London's orbit. Some of the Midland counties, too, had progressed in relative wealth, particularly Worcestershire, Leicestershire, Nottinghamshire and Oxfordshire, possibly because of the growth of industry. Certainly the presence of industry in a region that provided alternative or supplementary employment to agriculture made for wealthier communities than those depending solely on agriculture. In south Yorkshire, for example, in the late seventeenth century parishes in which the inhabitants were employed in metal-working as well as farming were less poor than purely agricultural neighbouring parishes. Generally speaking those regions of pre-industrial England possessing more diversified economies were more prosperous than those relying on agriculture alone.

Inequalities in the distribution of wealth among economic groups and individuals were more marked than the regional inequalities. Adopting the modern categories of incomes from rent, wages and

[1] Quoted by B. E. Supple, *Commercial Crisis and Change in England, 1600–1642,* 1959, pp. 3–4.

mixed incomes – including interest and profits – we find that wages accounted for a much smaller proportion of national income than they did in the nineteenth century. Gregory King's estimates suggest distribution of wealth as shown in Table 5.

TABLE 5   *The Distribution of Wealth, 1688*

		% of total population	% of personal incomes
Rents	Gentry	2·8	13
Mixed Incomes	Officeholders, Merchants, Lawyers, Clergy	5·5	14
	Persons in Science, Liberal Arts, Shopkeepers, Artisans, Handicraftsmen, Officers	9·7	13
	Freeholders and Farmers	31·4	39
Wages	Labourers, Outservants, Cottagers, Paupers, Seamen, Soldiers	50·7	21

Calculated from the figures of Gregory King, printed in P. Laslett, *The World We Have Lost*, 1965, pp. 32–3.

There is obviously a good deal of overlap between these categories. Some artisans were probably wage earners, and some labourers and others supplemented their wages by cultivating a small patch of land. Merchants owned land as well as business assets, and some members of the gentry were officeholders – and so on. Nevertheless King's calculations give a rough and ready indication of the distribution of wealth at the end of the seventeenth century. Another way of arranging King's figures shows that the family income of landowners averaged £1,230 per annum; mixed incomes ranged from £400 for families of prosperous overseas merchants to £40 for artisans and handicraftsmen; while the wage earning group received on average £10 per family per year.

There are no earlier calculations which may be compared with King's. On general grounds we should expect the proportion of incomes received in the form of rent to have been higher in earlier years because a greater proportion of the population owned land. During the inflationary decades before 1650 landlords, as a class, seem to have been able to increase their rents in pace with rising prices and so rent incomes at least held their proportion of total incomes. The chief beneficiaries of inflation were the recipients of mixed incomes, particularly copyholders paying fixed rents, and manufacturers whose prices were rising faster than labour costs. The losers were wage-earners whose numbers were increasing at the same time as the share of national income going to labour was falling. Trends in income distribution after 1650 are less clear. Rent incomes probably declined in relative importance, partly because the absolute level of rents in arable regions fell in the early eighteenth century, but mainly because of the growing importance of mixed incomes and wages. However the relative decline of rent incomes was accompanied by a concentration of landownership so that individual rent incomes were maintained, or even increased. The earners of mixed incomes increased their share of national income as trade and manufacture expanded in the late seventeenth and early eighteenth centuries. According to Joseph Massie's calculations of national income in 1760, mixed income accounted for more than 70 per cent of personal incomes compared with the 66 per cent estimated by King in 1688. Wage incomes increased in the late seventeenth and early eighteenth centuries in both money and real terms; but there is no evidence to suggest that incomes from wages were growing faster than total national income. In 1750 the national income was still very unequally distributed by modern standards. One of the less mentioned consequences of the industrial revolution is that the wealth of the country became much more equitably distributed among the community.

Within the various categories of rents, mixed incomes and wages, there were enormous variations in the incomes of individuals especially among the first two. No sufficient body of evidence is available to permit confident generalization about income levels over the whole period, but enough is known to indicate how great the differences were between rich and poor. Professor Stone has reckoned that in 1559 the average income of the peerage arising from their estates was £2,380 *per annum*; two peers received rent incomes over £5,000 a year but another six received less than £500. Similarly, in 1641, five peers had incomes from rents greater than £13,000 a year and twenty-two peers received less than £2,000. The estate incomes of non-titled landowners varied even more from individual to individual. In 1600 Thomas Wilson thought that most knights lived on £1,000 – £2,000 a year, some of them equalling 'the best Barons and come not much behind many Erles.'[1] Esquires according to Wilson lived on between £500 and £1,000 a year. However, many gentry received less than this. Only 73 gentry families in Yorkshire in 1642 received £1,000 or more a year; 244 had incomes between £250 and £1,000 and 362 under £250. In Kent between 1640 and 1660, the untitled gentry received, on average £270, Knights £873, baronets £1,405 and peers £4,089. The Kentish gentlemen were possibly wealthier than gentlemen in many other parts of the country; in Devon many of the Caroline gentry were worth no more than £100 or £200 a year.

The great disparities of wealth enjoyed by landowners arose basically from the size of individual estates. In the late sixteenth and early seventeenth centuries the largest landowners – and hence the wealthiest men in England – were those who had been able to add land bought from the incomes of public office to the estates they had inherited. Office holding was important in two ways: it enabled a man to be in the right place at the right time to buy,

[1] Thomas Wilson, *The State of England, A.D. 1600*, ed. F. J. Fisher, *Camden Miscellany*, vol. xvi, Camden Society, 1936, p. 23.

say, confiscated monastic land or estates entrusted to the Court
of Wards; and the profits of office could be used to buy land
coming on the market. The epitome of all office holders in the
early seventeenth century was Robert Cecil, first Earl of Salisbury.
Younger son of Lord Burghley, he was left estates by his father worth
between £1,600 and £1,800 a year – in this respect Cecil was
luckier than most younger sons of his generation who inherited
only 'that which the catt lefte on the malte heape' – and with this
inheritance, plus his ability and family connections, he amassed a
fortune. Successively as Secretary of State, Master of the Court of
Wards and Lord Treasurer he had unrivalled opportunities for
making money by fees, bribes, peculation and the acquisition of
land; at his death his income was probably at least £25,000 a
year. Lesser fish swam in the pool of royal patronage, picking up
minor offices with which to build up their landed estates. Indeed it
had become a grievance by the early seventeenth century among
gentry not possessing office that:

> it is impossible for a mere country gentleman ever to grow rich
> or raise his house. He must have some other vocation with his
> inheritance, as to be a courtier, lawyer, merchant or some other
> vocation ... By only following the plough he may keep his
> word and be upright, but he will never increase his fortune.[1]

For thousands of parish gentry the pickings of office were as
remote as London itself and their estates were held together, enlarged – or dissipated as the case may be – by careful or rash
management and the accidents of marriage, birth, death, politics
and religion. The first and the last two were indeed not entirely
random influences since a man could choose – or have chosen for
him – his wife, his politics and his creed and so avoid the dangers
of an unwise match, unpalatable opinions or the wrong religion.
But once chosen a wife might prove too fertile or else barren and
either alternative was likely to lend to the break-up of estates, the

---

[1] *A Royalists' Notebook, The Commonplace Book of Sir John Oglander of Nunwell,
1622–1652*, ed. F. Bamford, 1936, p. 75; quoted H. R. Trevor-Roper, *The
Gentry, 1540–1650, Econ. Hist. Rev. Suppl*, no. 1, 1953, p. 26.

former by creating too many claims on the family assets and the latter because of the absence of an heir. The wisest choice was a wife with a good dowry and the prospect of an inheritance who would produce a son to continue the line, but not too many younger sons or daughters.

The recipients of mixed incomes were an extremely heterogeneous group. In the countryside there were two main groups, owner-occupiers and tenant farmers. Outside agriculture profits and interest were earned by manufacturers and traders of all kinds. According to Gregory King owner-occupiers enjoyed annual family incomes averaging £84 for the better sort and £50 for the lesser sort; while gross incomes earned by tenant farmers were estimated at £44. But the regional variations were very large. Owner-occupiers near London in the late sixteenth century were often wealthier than parish gentry elsewhere, but others, especially in the north and west, were much poorer. A tenant farmer specializing in sheep on a large scale in the early seventeenth century might receive a gross income twenty times greater than the income of a small farmer producing crops for the market on thirty acres of common fields. No meaningful generalizations about farm incomes are possible. Neither can they be made about incomes earned in commerce and manufacture, except that trade was often more profitable than industry and overseas trade was the most profitable of all. King reckoned that overseas merchants earned between £200 and £400 a year compared with £45 for shopkeepers and tradesmen and £40 for manufacturers. He possibly underestimated the annual income of the richest London merchants who, according to Sir Josiah Child and Defoe in the late seventeenth and early eighteenth centuries, expected to receive between £1,200 and £1,500 a year.[1]

More information is available about the value of personal estates of businessmen as distinct from their annual income. An examina-

[1] Child suggested estates of £20,000 earning 6 per cent, and Defoe £25,000 at 6 per cent as adequate for wealthy London merchants. See R. Grassby, 'The Personal Wealth of the Business Community in Seventeenth Century England', *Econ. Hist. Rev.*, 2nd ser., vol. XXIII, no. 2, 1970, p. 228.

tion of a selection of inventories of London freemen shows that between 1586 and 1614 58 per cent left personal estates (excluding real property) of £500 or less; by 1666–77 the proportion had fallen to 39 per cent. The proportion of personal estates worth over £1,000 rose from 16 per cent to 25 per cent over the same periods. In terms of the annual incomes that such estates could yield the majority of London freemen were not rich and there was a large gap between the majority of merchants and traders with modest wealth and the small minority whose estates ran into five figures. The great accumulations of wealth at the end of the seventeenth century were owned by men such as Sir Josiah Child and Ambrose Crowley whose economic interests were very diversified, embracing land, commerce and manufacture. In the provinces the general level of mixed incomes was lower than in London. Traders and manufacturers rarely left personal estates exceeding three figures, even at the end of the seventeenth century.

Gregory King estimated annual incomes of wage-earners in 1688 at £20 for common seamen down to £6. 10s. for cottagers and paupers. Once again generalizations about earnings are made difficult by a shortage of information. However some features of the pre-industrial labour market are clear enough. The most remarkable was the relative stability of wage rates. In their study of builders' wage rates in southern England Professor Phelps Brown and Miss Hopkins found that craftsmen's wages were around 6d. a day for more than a century before the 1530s, and labourers' wages around 4d. a day in the same period. Then in the next thirty years money wage rates doubled, although they failed to keep pace with the rise in the cost of living. Money wages remained static once more until the 1630s, but between the 1630s and 1660s increased by 50 per cent until craftsmen's wages reached 18d. a day and labourers' rate 12d. Thereafter craftsmen's and labourers' wages drifted up slowly to 24d. and 16d. respectively by the mid-eighteenth century. From the little that is known of wages in other occupations it seems as though they moved in much the same way. In the short-term, of course, wage rates fluctuated according to the seasons and local demand and supply conditions, but these fluctuations seem to have been around a stable long-term trend. This stability cannot be attributed to the operation of the Statute of Artificers, for it had set in much earlier; indeed it is noticeable that that act was passed in a period of relatively rapid wage increases. The force of custom probably operated to keep wages fairly constant and market forces were not sufficiently strong to bring about major shifts over short periods, particularly as the supply of labour was probably increasing faster than employment opportunities until the mid-seventeenth century.

A second observable feature of the labour market was the differential rates received by skilled and unskilled men in the same craft. Once again, the differentials seem to have been very stable, with skilled men in the building industry consistently earning about 50 per cent more than the unskilled. Roughly the same gap was found in the leather crafts. Wiltshire justices in 1603 assess the wages of 'chief' workmen in various leather crafts at £2 a year and wages of 'common workmen' at £1 6s. 8d. In Middlesex in the 1660s curriers, shoemakers and turners of the 'best sort' were to receive £10 a year and the 'second sort' £6. Wages in the same occupations in Kent sixty years later were much lower: there the best workmen received £3 10s. od. and the common workmen £3 os. od. London wage-earners were probably among the aristocrats of the labour market; there was a constant demand for their services and the size of the market and the great variety of occupations encouraged the development of specialist skills that commanded a high price. On the other hand, the cost of living was probably higher in London and in real terms London wage earners may not have been so well off.

Little is known about differences in wage rates between different occupations. Leaving aside the handful of occupations such as sugar refining, glass manufacture or the boring of mines where workers possessed special skills and hired out their services on their own terms, the majority of wage-earners were semi-skilled or unskilled, with the result that wage rates for many occupations probably tended to be similar in the same district. Agricultural wage rates rose from roughly 4d. to 1s. a day between 1500 and 1640,

which was not greatly different from the daily rates paid to builders'
labourers. But there were higher rates for particular skills. On one
large Kent farm in the mid-seventeenth century annual wages
ranged from 20s. or 30s. to £15 and skilled tasks were rewarded
by special piece rates. Piece rates were common in many industries,
particularly those organized on some form of putting out. The
rates were often very low. Journeymen stocking-weavers in London
in the 1740s earned no more than nine or ten shillings a week.
Even so Londoners were better off than their provincial competi-
tors. Stocking knitters in Westmorland appear to have earned
about 2s. 6d. for making half a dozen pairs of stockings a week
in the 1760s and '70s. Knitting was a part-time occupation in this
district, done chiefly in the winter months and the earnings, meagre
as they were, supplemented the equally meagre incomes yielded
by the bleak northern farms.

Money wages are not the whole story of wage earnings. Many
labourers, especially in the countryside, also cultivated a patch of
land or enjoyed rights on the common land where they gathered
firewood or peat and kept a cow. Many craftsmen received payments in kind in addition to money wages. These were acknowledged in justices' wage assessments; in Lancaster, for example, in
1595 leather workers were awarded 3d. a day with meat and drink
or 6d. without. The existence of non-pecuniary earnings obviously
qualifies the picture of sharply falling real wages of labourers obtained by comparing money wages and prices between 1500 and
1650. On the other hand, day labourers rarely enjoyed a full
year's work. Apart from the statutory or customary holidays that
punctuated the working year, work was disrupted by bad weather,
bad trade, war and disease. The burden of depressed trade fell
directly on employees, particularly on out-workers who could be
laid off by an employer without any danger of his capital lying
idle. The irregular nature of employment was recognized by the
Statute of Artificers which insisted on annual hirings in many occupations and stipulated hours of work, but the law could do little to
alleviate irregularities caused in employment by climate or trade
fluctuations. Thus the majority of wage earners lived on wages that,

even in a full year, provided only a slim margin betwen a tolerable existence and destitution; and, in the nature of things, the pre-industrial economy seldom provided a full year's work.

The Disposal of Income

Personal wealth could be consumed, saved, or given away. The grossly unequal distribution of wealth, combined with the low level of personal incomes received by most people in pre-industrial England, resulted in a small number of potential net savers and a great mass of people with little income to spare beyond the needs of current consumption. As always we know less about the consumption habits of the anonymous masses than of the rich minority. Clearly, however, most of those on small incomes spent practically all their incomes on food, fuel, light, clothing and shelter. The bulk of the food was grain – barley for the most part but also oats, wheat and rye – perhaps mixed with peas, beans and lentils, or even tares and acorns in hard times. Bread was supplemented by cheese and butter and more rarely by meat – mainly bacon and pork in country districts where many labourers kept pigs. Fish was not much consumed by the poorest sections of the population except near the coast, but basic diets were varied with eggs, poultry, rabbits and vegetables where they were available. There were, of course, many regional differences in diet, and there was some improvement in the late seventeenth century when meat and dairy produce began to figure more prominently. Solid food was washed down with milk, ale and beer, and, by the early eighteenth century, even tea and chocolate sweetened with sugar.

In the middle decades of the seventeenth century prosperous employers were prepared to spend between £9 and £12 a year on boarding and lodging an adult male living-in servant. If these figures are representative of the cost of maintaining a person in the necessities of life at a modest standard, then it is evident that a wage earner maintaining a family on 8d. or even a shilling a day had precious little to spare for housing, clothing and what eighteenth century economists called the 'decencies' of life. Many farm labourers lived in cottages of one, two or three rooms and few aspired to anything better. Some fared even less well, even in the more prosperous days of the early eighteenth century. During his tours through England Defoe came across a lead-miner and his family living in a cave in Derbyshire, although the length and detail of Defoe's description suggests that it was an unusual sight. In the congested districts of London the miserable hovels of the poor were probably less desirable than the miner's cave. Household furnishings were poor and sparse, although inventory evidence suggests that the standard of comfort was improving for the better off, even when prices were rising before 1640. A bedstead, a table and a chair or two often completed the catalogue of furniture in poor households, and the poorest people of all made do with a straw mattress on the floor. Clothing was a small part of a wage earner's budget. Most of it was woollen or leather, and most people wore shoes: for all their poverty, the Englishman's leather footwear was the occasion for comment by more than one visitor from the continent and it distinguished him in the sixteenth century from his barbarian, barefooted neighbour in Ireland.

The spending patterns of artisans, farmers, and traders living on profits or other forms of income varied according to their degree of wealth. The 'average' farmer or manufacturer of Gregory King's calculations earning £40 – £50 a year was probably little better off than the wage-earning craftsman, for after paying rent and tithes, buying stocks of seed and materials and providing for depreciation of capital, there could not have been more than £10 – £15 a year remaining for food, clothing and household equipment. But as we move up the economic ladder we find people with more to spare, and spending becomes more selective and spread over a wider range of products. In contrast to the bread and cheese of seventeenth century farm labourers, yeomen farmers eat more substantially:

> Today or tomorrow, when he comes [a visitor] shall be welcome to bread, beer and beof, yeoman's fare; we have no kickshaws: full dishes, whole bellyfuls.[1]

[1] Quoted by M. Campbell, *The English Yeoman Under Elizabeth and the Early Stuarts,* 1942, p. 224.

Prosperous yeomen – and doubtless others similarly placed – supplemented English produce with imported foods. Thomas Taylor, a yeoman farmer at Witney in Oxfordshire, left among his possessions at his death in 1583 'a Brasen Spycemorter'. Some years later, in 1625, George Hoskyns, an East Devon yeoman, had 'five hogsheads wyne barrells' in his house. People such as Taylor and Hoskyns also spent more on clothing and furniture. Thomas Taylor's 'geasten chamber' was furnished with 'Venyce Carpitt Clothe' and 'three Silke quisshens' – likewise imported. His windows were glazed, his rooms well stocked with chairs, tables, cupboards and beds, and there were books on his shelves. His household linen was plentiful enough to be listed separately in his inventory and was valued at £13 12s. 8d. – the equivalent of a year's wages of a skilled craftsman. George Hoskyns also had his Bible and 'other little Bookes' as well as 'a treble viall' with which to while away dark nights. These men were not untypical of their class and income group at the time. The late sixteenth and early seventeenth centuries were years when persons living on mixed incomes, provided they possessed sufficient capital assets, improved their living standards, varied their diets and enlarged their houses. For yeomen farmers growing prosperity did not survive into the late seventeenth century, but expanding market opportunities continued to support enterprising tradesmen and manufacturers.

An unusually detailed picture of the expenditure of a mid-seventeenth century clergyman is provided by Dr Macfarlane's study of the diary of the Rev Ralph Josselin of Earls Colne in Essex.[1] Josselin's annual income ranged between £65 in the 1640s to £205 in the 1660s and during the main span of his working life averaged £145 a year. On this yearly income he was probably better off than all but the most prosperous farmers and tradesmen, and even many gentlemen. Half his income came from his ecclesiastical living, a third from farming and leasing land, and the rest from teaching and miscellaneous sources. Roughly 56 per cent of his earnings during his working years was spent on maintaining himself, wife,

[1] A. Macfarlane, *The Family Life of Ralph Josselin: A Seventeenth Century Clergyman*, 1970, pp. 38–54.

servant and children, of whom ten were born, two died in infancy, one in childhood, one at 19, and five survived to marriage. This family expenditure included education and the provision of dowries as well as the purchase of consumer goods. 20 per cent of his income went on capital formation – the purchase of land and buildings – and 15 per cent on rent, taxes and the running costs of his farm. If we regard the last item as the cost of maintaining his existing capital, then more than a third of his income went on gross capital formation. The remainder was spent on charities, books, entertainment, baptisms and other ceremonies. It would be unwise to claim that a puritan parson in mid-seventeenth century rural Essex was typical of other groups in other places and times, but his example suggests that there was ample scope among his income group for purchasing goods not strictly necessary for existence and also for devoting a considerable proportion of current income to capital formation.

At the higher social levels we find not only greater incomes but also different aspirations which dictated different patterns of spending. Gentlemen and those hoping to be gentlemen needed to behave like gentlemen and spend heavily on eating, drinking, clothes, entertaining and building. Gentry households were probably the closest in England to the extended family groupings found in parts of the under-developed world today. The more elevated the status, the larger the household. Peerage households averaged 40 persons according to Gregory King, and those of mere gentlemen only 8. The household of Sir Hugh Cholmley, a Yorkshire Knight, resembled a family hotel in the early seventeenth century:

> I had between thirty and forty in my ordinary family, a chaplain who said prayers every morning at six, and again before dinner and supper, a porter who merely attended the gates, which were ever shut up before dinner, when the bell rung to prayers, and not opened till one o'clock, except for strangers who came to dinner, which was ever fit to receive three or four besides my family, without any trouble ... Twice a week, a certain number of old people, widows and indigent persons,

were served at my gates with bread and good pottage made of beef. . . .[1]

The more aristocratic the establishment the greater the hospitality. At the same time as Sir Hugh was feeding his regular thirty or forty and the irregular strays, the Earl of Worcester was presiding over a company of 150 fed at three tables in two sittings. This was admittedly exceptional even in the pre-Civil War period, and vast college-like households became increasingly unusual as the seventeenth century wore on. Even so, the status of gentlemen continued to demand a certain style of hospitality and a large expenditure on home produced and imported foods. To take but a single example from a part of the country where the standards of gentry life were not up to the levels set in London, Humphrey Senhouse of Netherall in West Cumberland spent £210 16s. od. on housekeeping in 1727. £30 went on servants' wages, but the rest was spent on meat, fish, poultry, eggs, butter, fruit, vegetable, coal, soap, candles, wines, sugar and spices.

Gentry status also required large outlays on clothing, houses and furniture. Probably few classes or periods matched the Elizabethan and early Stuart aristocracy in the extravagance of their finery, for they had to keep up with the standards set by the monarch; and in a single year James 1 and his Queen spent £25,000 on their wardrobe. Nevertheless, provincial gentlemen had to look like gentlemen and not fall too far behind London fashions. Similarly, the prodigious building done by the peerage before 1640 was not matched in scale by the lesser gentry, although the urge to construct substantial houses stretched far down the social scale. The peak of aristocratic ostentation in building great family seats had passed by about 1620, but the wish to live graciously did not recede entirely and there is plenty of visual evidence remaining in England demonstrating that the wealthy devoted money – and taste – to building country houses and establishing gracious parks throughout the seventeenth and early eighteenth centuries.

[1] Quoted by J. T. Cliffe, *The Yorkshire Gentry from the Reformation to the Civil War*, 1969, p. 114.

The expenditure patterns of the wealthy were not without economic ramifications. Some of the large aristocratic households affected local agriculture in a manner similar to the demands of the royal court in the days of purveyance. In a single week in 1602 the household of the Earl of Shrewsbury consumed 23 sheep and lambs, one veal, 59 chickens, capons and pullets, five pigs, 24 pigeons and 54 rabbits, and agricultural specialisms such as the rearing of rabbits grew up to keep aristocratic tables well stocked. Gentry and merchant households were large consumers of manufactured goods and imported commodities, and their building activities supported many of the specialized building craftsmen whose occupations appear on freemen's rolls during the sixteenth century.

Maintaining the expenditure appropriate to the status of a gentleman bit deeply into resources. Some members of the upper classes, indeed, were able to keep up their style of living only by borrowing, which sometimes led eventually to the sale of land and the descent from gentility. Nevertheless, in spite of conspicuous consumption, the wealthy made substantial contributions to productive investment. We have already argued in Chapter Three that landlords assisted in the process of agricultural improvement by financing reorganization and buildings as well as by their leasing policies. They also developed the timber and mineral assets on their estates. Professor Stone has demonstrated the important contributions that the aristocracy made to the expansion of coal mining and iron-smelting before 1640; and if, as he claims, their initiative was inspired by a search for additional sources of income in order to live in aristocratic splendour and not by a strong sense of economic enterprise, the result was no less productive. The non-titular gentry, too, invested in mining and metallurgy. Sir William Slingsby claimed in 1623 to have spent £700 developing coalmines at Kippax in Yorkshire; while the gentry and nobility of Yorkshire together controlled practically the whole of the iron industry in the county before the Civil War. Wealth from land also found its way into urban development, transport, harbour improvements and overseas enterprise.

It is impossible to calculate what proportion of wealth earned in the form of rents was devoted to capital formation and the citing of particular instances may give an exaggerated picture of the importance of investment by the landed class as a whole. Possibly the bulk of capital formation was done by recipients of mixed incomes: by merchants, manufacturers and farmers who re-invested profits. This was certainly the pattern in the early stages of the industrial revolution and there is no reason for thinking it should have been greatly different in earlier periods when most kinds of business investment consisted of purchasing raw materials. It is true that raw materials were bought on credit, but eventually suppliers had to be paid, if only to assure additional credit in the future. The saving of income from current consumption was a practice that must have been found quite far down the income scale as small farmers kept back seed corn from consumption – or bought seed from suppliers – and spared cattle from the butchers' knife for breeding purposes. Borrowed capital for long-term development was required in two sets of conditions: when heavy initial outlays were required to finance fen drainage, to improve river navigation, or equip a ship for a voyage to the East Indies, for example; and when bad harvests or bad trade eroded modest trading profits and prevented the repayment of short-term loans.

One channel of expenditure – charity – has not so far been mentioned. In an age imbued with strong religious beliefs and an economy characterized by widespread poverty the wealthy were expected to show some concern for the less fortunate. The state itself sanctioned transfer payments for the relief of paupers and Gregory King's estimates of national income have enabled Miss Phyllis Deane to calculate that the parishes spent about £600,000 on poor relief in 1688; that is less than 2s. 6d. a year per head of population. Private charity took the form of gifts in kind – such as when Sir Hugh Cholmley fed the 'old people, widows and indigent persons' at his gate – monetary gifts, and bequests establishing schools, alms houses and other forms of charitable enterprise. The Rev Ralph Josselin devoted an estimated 6.6 per cent of his income to charity, hospitality and his library over his lifetime. As a clergyman he may have felt a particular obligation to relieve the poor, but the same obligation was felt by others. In a detailed analysis of English philanthropy between 1480 and 1660, Professor W. K. Jordan has shown that merchants were the most generous givers. Those in his sample gave 17 per cent of the gross value of their estates to charitable purposes; tradesmen gave 12 per cent and the gentry, artisans and yeomen just over 4 per cent. Merchants were richer than the other classes and could afford to give most. The cynical might also argue that in an age still suffering twinges of conscience about the ethics of profit maximization, giving to the poor in this life was a down payment on a satisfactory residence in the life hereafter. If so, the price of the premium was not very high in real terms and was falling. Over the period studied by Professor Jordan food prices increased seven-fold and the population doubled; although the money value of benefactions rose five-fold, real giving per head of population must have fallen. In one county, Kent, the identifiable capital value of endowments for charitable purposes between 1480 and 1660 was equivalent to 'an investment of just twopence-halfpenny per head per annum: or perhaps one-half of the daily wages of a Kentish plowboy.'[1] Resources, of course, were concentrated on the needy; even so, public and private charity together can have made only a little impact on poverty in pre-industrial England.

Poverty

Poverty is a relative concept and therefore difficult to identify. Late-Victorian Britain was shocked to discover that deep and inescapable poverty afflicted about one-third of the wage earning class, in spite of a century of economic advance. Every age has its own standard of poverty and it is difficult to judge how many people were poor in pre-industrial England according to the standards of the time. Gregory King believed that more than half the population were 'decreasing the wealth of the Kingdom' by spending annually more than they earned. Presumably these people

[1] A. M. Everitt, reviewing W. K. Jordan, *Social Institutions in Kent, 1480–1660*, (Kent Arch. Soc., 1961) in *Econ. Hist. Rev.*, 2nd ser., vol. xv, 1962, p. 377.

had to depend on public or private charity from time to time to make ends meet, although they were not necessarily all receiving relief at the same time. Indeed King also reckoned that in Lichfield those receiving charity totalled 17 per cent of the population. If we take the receipt of poor relief as the mark of pauperism then we may say that there was always roughly one-fifth of the population who were paupers by contemporary standards at the end of the seventeenth century and one-half of the population ran the risk of becoming paupers from time to time.

Another measure of poverty is exemption from taxation assessed on wealth, although this is not a precise indication since exemption reflected the attitudes of collectors as well as levels of wealth. In the early sixteenth century exemptions from the lay subsidies levied in the 1520s and 1540s ranged between one-third and one-half of the populations of Coventry, Exeter and Leicester. The growing unreality of taxation assessments in the sixteenth century deprive us of any comparable figures until the post-Restoration period. During the 1660s 31 per cent of the rural population of Kent was exempted on grounds of poverty from paying the hearth tax. The lowest proportion of exemptions was 26 per cent in north-west Kent where the proximity to London gave a prosperity to agriculture not enjoyed throughout the county. In central Kent the proportion was 32 per cent – the county average – and in the Weald it rose to 36 per cent. This was an area of numerous small holdings and the woollen industry, which had earlier offered a useful by-employment to agriculture, was in decay. The highest proportion of exemptions – 38 per cent – was in east Kent which was a region of large, consolidated farms containing a large proportion of landless labourers. In Leicestershire and Devon roughly one-third of householders were exempted from the hearth tax in 1670 and 1674; by contrast, in the south Yorkshire metal-working parishes of Ecclesfield and Sheffield, the exemptions were only 10 and 13 per cent respectively in 1672. In Westmorland 24 per cent of households in the Barony of Kendale were excused paying the hearth tax in 1669–72, but the proportions in individual villages varied between 5 per cent and 50 per cent. In the northern part of the county, the average figure was higher at 30 per cent. For the nation as a whole 55 per cent of the population was said by Gregory King to be excused or insolvent when the poll tax was collected in 1691.

To say that before 1750 between 20 and 50 per cent of the population were likely to become impoverished by contemporary standards is another way of saying that pre-industrial England was economically backward. The basic causes of poverty were to be found in the economic conditions of the country. Fundamentally poverty reflected the low productivity of labour which stemmed from the poor technology and organization existing in all branches of production. The stock of capital equipment available to be combined with labour was very small and much of it was primitive and although capital stocks were enlarged and techniques improved between 1500 and 1750 they remained inadequate. Poverty, that is, resulted from the smallness of the national income in relation to the size of the population and the slow rate of growth of production.

The problem of poverty was aggravated by weaknesses in economic organization. In agriculture particularly, but in other occupations as well, labour was often under-employed and average productivity was very low. The situation was usually better near towns which offered alternative employment opportunities and in rural regions where industrial employment was available to absorb surplus agricultural labour. Under-employment and unemployment were also caused by climatic fluctuations beyond the control of man. In winter bad weather could disrupt communications and bring production and trade to a halt with resulting poverty in town and countryside. However, poverty among the temporarily unemployed was only one part of the problem and the least intractable. The major problem in pre-industrial England was chronic poverty among those in work. When the city authorities in Norwich conducted a survey of their poor in the parish of St Stephen in 1570, a large proportion of the poor were found to be in employment but they earned too little to support themselves and their families.

Fluctuations in harvest conditions were an important contributory cause of pauperism. Dr A. L. Beier has shown that in Warwickshire there was a close positive correlation between food prices and the number of poor relief cases between 1630 and 1660. The highest number of cases came at the end of the 1640s when high corn prices coincided with a depression in trade. Warwickshire had little cloth manufacturing for export, but economic activity was generally depressed by the fall in the level of effective demand. At the national level there was a clear general relationship between corn prices and poverty. The great Elizabethan poor law itself was formulated during a decade of rising prices and mounting poverty. Again if the complaints of contemporaries are to be believed, the combination of high grain prices and trade depression in the early 1620s caused deepening poverty in the cloth manufacturing regions. In the barren upland regions there was always only a slim margin of comfort for most people and in bad seasons this vanished entirely; and in the parish of Greystoke in Cumberland, for example, people died 'for very want of food and maintenance to live' in 1623.

The problem of poverty was aggravated by the growth of population and the demographic structure of pre-industrial England. At least until 1650 population grew faster than the growth of employment opportunities and agricultural production. The most obvious consequence, as we have noted, was the chronic decline in real wages at the same time as the proportion of the population relying on wage-incomes was rising. As the population grew there was an overflow of people from the land. Some migrated to towns seeking employment, and although the urban areas probably offered more opportunities for work they also possessed their own forms of destitution. In the cities the dependence on money wages by labourers became absolute. In the countryside money earnings might be augmented by payments in kind, rights of common, or poaching. But in the towns the poor were at the mercy of the market: if it was easier to get a job in the town it was also easier to lose it when trade was slack. As towns grew they became full of unskilled people living on casual employment. Despite the slower rate of population growth in the country as a whole in the later seventeenth century the problem of urban poverty was not eased, since the population of towns like London, Manchester, Liverpool and Birmingham continued to grow rapidly as people migrated from the countryside in search of work. The successful found what they were looking for, but the less fortunate joined the ranks of the anonymous poor.

If the age structure of English population before 1750 in any way corresponded to that found in under-developed countries to-day then roughly 40 per cent of the population was under 15 years of age. Even allowing for extensive employment of children there was therefore a large dependent population. Poverty among those in regular employment was frequently found in families containing several young children. Many of the impoverished listed in the Norwich survey in 1570 were parents of young children; and 47 per cent of the pauperized population of Lichfield in 1695 were children under 15, whereas the same age group formed 37 per cent of the total population of the town. Children were an economic burden whose presence was likely to drag families of modest means below the poverty line. In these circumstances it is not surprising that children were commonly put to work at very young ages and that when economic circumstances were particularly difficult, people attempted to restrict their numbers by postponing marriage, *coitus interruptus,* or even abortion. It is also easy to see why infant mortality rates were so high in pre-industrial England. Such scattered evidence as exists suggests that infant mortality rates often ranged between 150 to 200 per 1,000, rising even higher in years of food shortage. This harvest of death was a major cause of the relatively small size of the average family in pre-industrial England: in the seventeenth century the average number was roughly 5. Many were born but few survived to endure the miseries of life.

Those who did survive into adult life ran the risk of succumbing to one of the many illnesses endemic in pre-industrial England and falling into poverty through sickness. The surplus of income enjoyed by most people was so small that it vanished almost as soon as sickness struck, leaving the victims dependent on the charity of their neighbours. Much is made by historians of plague as the scourge of pre-industrial societies; and, indeed, from time to time it drastically thinned out communities. But it was not the only epidemic with which men had to contend and it may be that unspectacular illnesses associated with, or made worse by, under-nourishment were a more insidious cause of destitution and death. If the main bread winner died, his dependants were likely to be left penniless. Even if sickness did not end in death is resulted in days lost to work and often left men and women unfit for manual labour. The productivity of labour was, in any case, low and it was made even lower by disease. There was thus a vicious circle of low productivity, low incomes, deficient diets, illness, and low productivity, all spiralling down to deep poverty.

Had the wealth of England been more equally distributed there might have been a little less poverty. Indeed it has been argued, on the basis of Gregory King's figures, that average incomes per head at the end of the seventeenth century, when translated into mid-twentieth century values, show that England was a rich country compared with many of today's underdeveloped nations. Nevertheless the poverty of pre-industrial England compared with the levels of wealth that were created in the nineteenth and twentieth centuries cannot be denied. It was not merely that Englishmen before 1750 had lower incomes than Englishmen later, but that the range of goods and services available to them was much narrower than in later years. By modern standards even the rich in pre-industrial England were poor in terms of the choice of commodities open to them. No amount of redistribution of national income could have increased the range of goods and services available for consumption; and a more equal distribution might even have retarded economic growth, since the unequal way in which wealth was shared at least made possible the accumulation of saving required for long-term capital formation.

If the concept of poverty is difficult to define because standards of poverty change from generation to generation, the reality was plain enough to the poor themselves before 1750. For them poverty meant a life expectancy at birth of less than 35; it meant receiving incomes too small to support existence without public or private charity. Poverty was the price of industrial innocence in pre-industrial England. During the early, turbulent, years of the industrial revolution, some writers looked back to the years before 1750 as an age of health and prosperity for labouring people. They looked back to an England that never existed. Before industrialization the material benefits of life were enjoyed by a small minority of the population, and most people did not live sufficiently long in sufficient leisure to benefit from the pleasures of rural society. The industrial revolution created dirt, ugliness and social tensions so obvious that they have often obscured the wealth that the industrial revolution also created. The pre-industrial economy had its own forms of dirt, ugliness and social tensions, less obvious through lurking in villages and cottages, but no less brutalizing and depressing to the human spirit than the environment of the factory town. But the pre-industrial economy also lacked the widespread wealth that comes from and ameliorates the disadvantages of industrial society.

BIBLIOGRAPHY

Works dealing with pre-industrial England frequently discuss several facets of the economy. Thus a book ostensibly on, say, industry will often contain information on agriculture, trade and entrepreneurship as well. In the following bibliography I have tried to list the books and articles I found useful under sections where they were most helpful, but some works will be seen to have performed sterling service in several fields.

The following abbreviations are used:

AgHEW   *The Agrarian History of England and Wales*, gen. ed. H. P. R. Finberg, vol. IV, *1500–1640*, ed. J. Thirsk, 1967

AgHR   *Agricultural History Review*

BIHR   *Bulletin of the Institute of Historical Research*

Carus-Wilson   *Essays in Economic History*, ed. E. M. Carus-Wilson, vol. I., 1954, vols. II and III, 1962

EcHR   *Economic History Review*

EHR   *English Historical Review*

Fisher   *Essays in the Economic and Social History of Tudor and Stuart England in Honour of R. H. Tawney*, ed. F. J. Fisher, 1961

JEcH   *Journal of Economic History*

PP   *Past and Present*

Pressnell   *Studies in the Industrial Revolution presented to T. S. Ashton*, ed. L. S. Pressnell, 1960

Provincial England   W. G. Hoskins, *Provincial England: Essays in Economic and Social History, 1963*

TRHS   *Transactions of the Royal Historical Society*

I   THE STRUCTURE OF THE ECONOMY, 1500–1750

(i) General Economic History

F. J. FISHER 'The Sixteenth and Seventeenth Centuries: The Dark Ages of English Economic History?', *Economica*, n.s. vol. XXIV, 1957

F. J. FISHER 'Tawney's Century', Fisher

C. HILL *Reformation to Industrial Revolution: British Economy and Society, 1530–1780*, 1967

E. LIPSON *Economic History of England*, vols. II, III, 6th ed., 1956

P. RAMSEY *Tudor Economic Problems*, 1963

B. E. SUPPLE 'Economic History and Economic Underdevelopment', *Canadian Journal of Economics and Political Science*, vol. XXVII, no. 4, 1961

C. WILSON *England's Apprenticeship, 1603–1763*, 1965

(ii) General Economic Development

A. N. AGARWALA and s. p. SINGH (eds.) *The Economics of Development*, 1958

P. BAUER and B. S. YAMEY *The Economics of Underdeveloped Countries*, 1957

SIR JOHN HICKS *A Theory of Economic History*, 1969

C. P. KINDLEBERGER *Economic Development*, 2nd ed., 1965

W. A. LEWIS *The Theory of Economic Growth*, 1955

R. NURKSE *Problems of Capital Formation in Underdeveloped Countries*, 1953

2 THE ENVIRONMENT OF CHANGE

(i) Geography and Resources

T. S. ASHTON *Economic Fluctuations in England, 1700–1800*, 1959, ch. 1, 'The Elements'

E. L. JONES *Seasons and Prices: the Role of the Weather in English Agricultural History*, 1964

(ii) The Growth of Population

J. D. CHAMBERS *The Vale of Trent, 1670–1800*, EcHR, Suppl., 1957

J. D. CHAMBERS 'Population Changes in a Provincial Town: Nottingham 1700–1800', Pressnell

J. CORNWALL 'English Population in the Early Sixteenth Century', *EcHR*, 2nd ser., vol. XXIII, 1970

M. DRAKE 'An Elementary Exercise in Parish Register Demography', *EcHR*, 2nd ser., vol. XIV, 1962

A. D. DYER 'The Economy of Tudor Worcester', *Univ. of Birmingham Hist. Journ.*, vol X, no. 2, 1966

F. J. FISHER 'Influenza and Inflation in Tudor England', *EcHR*, 2nd ser., vol. XVIII, 1965

D. V. GLASS 'Gregory King's Estimate of the Population of England and Wales, 1695', *Population Studies*, vol. III, 1949

W. G. HOSKINS 'The Population of an English Village, 1086–1801: A Study of Wigston Magna', *Provincial England*

W. G. HOWSON 'Plague, Poverty and Population in Parts of North-West England, 1580–1720', *Trans. Hist. Soc. of Lancs. and Cheshire*, 1960

P. E. JONES and A. V. JUDGES 'London Population in the Late Seventeenth Century', *EcHR*, vol. VI, 1935

P. LASLETT and J. HARRISON 'Clayworth and Cogenhoe', *Historical Essays Presented to David Ogg*, ed. H. E. Bell and R. L. Ollard, 1963

W. A. LEWIS 'Economic Development with Unlimited Supplies of Labour', in A. N. Agarwala and S. P. Singh (eds.), *The Economics of Development*, 1958

E. E. RICH 'The Population of Elizabethan England', *EcHR*, 2nd ser., vol. II, 1949–50

J. C. RUSSELL *British Medieval Population*, 1948

G. S. L. TUCKER 'English Pre-Industrial Population Trends', *EcHR*, 2nd ser., vol. XVI, 1963

E. A. WRIGLEY 'Family Limitation in Pre-Industrial England', *EcHR*, 2nd ser., vol. XIX, 1966

E. A. WRIGLEY 'A Simple Model of London's Importance in Changing English Society and Economy, 1650–1750', *PP*, no. 37, 1967

E. A. WRIGLEY 'Mortality in Pre-industrial England: the Example of Colyton, Devon over Three Centuries', *Daedalus*, vol. 97, no. 2, 1968

E. A. WRIGLEY *Population and History*, 1969

(iii) The Long-term Movement of Prices

Y. S. BRENNER 'The Inflation of Prices in Early Sixteenth-Century England', *EcHR*, 2nd ser., vol. XIV, 1961

Y. S. BRENNER 'The Inflation of Prices in England 1551–1650', *EcHR*, 2nd ser., vol. XV, 1962

J. D. GOULD 'The Price Revolution Reconsidered', *EcHR*, 2nd ser., vol. XVII, 1964

E. J. HAMILTON 'American Treasure and the Rise of Capitalism', *Economica*, vol. XXVII, 1929

I. HAMMARSTRÖM 'The "Price Revolution" of the Sixteenth Century: Some Swedish Evidence', *Scandinavian Econ. Hist. Rev.*, vol. V, 1957

R. B. OUTHWAITE *Inflation in Tudor and Early Stuart England*, 1969

(iv) The Political and Social Framework

A. EVERITT 'Social Mobility in Early Modern England', PP, no. 33, 1966

M. W. FLINN *Men of Iron: The Crowleys in the Early Iron Industry*, 1962

T. H. HOLLINGSWORTH *The Demography of the British Peerage*, suppl. to *Population Studies*, vol. XVIII, 1965

P. LASLETT *The World We Have Lost*, 1965

P. LASLETT 'Size and Structure of the Household in England over Three Centuries', *Population Studies*, vol. XXIII, pt. 2, 1969

N. ROSENBERG 'Capital Formation in Underdeveloped Countries', *American Econ. Rev.*, vol. L, 1960

W. A. SPECK 'Social Status in Late Stuart England', PP, no. 34, 1966

L. STONE *Social Change and Revolution in England, 1540–1640*, 1965

L. STONE *The Crisis of the Aristocracy, 1558–1641*, 1965, ch. II.

L. STONE 'Social Mobility in England, 1500–1700', PP, no. 33, 1966

P. STYLES 'The Social Structure of Kineton Hundred in the Reign of Charles II', *Birmingham Arch. Soc. Trans.*, vol. LXXVIII, 1962

J. THIRSK 'Younger Sons in the Seventeenth Century', *History*, vol. LIV, 1969

D. M. WOODWARD 'Robert Brerewood: An Elizabethan Master Craftsman', *Cheshire Round*, vol. I, no. 9, 1968

(v) Attitudes towards Economic Development

D. C. COLEMAN 'Labour in the English Economy of the Seventeenth Century', *EcHR*, 2nd ser., vol. VIII, 1956; repr. in Carus-Wilson, vol. II

R. W. GREEN (ed.) *Protestantism and Capitalism: The Weber Thesis and its Critics*, 1959

C. HILL 'Protestantism and Capitalism', Fisher

W. A. LEWIS *The Theory of Economic Growth*, 1955; ch. II, 'The Will to Economize'

R. H. TAWNEY *Religion and the Rise of Capitalism*, Penguin ed., 1938

R. C. WILES 'The Theory of Wages in Later English Mercantilism', *EcHR*, 2nd ser., vol. XXI, 1968

C. WILSON 'The Other Face of Mercantilism', *TRHS*, 5th ser., vol. IX, 1959; repr. in D. C. Coleman (ed.), *Revisions in Mercantilism*, 1969, and in C. Wilson, *Economic History and the Historian: Collected Essays*, 1969

BIBLIOGRAPHY

3 AGRICULTURE

(*i*) *The Demand for Agricultural Products*

P. DEANE 'The Output of the British Woollen Industry in the Eighteenth Century', *JEcH*, vol. XVII, no. 2, 1957

A. EVERITT 'The Marketing of Agricultural Produce', *AgHEW*

A. EVERITT 'The Food Markets of the English Town, 1660–1760', *3rd Int. Conf. of Econ. Hist.*, 1968

F. J. FISHER 'The Development of the London Food Market, 1540–1640', *EcHR*, vol. VII, 1937; repr. in Carus-Wilson, vol. I

M. W. FLINN 'The Growth of the English Iron Industry, 1660–1760', *EcHR*, 2nd ser., vol. XI, 1958

P. MATHIAS *The Brewing Industry in England*, 1700–1830, 1959

E. H. PHELPS BROWN and S. V. HOPKINS 'Seven Centuries of the Prices of Consumables, Compared with Builders' Wage Rates', *Economica*, n.s., vol. XXIII, 1956; repr. in Carus-Wilson, vol. II

E. H. PHELPS BROWN and S. V. HOPKINS 'Wage Rates and Prices: Evidence for Population Pressure in the Sixteenth Century', *Economica*, n.s., vol. XXIV, 1957

(*ii*) *Supply Conditions: the Land and its Uses*

F. EMERY 'The Farming Regions of Wales', *AgHEW*

M. A. HAVINDEN 'Agricultural Progress in Open-field Oxfordshire', *AgHR*, vol. IX, 1961; repr. in E. L. Jones (ed.), *Agriculture and Economic Growth in England, 1650–1815*, 1967

W. G. HOSKINS 'The Leicestershire Farmer in the Sixteenth Century', *Essays in Leicestershire History*, 1950

W. G. HOSKINS, 'The Leicestershire Farmer in the Seventeenth Century', *Provincial England*

E. KERRIDGE *The Agricultural Revolution*, 1967, ch. II

JOAN THIRSK 'The Common Fields', PP, no. 29, 1964

JOAN THIRSK 'Farming Techniques', *AgHEW*

JOAN THIRSK 'The Farming Regions of England', *AgHEW*

(*iii*) *Supply Conditions: New Techniques*

E. L. JONES 'Agriculture and Economic Growth in England 1660–1750: Agricultural Change', *JEcH*, vol. XXV, 1965; repr. in E. L. Jones (ed.), *Agriculture and Economic Growth in England 1650–1815*, 1967

E. KERRIDGE *The Agricultural Revolution*, 1967, chs. III–IX

(*iv*) *Supply Conditions: Re-organisation and the Extension of Cultivation*

J. THIRSK 'Enclosing and Engrossing', *AgHEW*

(*v*) *Enterprise and Finance*

G. BATHO and J. YOUINGS 'Landlords in England', *AgHEW*

M. CAMPBELL *The English Yeoman Under Elizabeth and the Early Stuarts*, 1942

J. P. COOPER 'The Social Distribution of Land and Men in England, 1436–1700', *EcHR*, 2nd ser., vol. XX, 1967

H. J. HABAKKUK 'English Landownership, 1680–1740', *EcHR*, vol. X, 1940

H. J. HABAKKUK 'Economic Functions of Landowners in the Seventeenth and Eighteenth Centuries', *Explorations in Entrepreneurial History*, vol. VI, 1952

H. J. HABAKKUK 'The English Land Market in the Eighteenth Century', J. S. Bromley and E. H. Kossman (eds.), *Britain and the Netherlands*, 1960

E. KERRIDGE *Agrarian Problems in the Sixteenth Century and After*, 1969

G. E. MINGAY 'The Size of Farms in the Eighteenth Century', *EcHR*, 2nd ser., vol. XIV, 1962

G. E. MINGAY *English Landed Society in the Eighteenth Century*, 1963

L. A. PARKER 'The Agrarian Revolution at Cotesbach, 1501–1612', *Studies in Leicestershire Agrarian History. Leics. Arch. Soc.*, vol. XXIV, 1948

L. STONE *The Crisis of the Aristocracy, 1558–1641*, 1965, ch. VI.

R. H. TAWNEY *The Agrarian Problem in the Sixteenth Century*, 1912

R. H. TAWNEY 'The Rise of the Gentry, 1558–1640', *EcHR*, vol. XI, 1941; repr. in Carus-Wilson, vol. I

F. M. L. THOMPSON 'The Social Distribution of Landed Property in England since the Sixteenth Century', *EcHR*, vol. XX, 1967

(*vi*) *The Achievement and its Consequences*

P. J. BOWDEN 'Agricultural Prices, Farm Profits, and Rents', *AgHEW*

P. DEANE and W. A. COLE *British Economic Growth 1688–1959*, 1962, ch. II, section 3

M. W. FLINN 'Agricultural Productivity and Economic Growth: a Comment', *JEcH*, vol. XXVI, 1966

W. G. HOSKINS 'Harvest Fluctuations and English Economic History, 1480–1619', *AgHR*, vol. XII, 1964

W. G. HOSKINS 'Harvest Fluctuations and English Economic History, 1620–1759', *AgHR*, vol. XVI, 1968

E. L. JONES (ed.) 'Introduction' to *Agriculture and Economic Growth in England, 1650–1815*, 1967

E. L. JONES 'The Condition of English Agriculture, 1500–1640', *EcHR*, 2nd ser., vol. XXI, 1968

A. H. JOHN 'Aspects of English Economic Growth in the First Half of the Eighteenth Century', *Economica*, n.s., vol. XXVIII, 1961; repr. in Carus-Wilson, vol. II

A. H. JOHN 'Agricultural Productivity and Economic Growth in England, 1700–1760', *JEcH*, vol. XXV, 1965; repr. in E. L. Jones (ed.), *Agriculture and Economic Growth in England, 1650–1815*, 1967

E. KERRIDGE *The Agricultural Revolution*, 1967, ch. X

J. THIRSK 'Seventeenth Century Agriculture and Social Change', *AgHR*, *Suppl.*, 1970

4 INDUSTRY

(*i*) *The Composition of the Industrial Sector*

K. J. ALLISON 'The Norfolk Worsted Industry in the Sixteenth and Seventeenth Centuries', *Yorks. Bulletin*, vol. XII, 1960, vol. XVI, 1961

E. K. BERRY 'The Borough of Droitwich and its Salt Industry, 1215–1700', *Univ. of Birmingham Hist. Journal*, vol. v, 1957–8

E. J. BUCKATZCH 'Occupations in the Parish Registers of Sheffield, 1655–1719', *EcHR*, 2nd ser., vol. I, 1949

M. CASH (ed.) *Devon Inventories in the Sixteenth and Seventeenth Centuries*, Devon and Cornwall Record Society, n.s., vol. XI, 1966

C. W. CHALKLIN *Seventeenth Century Kent: A Social and Economic History*, 1965

J. D. CHAMBERS *Nottinghamshire in the Eighteenth Century*, 2nd ed., 1966

L. A. CLARKSON 'The Leather Crafts in Tudor and Stuart England', *AgHR*, vol. XIV, 1966

D. C. COLEMAN 'Naval Dockyards under the Later Stuarts', *EcHR*, 2nd ser., vol. VI, 1953

D. C. COLEMAN *The British Paper Industry, 1495–1860*, 1958

F. COLLINS (ed.) *Register of the Freemen of York*, vol. II, *1559–1579*, Surtees Society, vol. CII, 1899

J. CORNWALL 'English Country Towns in the Fifteen-Twenties', *EcHR*, 2nd ser., vol. XV, 1962

W. H. B. COURT *The Rise of the Midland Industries*, 1938

R. DAVIS *The Rise of the English Shipping Industry in the Seventeenth and Eighteenth Centuries*, 1962

M. W. FLINN 'The Growth of the English Iron Industry, 1660–1760', *EcHR*, 2nd ser., vol. XI, 1958

M. A. HAVINDEN (ed.) *Household and Farm Inventories in Oxfordshire, 1550–1590*, 1965

H. HEATON *The Yorkshire Woollen and Worsted Industries*, 2nd ed., 1965

W. G. HOSKINS 'English Provincial Towns in the Early Sixteenth Century', *Provincial England*

W. G. HOSKINS, 'An Elizabethan Provincial Town: Leicester', *Provincial England*

W. G. HOSKINS 'The Rebuilding of Rural England, 1570–1640', *Provincial England*

G. H. KENYON 'Kirdford Inventories, 1611–1776', *Sussex Archaeol. Collns*, vol. 93, 1954

G. H. KENYON *The Glass Industry of the Weald*, 1967

G. R. LEWIS *The Stanneries: A Study of the English Tin Mines*, 1907

P. MATHIAS *The Brewing Industry in England, 1700–1800*, 1959

J. U. NEF *The Rise of the British Coal Industry*, 2 vols., 1932

P. A. J. PETTIT *The Royal Forests of Northants: A Study in their Economy, 1558–1714*, Northants R. S., vol. XXIII, 1968

J. F. POUND 'The Social and Trade Structure of Norwich, 1525–1575', *PP*, no. 34, 1966

G. D. RAMSAY *The Wiltshire Woollen Industry in the Sixteenth and Seventeenth Centuries*, 2nd ed., 1965

W. REES *Industry Before the Industrial Revolution*, 2 vols., 1968

J. S. ROPER (ed.) *Dudley Probate Inventories*, 1st ser., *1544–1603*, 2nd ser., *1605–1685*, 3rd ser. *1601–1650*, 1965, 1966, 1968

J. S. ROPER (ed.) *Stourbridge Probate Inventories, 1541–1558*, 1966

J. S. ROPER (ed.) *Sedgley Probate Inventories, 1614–1787*, 1966

H. R. SCHUBERT *History of the British Iron and Steel Industry*, 1957

F. W. STEER (ed.) *Farm and Cottage Inventories of Mid-Essex, 1634–1749*, Essex Record Office Publication, no. 8, 1950

E. STRAKER *Wealden Iron*, 1931

A. J. and R. H. TAWNEY 'An Occupational Census of the Seventeenth Century', *EcHR*, vol. V, 1934

G. UNWIN 'The Suffolk Cloth Industry', *Studies in Economic History: The Collected Papers of George Unwin*, ed. R. H. Tawney, 1927

J. WEST *Village Records*, 1962

D. M. WOODWARD 'The Chester Leather Industry, 1558–1625', *Trans. Hist. Soc. of Lancs. and Cheshire*, vol. 119, 1967

(ii) The Location of Industries

R. BRAUN 'The Impact of Cottage Industry in an Agricultural Population', in D. Landes (ed.), *The Rise of Capitalism*, 1966

A. EVERITT 'Farm Labourers', *AgHEW*

E. MILLER 'The Fortunes of the English Textile Industry during the Thirteenth Century', *EcHR*, 2nd ser., vol. XVIII, 1965

P. R. MOUNFIELD 'The Footwear Industry of the East Midlands', *East Midland Geographer*, vol. 3, 1964–1965, vol. 4, 1966

J. THIRSK 'Industries in the Countryside', Fisher

(iii) Industrial Organisation

K. BURLEY 'An Essex Clothier of the Eighteenth Century', *EcHR*, 2nd ser., vol. XI, 1958

L. A. CLARKSON 'The Organisation of the English Leather Industry in the Late Sixteenth and Seventeenth Centuries', *EcHR*, 2nd ser., vol. XIII, 1960

D. W. CROSSLEY 'The Management of a Sixteenth Century Ironworks', *EcHR*, 2nd ser., vol. XIX, 1966

F. J. FISHER 'Some Experiments in Company Organisation in the Early Seventeenth Century', *EcHR*, vol. IV, 1933

M. W. FLINN *Men of Iron: The Crowleys in the Early Iron Industry*, 1962

I. V. HALL 'John Knights, Jnr.: Sugar Refiner . . . (1654–1679)', *Trans. Bristol and Glos. Arch. Soc.*, vol. LXVIII, 1949

B. C. L. JOHNSON 'The Foley Partnerships', *EcHR*, 2nd ser., vol. IV, 1952

J. R. KELLETT 'The Breakdown of Gild and Corporation Control over the Handicrafts and Retail Trades in London', *EcHR*, 2nd ser., vol. X, 1958

S. KRAMER *The English Craft Gilds*, 1927

D. LANDES (ed.) 'Introduction' to *The Rise of Capitalism*, 1966

J. DE L. MANN 'A Wiltshire Family of Clothiers: George and Hester Winsey, 1683–1714', *EcHR*, 2nd ser., vol. IX, 1956

A. RAISTRICK and E. ALLEN 'The South Yorkshire Ironmasters (1690-1750)', *EcHR*, vol. IX, 1939

R. S. SMITH 'Huntington Beaumont: Adventurer in Coalmines', *Renaissance and Modern Studies*, vol. I, 1957

G. UNWIN *Industrial Organization in the Sixteenth and Seventeenth Centuries*, 1904

G. UNWIN *The Gilds and Companies of London*, 1908

(iv) The Expansion of Industry

P. J. BOWDEN 'Wool Supply and the Woollen Industry', *EcHR*, 2nd ser., vol. IX, 1956

J. D. CHAMBERS 'The Rural Domestic Industries during the Period of Transition to the Factory System, with Special Reference to the Midland Counties of England', *2nd Int. Conf. Econ. Hist.*, Aix-en-Provence, 1962

D. C. COLEMAN 'Technology and Economic History, 1500–1750', *EcHR*, 2nd ser., vol. XI, 1959

D. C. COLEMAN 'An Innovation and its Diffusion: The "New Draperies" ', *EcHR*, 2nd ser., vol. XXII, 1969

W. CUNNINGHAM *Alien Immigrants to England*, 1897

M. B. DONALD *Elizabethan Copper: The History of the Company of Mines Royal, 1568–1605*, 1955

M. B. DONALD *Elizabethan Monopolies: The History of the Company of Mineral and Battery Works from 1565 to 1604*, 1961

J. W. GOUGH *The Rise of the Entrepreneur*, 1969

P. MANTOUX *The Industrial Revolution in the Eighteenth Century*, new ed., 1964

W. E. MINCHINTON 'The Diffusion of Tinplate Manufacture', *EcHR*, 2nd ser., vol. IX, 1956

E. MOIR, 'Benedict Webb, Clothier', *EcHR*, 2nd ser., vol. X, 1957

J. U. NEF 'The Progress of Technology and the Growth of Large-Scale Industry in Great Britain, 1540–1640', *EcHR*, vol. V, 1934; repr. in Carus-Wilson, vol. I

J. U. NEF 'Prices and Industrial Capitalism in France and England, 1540–1640', *EcHR*, vol. VII, 1937; repr. in Carus-Wilson, vol. I

J. E. PILGRIM 'The Rise of the "New Draperies" in Essex', *Univ. of Birmingham Hist. Journal*, vol. VII, 1959–60

W. C. SCOVILLE 'Minority Migrations and the Diffusion of Technology', *JEcH*, vol. XI, 1951

W. C. SCOVILLE 'The Huguenots and the Diffusion of Technology', *J. Polit. Econ.*, vol. LX, 1962

A. P. WADSWORTH and J. DE L. MANN *The Cotton Trade and Industrial Lancashire, 1600–1780*, 1931

(v) The Achievement

T. S. ASHTON *An Economic History of England: The Eighteenth Century*, 1955

L. A. CLARKSON 'An Industrial Revolution in the Sixteenth and Seventeenth Centuries?' *Melbourne Hist. Rev.* (Univ. of Melbourne), no. 2, 1962

D. C. COLEMAN 'Industrial Growth and Industrial Revolutions', *Economica*, n.s., vol. XXIII, 1956; repr. in Carus-Wilson, vol. III

J. U. NEF 'Industrial Growth in France and England, 1540–1640', *J. Polit. Econ.* vol. XLIV, 1936

J. U. NEF *Cultural Foundations of Industrial Civilization*, 1958

5 COMMERCE AND COMMUNICATIONS

(i) Internal Trade (most of the references on industry—above, ch. 4 (i)—also contain material on internal trade)

T. S. ASHTON *An Economic History of England: The Eighteenth Century*, 1953, ch. III

P. J. BOWDEN *The Wool Trade in Tudor and Stuart England*, 1962

L. A. CLARKSON *The English Leather Industry in the Sixteenth and Seventeenth Centuries*, Nottingham Univ. Ph.D. thesis, 1960, ch. 3, 4

A. EVERITT 'The Marketing of Agricultural Produce', *AgHEW*

F. J. FISHER 'The Development of the London Food Market, 1540–1640', *EcHR*, vol. VII, 1937; repr. in Carus-Wilson, vol. I

F. J. FISHER 'The Development of London as a Centre of Conspicuous Consumption in the Sixteenth and Seventeenth Centuries', *TRHS*, 4th ser., vol. XXX, 1948, repr. in Carus-Wilson, vol. II

N. S. B. GRAS *Evolution of the English Corn Market*, 1926

T. C. MENDENHALL *The Shrewsbury Drapers and the Welsh Wool Trade in the XV and XVI Centuries*, 1953

C. SKEEL 'The Cattle Trade Between Wales and England . . .', *TRHS*, 4th ser., vol. IX, 1921

E. A. WRIGLEY 'A Simple Model of London's Importance in Changing English Society and Economy, 1650–1750', *PP*, no. 37, 1967

(ii) Overseas Trade

R. DAVIS 'English Foreign Trade, 1660–1700', *EcHR*, 2nd ser., vol. VII, 1954; repr. in Carus-Wilson, vol. II, and in W. E. Minchinton (ed.), *The Growth of English Overseas Trade in the Seventeenth and Eighteenth Centuries*, 1969

R. DAVIS 'English Foreign Trade, 1700–1774', *EcHR*, 2nd ser., vol. XV, 1962; repr. in W. E. Minchinton (ed.), *The Growth of English Overseas Trade in the Seventeenth and Eighteenth Centuries*, 1969

R. DAVIS *A Commercial Revolution: English Overseas Trade in the Seventeenth and Eighteenth Centuries*, Historical Association, 1969

R. DAVIS 'England and the Mediterranean, 1570–1670', Fisher

F. J. FISHER 'Commercial Trends and Policy in Sixteenth Century England', *EcHR*, vol. X, 1940; repr. in Carus-Wilson, vol. I

F. J. FISHER 'London's Export Trade in the Early Seventeenth Century', *EcHR*, 2nd ser., vol. III, 1950; repr. in W. E. Minchinton (ed.), *The Growth of English Overseas Trade in the Seventeenth and Eighteenth Centuries*, 1969

H. E. S. FISHER 'Anglo-Portuguese Trade, 1700–1770', *EcHR*, 2nd ser., vol. XVI, 1963; repr. in W. E. Minchinton (ed.), *The Growth of English Overseas Trade in the Seventeenth and Eighteenth Centuries*, 1969

J. D. GOULD 'The Crisis in the Export Trade, 1586–1587', *EHR*, vol. LXXI, 1961

J. D. GOULD *The Great Debasement: Currency and the Coinage in Mid-Tudor England*, 1970, ch. 6

W. E. MINCHINTON (ed.) 'Introduction' to *The Growth of English Overseas Trade in the Seventeenth and Eighteenth Centuries*, 1969

G. D. RAMSAY *English Overseas Trade during the Centuries of the Emergence*, 1957

P. RAMSEY 'Overseas Trade in the Reign of Henry VIII: The Evidence of the Customs Accounts', *EcHR*, 2nd ser., vol. VI, 1953

E. B. SCHUMPETER *English Overseas Trade Statistics, 1697–1808*, 1960

W. B. STEPHENS 'The Cloth Exports of the Provincial Ports, 1600–1640', *EcHR*, 2nd ser., vol. XXII, 1969

L. STONE 'State Control in Sixteenth Century England', *EcHR*, vol. XVII, 1947

L. STONE 'Elizabethan Overseas Trade', *EcHR*, 2nd ser., vol. II, 1949

B. E. SUPPLE *Commercial Crisis and Change in England, 1600–1642*, 1959

T. S. WILLAN *Studies in Elizabethan Foreign Trade*, 1959

C. WILSON 'Cloth Production and International Competition in the Seventeenth Century', *EcHR*, 2nd ser., vol. XIII, 1960

(*iii*) *Overseas Trade and the Home Economy*

K. N. CHAUDHURI 'The East India Company and the Export of Treasure in the Early Seventeenth Century', *EcHR*, 2nd ser., vol. XVI, 1963

K. N. CHAUDHURI 'Treasure and Trade Balances: The East India Company's Export Trade', *EcHR*, 2nd ser., vol. XXI, 1968

P. DEANE and W. A. COLE *British Economic Growth, 1688–1959*, 1962, ch. II

A. W. DOUGLAS 'Cotton Textiles in England: the East India Company's Attempt to Exploit Developments in Fashion', *Journal of British Studies*, vol. VIII, 1969

E. F. HECKSHER 'Multilateralism, Baltic Trade and the Mercantilist,' *EcHR*, 2nd ser., vol. III, 1950

R. W. K. HINTON 'The Mercantile System in the Time of Thomas Mun', *EcHR*, 2nd ser., vol. VII, 1955

A. H. JOHN 'Aspects of English Economic Growth in the first Half of the Eighteenth Century', *Economica*, n.s., vol. XXVIII, 1961; repr. in Carus-Wilson, vol. II

W. E. MINCHINTON 'Bristol—Metropolis of the West in the Eighteenth Century', *TRHS*, 5th ser., IV, 1954

J. SPERLING 'The International Payments Mechanism in the Seventeenth and Eighteenth Centuries', *EcHR*, 2nd ser., vol. XIV, 1962

C. WILSON 'Treasure and Trade Balances: the Mercantilist Problem', *EcHR*, 2nd ser., vol. II, 1949

C. WILSON, 'Treasure and Trade Balances: Further Evidence', *EcHR*, 2nd ser., vol. IV, 1951

(*iv*) *Commercial Institutions: Markets, Middlemen and Merchants*

T. S. ASHTON *An Economic History of England: The Eighteenth Century*, 1955, ch. V

K. N. CHAUDHURI *The East India Company: the Study of an Early Joint-Stock Company*, 1965

K. G. DAVIES *The Royal Africa Company*, 1957

A. FRIIS *Alderman Cockayne's Project and the Cloth Trade*, 1927

R. W. K. HINTON *The Eastland Trade and the Common Weal in the Seventeenth Century*, 1959

W. G. HOSKINS 'Elizabethan Merchants of Exeter', in S. T. Bindoff *et al.* (eds.), *Elizabethan Government and Society*, 1961

W. E. MINCHINTON 'The Merchants in England in the Eighteenth Century', *The Entrepreneur: Annual Conf. of Econ. Hist. Soc.*, 1957

P. MCGRATH (ed.) *Merchants and Merchandise in Seventeenth Century Bristol*, Bristol Record Society Publications XIX, 1955

R. H. TAWNEY *Business and Politics under James I: Lionel Cranfield as Merchant and Minister,* 1958

G. UNWIN 'The Merchant Adventurers Company in the Reign of Elizabeth', *Studies in Economic History: The Collected Papers of George Unwin,* ed. R. H. Tawney, 1927

R. B. WESTERFIELD 'Middlemen in English Business, particularly between 1660 and 1760', *Trans. Connecticut Academy of Arts and Sciences,* vol. IX, 1915; repr. 1968

T. S. WILLAN *The Early History of the Russia Company, 1553–1603,* 1956

T. S. WILLAN *An Eighteenth Century Shopkeeper: Abraham Dent of Kirkby Stephen,* 1970

N. J. WILLIAMS 'Tradesmen in Early Stuart Wiltshire', *Wilts. Arch. and Nat. Hist. Soc.,* Records Branch, vol XV (1959), 1960

A. C. WOOD *A History of the Levant Company,* 1935

(v) Commercial Institutions—Currency and Credit

T. S. ASHTON *An Economic History of England: The Eighteenth Century,* 1955, ch. VI

C. E. CHALLIS 'The Debasement of the Coinage, 1542–1551', *EcHR,* 2nd ser., vol. XX, 1967

SIR JOHN CLAPHAM *The Bank of England: a History,* 1944, vol. I

D. C. COLEMAN 'London Scriveners and the Estate Market in the Later Seventeenth Century', *EcHR,* 2nd ser., vol. IV, 1951

SIR JOHN CRAIG *The Mint: a History of the London Mint from A.D. 287 to 1948,* 1953

K. G. DAVIES 'Joint-Stock Investment in the Later Seventeenth Century', *EcHR,* 2nd ser., vol. IV, 1952; repr. in Carus-Wilson, vol. II

R. DE ROOVER *Gresham on Foreign Exchange,* 1949

A. FEAVEARYEAR *The Pound Sterling,* 2nd ed., revised by E. V. Morgan, 1963

J. D. GOULD 'The Royal Mint in the Early Seventeenth Century', *EcHR,* 2nd ser., vol. V, 1952

J. D. GOULD *The Great Debasement: Currency and the Economy in Mid-Tudor England,* 1970

H. J. HABAKKUK 'The Long-term Rate of Interest and the Price of Land in the Seventeenth Century', *EcHR,* 2nd ser., vol. V, 1952

J. K. HORSEFIELD *British Monetary Experiments, 1650–1710,* 1960

D. M. JOSLIN 'London Private Bankers, 1720–1785', *EcHR,* 2nd ser., vol. VII, 1954; repr. in Carus-Wilson, vol. II

L. S. PRESSNELL *Country Banking in the Industrial Revolution,* 1956

T. K. RABB *Enterprise and Empire: Merchant and Gentry Investment in the Expansion of England, 1575–1630,* 1967

R. D. RICHARDS *The Early History of Banking in England,* 1929

L. STONE *The Crisis of the Aristocracy, 1558–1641,* 1965, ch. IX

B. E. SUPPLE 'Currency and Commerce in the Early Seventeenth Century', *EcHR,* 2nd ser., vol. X, 1957

T. WILSON *A Discourse Upon Usury,* ed. R. H. Tawney, 1925

(vi) The Means of Transport

T. C. BARKER 'The Beginnings of the Canal Age', Pressnell

J. CROFTS *Packhorse, Waggon and Post: Land Carriage and Communications under the Tudors and Stuarts*, 1967

R. DAVIS *The Rise of the English Shipping Industry in the Seventeenth and Eighteenth Centuries*, 1962

D. DEFOE *A Tour Through England and Wales*, 2. vols., ed. G. D. H. Cole, 1928

H. J. DYOS and D. H. ALDCROFT *British Transport: An Economic Survey from the Seventeenth to the Twentieth Centuries*, 1969

C. H. HUGHES *The Story of the Roads*, 1927

W. B. STEPHENS 'The Exeter Lighter Canal, 1566–1698', *Journal of Transport History*, vol. III, 1957

D. SWANN 'The Pace and Progress of Port Investment in England, 1660–1830', *Yorkshire Bulletin*, vol. XII, 1960

T. S. WILLAN *River Navigations in England 1600–1750*, 1936

T. S. WILLAN *The English Coasting Trades*, 1938

T. S. WILLAN *The Early History of the Don Navigation*, 1965

6 THE GOVERNMENT AND THE ECONOMY

(*i*) *The Government as Producer and Consumer*

G. E. AYLMER 'The Last Years of Purveyance, 1610–1660', *EcHR*, 2nd ser., vol. X, 1957

SIR W. BEVERIDGE *Prices and Wages in England*, vol. I, 1939

D. C. COLEMAN 'Naval Dockyards under the Later Stuarts', *EcHR*, 2nd ser., vol. VI, 1953

C. S. L. DAVIES 'Provisions for Armies, 1509–60, a Study in the Effectiveness of Early Tudor Government', *EcHR*, 2nd ser., vol. XVII, 1964

M. W. FLINN *Men of Iron: The Crowleys in the Early Iron Industry*, 1962

A. H. JOHN 'War and the English Economy, 1700–1763', *EcHR*, 2nd ser., vol. VII, 1955

B. PEARCE 'Elizabethan Food Policy and the Armed Forces', *EcHR*, vol. XII, 1942

W. H. PRICE *The English Patents of Monopoly*, 1913

W. R. SCOTT *The Constitution and Finance of English, Scottish and Irish Joint-Stock Companies, to 1720*, 3 vols., 1912, vols. II–III

A. WOODWORTH 'Purveyance for the Royal Household in the Reign of Queen Elizabeth', *American Philosophical Society*, n.s., vol. XXXV, 1946

(*ii*) *The Government as Regulator—Control of the Factor Markets*

D. G. BARNES *A History of the English Corn Laws, 1660–1846*, 1930

M. W. BERESFORD *The Lost Villages of England*, 1954

M. W. BERESFORD 'Habitation v. Improvement: The Debate on Enclosure by Agreement', Fisher

S. T. BINDOFF 'The Making of the Statute of Artificers', S. T. Bindoff, *et al.* (eds.), *Elizabethan Government and Society*, 1961

C. S. L. DAVIES 'Slavery and Protector Somerset: The Vagrancy Act of 1547', *EcHR*, 2nd ser., vol. XIX, 1966

M. G. DAVIES *The Enforcement of English Apprenticeship: A study in Applied Mercantilism, 1563–1642*, 1956

R. DE ROOVER *Gresham on Foreign Exchange*, 1949

G. R. ELTON 'An Early Tudor Poor Law', *EcHR*, 2nd ser., vol. VI, 1953

N. S. B. GRAS *The Evolution of the English Corn Market*, 1926

F. J. FISHER 'Influenza and Inflation in Tudor England', *EcHR*, 2nd ser., vol. XVIII, 1965

M. JAMES *Social Problems and Policy during the Puritan Revolution, 1640–1660*, 1930

R. K. KELSALL *Wage Regulation under the Statute of Artificers*, 1938

E. M. LEONARD 'The Inclosure of Common fields in the Seventeenth Century', *TRHS*, n.s., vol. XIX, 1905; repr. in Carus-Wilson, vol. II

E. M. LEONARD *The Early History of English Poor Relief*, 1900

D. MARSHALL *The English Poor in the Eighteenth Century*, 1926

D. MARSHALL 'The Old Poor Law, 1662–1795', *EcHR*, vol. VIII, 1937; repr. in Carus-Wilson, vol. I

V. PONKO, JR. 'N. S. B. Gras and Elizabethan Corn Policy: a Re-examination of the Problem', *EcHR*, 2nd ser., vol. XVII, 1964

R. H. TAWNEY *The Agrarian Problem in the Sixteenth Century*, 1912

R. H. TAWNEY 'The Assessment of Wages on England by the Justices of the Peace', *Vierteljahrschrift für Sozial- und Wirtschaftgeschichte*, vol. XI, 1914

J. THIRSK 'Enclosing and Engrossing', *AgHEW*

T. WILSON *A Discourse Upon Usury*, ed. R. H. Tawney, 1925

(iii) *The Government as Regulator—Control of the Product Markets*

P. J. BOWDEN *The Wool Trade in Tudor and Stuart England*, 1962

L. A. CLARKSON 'English Economic Policy in the Sixteenth and Seventeenth Centuries: The case of the Leather Industry', *BIHR*, vol. XXXVIII, 1965

C. A. EDIE 'The Irish Cattle Bills: A Study in Restoration Politics', *Trans. American Philosophical Soc.*, n.s., vol. LX, pt. 2, 1970

A. EVERITT 'The Marketing of Agricultural Produce', *AgHEW*

H. HEATON *The Yorkshire Woollen and Worsted Industries*, 2nd ed., 1965

G. D. RAMSAY *The Wiltshire Woollen Industry*, 2nd ed., 1965

A. S. C. ROSS 'The Assize of Bread', *EcHR*, 2nd ser., vol. IX, 1956

W. M. STERN 'Control v. Freedom in Leather Production from the Early Seventeenth to the Early Nineteenth Centuries', *Guildhall Miscellany*, vol. II, no. 10, 1968

(iv) *The Government as Regulator—the Control of Overseas Trade*

M. P. ASHLEY *Economic and Financial Policy under the Commonwealth and Protectorate*, 1934

G. L. BEER *The Origins of the British Colonial System, 1578–1660*, 1908

G. L. BEER *The Old Colonial System, 1660–1754*, 2 vols, 1912

R. DAVIS 'The Rise of Protection in England, 1668–1786', *EcHR*, 2nd ser., vol. XIX, 1966

J. E. FARNELL 'The Navigation Act of 1651, The First Dutch War and the London Merchant Community', *EcHR*, 2nd ser., vol. XVI, 1964

L. A. HARPER *The English Navigation Laws*, 1939

R. W. K. HINTON *The Eastland Trade and the Common Weal in the Seventeenth Century*, 1959

E. LIPSON *The Economic History of England*, vols. II and III, 'The age of Mercantilism', 6th ed., 1956

T. S. WILLAN (ed.) *A Tudor Book of Rates*, 1962

(v) Public Finance

ROBERT ASHTON 'Revenue Farming under the Early Stuarts', *EcHR*, 2nd ser., vol. VIII, 1956

ROBERT ASHTON 'Deficit Finance in the Reign of James I', *EcHR*, 2nd ser., vol. X, 1957

ROBERT ASHTON *The Crown and the Money Market, 1603–1640*, 1960

F. C. DIETZ *English Public Finance, 1558–1641*, 1932

P. G. M. DICKSON *The Financial Revolution in England: A Study in the Development of Public Credit*, 1967

J. HURSTFIELD 'The Profits of Fiscal Feudalism, 1541–1602', *EcHR*, 2nd ser., vol. VIII, 1955

J. HURSTFIELD *The Queen's Wards: Wardship and Marriage Under Elizabeth*, 1958

W. KENNEDY *English Taxation, 1640–1799*, 1913

P. MATHIAS *The First Industrial Nation: An Economic History of Britain 1700–1914*, 1969, appendix, tables, 12–13

D. OGG *England in the Reign of Charles II*, 2 vols, 1934

D. OGG *England in the Reigns of James II and William III*, 1955

R. B. OUTHWAITE 'The Trials of Foreign Borrowing: the English Crown and the Antwerp Money Market in the Mid-Sixteenth Century', *EcHR*, 2nd ser., vol. XIX, 1966

H. ROSEVEARE *The Treasury*, 1969

W. R. SCOTT *The Constitution and Finance of English, Scottish and Irish Joint-Stock Companies to 1720*, 1912, vols. I, III

G. UNWIN 'The Merchant Adventurers and the National Finances', *Studies in Economic History: The Collected Papers of George Unwin*, ed. R. H. Tawney, 1927

T. S. WILLAN (ed.) *A Tudor Book of Rates*, 1962

(vi) The Aims and Formulation of Economic Policy

A. W. COATS 'In Defence of Eli Heckscher and the Idea of Mercantilism', *Scandinavian EcHR*, vol. V, 1957

D. C. COLEMAN 'Eli Heckscher and the Idea of Mercantilism', *Scandinavian EcHR*, vol. V, 1957; repr. in D. C. Coleman (ed.) *Revisions in Mercantilism*, 1969

D. C. COLEMAN 'Labour in the English Economy of the Seventeenth Century', *EcHR*, 2nd ser., vol. VIII, 1956; repr. in Carus-Wilson, vol. II

D. C. COLEMAN 'Introduction' to D. C. Coleman (ed.), *Revisions in Mercantilism*, 1969

G. E. ELTON 'State Planning in Early Tudor England', *EcHR*, 2nd ser., vol. XIII, 1961

F. J. FISHER 'Commercial Trends and Policy in Sixteenth-Century England', *EcHR*, vol. X, 1940; repr. in Carus-Wilson, vol. I

A. FRIIS *Alderman Cockayne's Project and the Cloth Trade: Commercial Policy of England in the Main Aspects, 1603–1625*, 1927

E. FURNESS *The Position of the Laborer in a System of Nationalism*, 1920

J. D. GOULD 'The Trade Crisis of the Early 1620s and English Economic Thought', *JEcH*, vol. XV, 1955

R. C. GWILLIAM 'The Chester Tanners and Parliament, 1711–1717', *Chester Arch. Soc. J.*, vol. XLIV, 1957

H. HEATON 'Heckscher on Mercantilism', *J. Pol. Econ.*, vol. XLV, 1937

E. F. HECKSCHER 'Mercantilism', *EcHR*, vol. VII, 1937; repr. in D. C. Coleman (ed.), *Revisions in Mercantilism*, 1969

E. F. HECKSCHER *Mercantilism*, 2nd ed., 1965

A. V. JUDGES 'The Idea of a Mercantile State', *TRHS* 4th ser., vol. XXI, 1939

H. F. KEARNEY 'The Political Background to English Mercantilism, 1695–1700', *EcHR*, 2nd ser., vol. XI, 1959

J. E. NEALE *The Elizabethan House of Commons*, 1949

V. PONKO, JR. 'The Privy Council and the Spirit of Elizabethan Economic Management, 1558–1603', *Trans. of American Philosophical Soc. n.s.*, vol. LVIII, pt. 4, 1968

G. D. RAMSAY 'Industrial Laisser-Faire and the Policy of Cromwell', *EcHR*, vol. XVI, 1946

ADAM SMITH *An Inquiry into the Nature and Causes of the Wealth of Nations*, 1776, Everyman ed. 1910, Book IV

J. J. SPENGLER 'Mercantilist and Physiocratic Growth Theory', in B. Hoselitz et al., *Theories of Economic Growth*, 1960

L. STONE 'State Control in Sixteenth Century England', *EcHR*, vol. XVII, 1947

B. E. SUPPLE *Commercial Crisis and Change in England, 1600–1642*, 1959

R. H. TAWNEY *Business and Politics under James I: Lionel Cranfield as Merchant and Minister*, 1958

C. WILSON ' "Mercantilism": Some Vicissitudes of an Idea', *EcHR*, 2nd ser., vol. X, 1957; repr. in C. Wilson, *Economic History and the Historian: Collected Essays*, 1969

C. WILSON 'The Other Face of Mercantilism', *TRHS*, 5th ser., vol. IX, 1959; repr. in D. C. Coleman (ed.), *Revisions in Mercantilism*, 1969; and in C. Wilson, *Economic History and the Historian: Collected Essays*, 1969

C. WILSON 'Government Policy and Private Interest in Modern English History', in C. Wilson, *Economic History and the Historian: Collected Essays*, 1969

(vii) *Enforcement and Effectiveness*

M. W. BERESFORD 'The Common Informer, the Penal Statutes and Economic Regulation', *EcHR*, 2nd ser., vol. X, 1957

E. G. DOWDELL *A Hundred Years of Quarter Sessions*, 1932

G. R. ELTON 'Informing for Profit', *Cambridge Hist. J.*, vol. IX, 1954

E. E. HOON *The Organization of the English Customs System 1696–1786*, 1938

E. HUGHES *Studies in Administration and Finance, 1558–1825*, 1934

E. MOIR *The Justice of the Peace*, 1969

D. O. WAGNER 'Coke and the Rise of Economic Liberalism', *EcHR*, vol. VI, 1935

N. J. WILLIAMS 'Tradesmen in Early Stuart Wiltshire', *Trans. Wilts. Arch. and Natural Hist. Soc.*, Records Branch, vol. xv (1959), 1960

7   WEALTH AND POVERTY IN PRE-INDUSTRIAL ENGLAND

(i) *The Growth of Wealth* (many of the references for Chapters 3–6 are also concerned with the growth of wealth)

P. DEANE 'The Implications of Early National Income Estimates for the Measurement of Long-term Growth in the United Kingdom', *Econ. Dev. and Cult. Change*, vol. IV, 1955–6.

R. M. HARTWELL 'Economic Growth in England before the Industrial Revolution: Some Methodological Issues', *JEcH*, vol. XXIX, 1969

S. KUZNETS 'Capital Formation in Modern Economic Growth, and Some Implications for the Past', *3rd Int. Conf. Econ. Hist.*, Paris, 1968

L. SOLTOW 'Long Run Changes in British Income Inequality', *EcHR*, 2nd ser., vol. XXI, 1968

(ii) *The Distribution of Wealth*

E. J. BUCKATZCH 'The Geographical Distribution of Wealth in England, 1086–1843', *EcHR*, 2nd ser., vol. III, 1950

P. J. BOWDEN 'Agricultural Prices, Farm Profits, and Rents', *AgHEW*

M. CAMPBELL *The English Yeoman Under Elizabeth and the Early Stuarts*, 1942

J. T. CLIFFE *The Yorkshire Gentry From the Reformation to the Civil War*, 1969

J. P. COOPER 'The Social Distribution of Land and Men in England, 1436–1700', *EcHR*, 2nd ser., vol. XX, 1967

J. CORNWALL 'The Early Tudor Gentry', *EcHR*, 2nd ser., vol. XVII, 1965

A. EVERITT *The Community of Kent at the Great Rebellion, 1640–1660*, 1966

M. E. FINCH *The Wealth of Five Northamptonshire Families*, Northants Record Society, vol. XIX, 1956

R. GRASSBY 'The Personal Wealth of the Business Community in Seventeenth Century England', *EcHR*, 2nd ser., vol. XXIII, 1970

D. G. HAY 'A Dual Economy in South Yorkshire', *AgHR*, vol. XVII, no. 1, 1970

W. G. HOSKINS and H. P. R. FINBERG *Devonshire Studies*, 1952

E. KERRIDGE 'The Movement of Rent, 1540–1640', *EcHR*, 2nd ser., vol. VI, 1953; repr. in Carus-Wilson, vol. II

P. MATHIAS 'The Social Structure in the Eighteenth Century: a Calculation by Joseph Massie', *EcHR*, 2nd ser., vol. X, 1957

E. H. PHELPS BROWN and S. V. HOPKINS 'Seven Centuries of Building Wages', *Economica*, n.s., vol. XXII, 1955; repr. in Carus-Wilson, vol. II

R. S. SCHOFIELD 'The Geographical Distribution of Wealth in England, 1334–1649', *EcHR*, 2nd ser., vol. XVIII, 1965

A. SIMPSON *The Wealth of the Gentry, 1540–1660: East Anglian Studies*, 1961

L. STONE 'The Fruits of Office: The Case of Robert Cecil, first Earl of Salisbury, 1596–1612', Fisher

L. STONE *The Crisis of the Aristocracy, 1558–1641*, 1965

F. M. L. THOMPSON 'The Social Distribution of Landed Property in England since the Sixteenth Century', *EcHR*, 2nd ser., vol. XIX, 1966

BIBLIOGRAPHY

H. R. TREVOR-ROPER *The Gentry, 1540–1640, Economic History Review*, Suppl. no. 1, 1953

T. WILSON *The State of England Anno Dom. 1600*, ed. F. J. Fisher, *Camden Miscellany*, vol. XVI, 1936

(iii) The Disposal of Income

M. W. BARLEY 'Rural Housing in England', *AgHEW*

C. M. L. BOUCH and G. P. JONES *The Lake Counties, 1500–1830*, 1961

M. A. HAVINDEN (ed.) *Household and Farm Inventories in Oxfordshire, 1500–1590*, 1965

E. HUGHES *North Country Life in the Eighteenth Century*, II. *Cumberland and Westmorland 1700–1830*, 1965

W. K. JORDAN *Philanthropy in England 1480–1660*, 1959

A. MACFARLANE *The Family Life of Ralph Josselin: A Seventeenth Century Clergyman*, 1970

E. H. PHELPS BROWN and S. V. HOPKINS 'Seven Centuries of the Price of Consumables, Compared with Builders' Wage Rates', *Economica*, n.s., vol. XXIII, 1956; repr. in Carus-Wilson, vol. II

F. W. STEER (ed.) *Farm and Cottage Inventories of Mid-Essex, 1634–1749*, Essex Record Office Publications, no. 8, 1950

(iv) Poverty

A. L. BEIER 'Poor Relief in Warwickshire, 1630–1660', *PP*, no. 35, 1966

C. W. CHALKLIN *Seventeenth Century Kent: A Social and Economic History*, 1965

J. D. CHAMBERS *Nottinghamshire in the Eighteenth Century*, 2nd ed., 1966

D. C. COLEMAN 'Labour in the English Economy of the Seventeenth Century' *EcHR*, 2nd ser., vol. VIII, 1956; repr. in Carus-Wilson, vol. II

M. D. GEORGE *London Life in the Eighteenth Century*, 1925

W. G. HOSKINS, 'English Provincial Towns in the Early Sixteenth Century', *Provincial England*

W. G. HOSKINS 'An Elizabethan Provincial Town: Leicester', *Provincial England*

W. G. HOSKINS 'Harvest Fluctuations and English Economic History, 1480–1619', *AgHR*, vol. XII, 1964

W. G. HOSKINS 'Harvest Fluctuations and English Economic History, 1620–1759', *AgHR*, vol. XVI, 1968

P. LASLETT *The World We Have Lost*, 1965

E. M. LEONARD *The Early History of English Poor Relief*, 1900

J. F. D. SHREWSBURY *A History of Bubonic Plague in the British Isles*, 1970

R. H. TAWNEY and E. POWER (eds.) *Tudor Economic Documents*, 3 vols., 1924; 'Regulations for the Relief of the Poor at Norwich, 1570', vol. II, pp. 313–6

255